CITY SCRIPTS

CITY SCRIPTS

NARRATIVES OF POSTINDUSTRIAL URBAN FUTURES

Edited by Barbara Buchenau,
Jens Martin Gurr, and Maria Sulimma

THE OHIO STATE UNIVERSITY PRESS
COLUMBUS

Copyright © 2023 by The Ohio State University.
All rights reserved.

Funded by the Volkswagen Foundation (Project number Az 93500)

Library of Congress Cataloging-in-Publication Data
Names: Buchenau, Barbara, editor. | Gurr, Jens Martin, 1974– editor. | Sulimma, Maria, 1985– editor.
Title: City scripts : narratives of postindustrial urban futures / edited by Barbara Buchenau, Jens Martin Gurr, and Maria Sulimma.
Description: Columbus : The Ohio State University Press, [2023] | Includes bibliographical references and index. | Summary: "Analyzes the past, present, and future of postindustrial cities in Germany and the US through assemblages of narrative, media, performance, and urban matter"—Provided by publisher.
Identifiers: LCCN 2023013586 | ISBN 9780814215524 (cloth) | ISBN 0814215521 (cloth) | ISBN 9780814283103 (ebook) | ISBN 0814283101 (ebook)
Subjects: LCSH: City planning. | Cities and towns in literature. | Cities and towns—History. | Narration (Rhetoric)—Social aspects. | Urbanization—Social aspects—United States. | Urbanization—Social aspects—Germany.
Classification: LCC PN56.C55 C55 2023 | DDC 307.76—dc23
LC record available at https://lccn.loc.gov/2023013586
Other identifiers: ISBN 9780814258866 (paper) | ISBN 0814258867 (paper)

Cover design by Larry Nozik
Text composition by Stuart Rodriguez
Type set in Minion Pro

♾ The paper used in this publication meets the minimum requirements of the American National Standard for Information Sciences—Permanence of Paper for Printed Library Materials. ANSI Z39.48-1992.

In memory of Josef Raab

CONTENTS

List of Illustrations   ix

Acknowledgments   xi

INTRODUCTION   City Scripts in Urban Literary and Cultural Studies
MARIA SULIMMA, BARBARA BUCHENAU, AND JENS MARTIN GURR   1

PART 1 • URBAN SPACES

CHAPTER 1   Black Lives Matter Graffiti and Creative Forms of Dissent: Two Sites of Counterscripting in Denver, Colorado
FLORIAN DECKERS AND RENEE M. MORENO   27

CHAPTER 2   Walking Down Woodward: (Re)Telling a City's Stories through Urban Figures
JULIANE BOROSCH AND BARBARA BUCHENAU   44

CHAPTER 3   Tiny Architecture and Narrative: Scripting Minimal Urban Living Spaces
KATHARINA WOOD AND RANDI GUNZENHÄUSER   69

CHAPTER 4   Narrative Path Dependencies in Sustainable and Inclusive Urban Planning: Portland's Albina Neighborhoods
ELISABETH HAEFS AND JENS MARTIN GURR   87

PART 2 • URBAN LITERATURE

CHAPTER 5   Scripting the Inclusive City, Narrating the Self: Contemporary Rust Belt Memoirs in Poetry and Prose
CHRIS KATZENBERG AND KORNELIA FREITAG   105

CHAPTER 6   Whose Detroit? Fictions of Land Ownership and Property in Postindustrial America
JULIA SATTLER   122

CHAPTER 7   To the Bodega or the Café? Microscripts of Gentrification in Contemporary Fiction
MARIA SULIMMA   138

CHAPTER 8   Redemptive Scripts in the City Novel
LIEVEN AMEEL   156

PART 3 • URBAN HISTORIES OF IDEAS

CHAPTER 9   Patterned Pasts and Scripted Futures: Cleveland's Waterfronts and Hopes of Changing the Narrative
JOHANNES MARIA KRICKL AND MICHAEL WALA   175

CHAPTER 10   The Creative Democracy: A Critique of Concepts of Creativity in Contemporary Urban Discourse
HANNA RODEWALD AND WALTER GRÜNZWEIG   193

CHAPTER 11   Forms, Frames, and Possible Futures
BARBARA ECKSTEIN AND JAMES A. THROGMORTON   212

List of Contributors   227

Index   231

ILLUSTRATIONS

FIGURE 1.1	Elijah McClain mural by artists Thomas "Detour" Evans, Hiero Veiga, and "TukeOne"	31
FIGURE 2.1	Conrad Kickert's map of the 1911 remnants of Augustus B. Woodward's design	50
FIGURE 2.2	Figural sculptures on Woodward Avenue, downtown Detroit	52
FIGURE 2.3	Hubert Massey's *Power to the People*	55
FIGURE 2.4	Marshall Fredericks's *The Spirit of Detroit*	57
FIGURE 2.5	Robert Graham's *Monument to Joe Louis,* with David Barr and Sergio De Giusti's *Transcending* in the background	60
FIGURE 2.6	William Kieffer and Ann Feeley's *Antoine de la Mothe Cadillac*	63
FIGURE 2.7	Ed Dwight's *Gateway to Freedom: International Memorial to the Underground Railroad*	64
FIGURE 3.1	An explosion drawing of the Didden village	76
FIGURE 3.2	33 Logements à Poissy	80
FIGURE 3.3	A prototypical Wohnwagon	81
TABLE 8.1	Features of a redemptive plot	159
FIGURE 9.1	Blazing Paddles Paddlefest logo	187
FIGURE 10.1	Janna Banning's "Art is only for the rich"	208

ACKNOWLEDGMENTS

This book would have been unthinkable without the passionate input of our critical interlocutors, who have shaped our argument at various stages. Special thanks go to Stephanie Leigh Batiste, Michael Batty, Alex Blue V., Bocafloja, Diane van Buren, Stefan Dierkes, Oliver Dörmann, Iris Dzudzek, Florian Freitag, Sage Gerson, Julika Griem, Dieter Hassenpflug, Jon Hegglund, Victoria Hegner, Thomas Heise, Hanna Henryson, Stefan Höhne, Arun Jain, Norman Klein, Kai Lipsius, Lena Mattheis, Dietmar Meinel, Courtney Moffett-Bateau, Paula M. L. Moya, Hajo Neis, Simone Raskob, Thomas Rühle, Ramón Saldívar, Sebastian Schlecht, Heike Steinhoff, Ulrike Sommer, Boris Vormann, and Ernest Zachary for their unwavering support and their expertise. Early on, the financial and institutional support of the Mercator Research Center Ruhr for a research project directed by Walter Grünzweig and coordinated by Julia Sattler allowed many of us to jointly venture into the field of literary urban studies. Three anonymous reviewers of an unsuccessful research initiative on historical North American city scripts directed by Barbara Buchenau provided useful feedback. This temporary failure sparked our interest in narrativity in postindustrial cities in the US and Germany that are rescripting the pragmatic functions of storytelling. The Volkswagen Foundation supported this collaborative research extensively: It funded a sustained systematic exchange between urban planning and American studies called Scripts for Postindustrial Urban Futures: American Models, Transatlantic Interventions (2018–23, directed by

Barbara Buchenau, codirected by Jens Martin Gurr, coordinated by Maria Sulimma). This research group has served as the intellectual hub or homebase for the authors assembled here. We particularly thank the teams at Zachary & Associates, Detroit; Ruhrfutur; the City of Essen; lala Ruhr; the world heritage site Zeche Zollverein; Ökozentrum NRW; and the Dortmunder U—Zentrum für Kunst und Kreativität for critical feedback and great opportunities to discuss our work with urban professionals. At the Volkswagen Foundation, Cornelia Soetbeer, Pierre Schwidlinski, Barbara Neubauer, and Jeana Thilla have been unwavering in their support of our endeavor. Christine Vennemann and Phillip Grider offered time and critical acumen to assemble the argument in its present form. Two anonymous readers provided extremely valuable feedback. It has been magic to experience the guidance of Ana Maria Jimenez-Moreno, Elizabeth Zaleski, and everyone else at The Ohio State University Press throughout the editorial process.

INTRODUCTION

City Scripts in Urban Literary and Cultural Studies

MARIA SULIMMA, BARBARA BUCHENAU, AND JENS MARTIN GURR

Have we come to a new era of narrating the city in Western democracies? And is narration an appropriate technique to influence powerful transformations? In a video statement announcing the United Nations Policy Brief "Covid-19 in an Urban World" in July 2020, UN Secretary-General António Guterres evoked stories of atomic wars and 9/11 alike when he described cities as "ground zero" of the global pandemic (United Nations). Like Guterres, many politicians, activists, scientists, and journalists framed the COVID-19 pandemic as a decidedly urban phenomenon, challenging their listeners to understand the spread of the virus as a fundamental threat to their cities. Urban dwellers, infrastructures, and lifestyles were registered by the media as the first and foremost victims. Simultaneously, public discourse and the professional fields of urban management and urban planning picked up on the added sense of opportunity and futurity that emerged from this multiauthored narrative documentation: The pandemic was seized as an incentive to rethink and restructure urban communities. Between 2020 and 2022, several factual as well as fictionalized narratives surrounding cities and pandemics surfaced in newspapers, statements of politicians, or social media posts from around the world. These texts contributed to the recrafting of the canonical and starkly racialized scripts of *urban flight* and *deserted cities*.

Urban flight, deserted cities: each a pas de deux that refers readers back to a contingent, albeit conspicuous, assemblage of narrative techniques, performing characters, medial frames, and figural interpretation. They recall past crises, sketch present urban isolation, and call for future urban action. They are especially familiar descriptors for transformational processes in so-called "legacy cities" adapting to major global shifts in the heavy industries (Mallach and Brachman). Most importantly for the volume at hand, they are scripts—consequential, but rather terse and stereotyping placemaking strategies at the intersections between textuality, urban space, mediality, performativity, and materiality. Drawing on mental schemata and conceptual models, scripts tend to renew outdated explanations of social transformations to pitch story arcs forward into the future. This new pandemic life given to two well-worn abbreviations of urban change is one example of *city scripts* (see Mahler) as highly condensed, and yet expansive in scope, dynamic storytelling phenomena to be methodically analyzed in this book.

As the example of the compressed yet complex storytelling sparked by the rise of a pandemic demonstrates, factual and fictional stories affect how we imagine our cities and life within them. Two contrapuntal fields of urban practices equally depend on this ability to invent plausible stories of collective action, partial cohesion, and selective connectedness: political activism and urban planning. This volume suggests the *city script* as a methodological and conceptual framework to better analyze and understand such future-oriented storytelling. The conceptualization of scripts as much as the observation of material practices of scripting and the performative dimension of "scriptivity" permit innovative insights into the transgressive overlap and interdependence of fictional, factual, and real-life modes of urban and anti-urban imaginaries.[1]

City Scripts responds to calls by literary theorists such as Rita Felski in *Hooked: Art and Attachment* (2020) and Paula M. L. Moya in *The Social Imperative* (2016) to develop methods for a new kind of narrative analysis that recalibrates close reading and interpretation to the multiple ways in which narratives "do things" (Felski 42) by, for instance, allowing their readers to enter into emotionally and epistemically transformative "interracial friendship[s]" (Moya 51) with literary characters and with the narrative progression that can and will "prompt a reader to question and then revise some of her assumptions about structures of racial and economic inequality" (Moya

---

1. Within the field of performance studies, "scriptivity" is defined as "the moment when dramatic narrative and movement through space are in the act of becoming each other" (Bernstein 89). It blends word and action, doing and telling. See chapter 2 by Borosch and Buchenau for a discussion of scriptivity.

58).[2] We are particularly interested in how narratives take action in everyday life. This book will analyze polysemic assemblages of narrative, media, and poetics with their multiplying and contesting temporal, spatial, and material groundings. We define *scripts* as "artful combinations of narrative, medial as well as figural acts of framing, inscription, description and prescription [that . . .] establish contingent connective tissues between the past, the present and the future" of cities and their frequently anti-urban constituents and contexts (Buchenau and Gurr, "Urban Development" 142). This colloquial art of crafting connective tissues between an emotionally charged past, a contentious present, and an anticipated future is especially prominent in scenarios of massive deindustrialization and selective reindustrialization experienced in many second cities across the United States and Germany, the regional foci of our examination.[3]

In the US-American Northeast and Midwest, and in the German Ruhr region, where many of our authors are based,[4] stories past and passing by have breathed new life into images of *rust belts* and *transformation engines*. On both sides of the Northern Atlantic, the former heartlands of the steel, coal, and car industries are producing countless stories—old and new—of (post)industrial labor and exploitation. These stories of a very special kind of urban setting are "building character," as architectural historian Charles L. Davis II would call it (see 6–9), in the shape of divisive urban architecture, racialized social orders, and regional, national as well as transatlantic interpretations of histori-

---

2. Rita Felski draws on Actor Network Theory and criticizes the ideological exhaustion of surface as well as strong readings, arguing that "our critical languages need to become more attuned to their objects" (135). Paula Moya builds on the work of social and cultural psychology to indicate how a revised employment of close reading techniques can enhance our understanding of narrative agency and help "to build racial literacy" (31). Moya also asks for a new "conceptual vocabulary capable of registering [. . .] the linkages between [a wide variety of schemas developed and employed by a large number of diverse readers,] institutional structures of power and literary 'value'" (27). See also Marie-Laure Ryan who moves forward from the most prominent trends in postclassical narratology to emphasize the foundational sequence-building, cross-medial, and material interactivity afforded and required by narrative (3, see also 183).

3. Ryberg-Webster and Tighe indicate the extent to which these cities appear to be defined by a past forever lost and a future that is hard to bring into action: "Legacy cities, also commonly referred to as shrinking, Rust Belt, or postindustrial cities, are places that have experienced sustained population loss and economic contraction" (3). They emphasize that "the reality on the ground is a nuanced landscape of racial segregation, industrial decline, vacancy and abandonment, revitalized neighborhoods, vibrant downtowns, and so forth" (6).

4. The volume presents chapters cowritten by members and collaborators of the research group Scripts for Postindustrial Urban Futures: American Models, Transatlantic Interventions (www.cityscripts.de; 2018–23), funded by the Volkswagen Foundation and based at three universities in the German metropolitan Ruhr region.

cal meaning. In *Remaking the Rust Belt* (2016) Tracy Neumann has pointed to the paradigmatic status of so-called rust belts: City-makers in deindustrializing cities are crafting an imaginary for their urban future that engages "local variants of larger social, political, and economic processes that affect[ ] many North American and Western European cities" (3). In the view of Neumann, these spaces have been experiencing a "shift from manufacturing to services" not because of global market forces, but because "growth coalitions composed of local political and business elites [assisted by] international consultants" envision and craft the transition to the lower-paying service industry while seeking to attract members of the new middle class (3). This is a future-oriented narrative at work in a quite literal sense.

City scripts such as these harness the powers of both story (as a sequentialized ordering of events) and narrative (as past and potential lived experiences).[5] In doing so, they impact the social worlds of those who actively *read* or unconsciously come into contact with them. These scripts challenge analysts and theoreticians of narrative to contribute to the development of a transdisciplinary narratology that is commensurate to the centrality of narrativity for factual, nonliterary sensemaking and world-building activities.[6] Because colloquial storytelling and professional narrativization become the touted and increasingly ritualized practices of politicians, businesspeople, and city-makers, it is time for narrative theory to account for the growing importance of a new, fragmented kind of narrativity in the public and the private sphere. Adopting terminology of the study of popular seriality, we want to draw attention to the "proliferation" and "sprawl" of both terse and extended forms of narrative in and for the conceptualization of urban space.[7]

This book uses our practice-oriented work at the intersection of literature, media, and urban development as a growing archive, which will need a

---

5. This distinction is roughly in line with Albrecht Koschorke's discussion of the abundance of storytelling and narration in everyday life. He understands "narrative" as "a multistoried construct" (10). Stories resemble the "events and actions with episodes"; they are "subunits of the narrative sequence" (10). Koschorke speaks of the "dynamization" inherent in storytelling (11), emphasizing the "universality" of narrative as "a creative process of appropriation" of the world (12).

6. One handbook and two edited collections sketch the emerging field: Huber and Schmid's handbook (2018) points at the anthropological base of human narrativity; Strohmaier's collection (2013) on transdisciplinary narratological research is particularly interested in the generative capacities of storytelling. Finally, Gamper and Mayer's collection is a media history of short and terse everyday narrative in journalism, literature, and the public (and publicized private) sphere (2017). Koschorke's general theory of narrative lays a useful foundation.

7. In *Serial Agencies* (2014), Frank Kelleter uses these concepts to describe repetitive patterns in televised popular urban seriality. Both terms are equally well established in the description of phenomena in urban infrastructure.

broader methodological toolkit if interdisciplinary scholarship on narrative is to provide adequate and meaningful analyses of story-driven scripts.

URBAN ANALYSIS AS A CHALLENGE FOR LITERARY AND CULTURAL STUDIES

In the past years, urban studies as a discipline has increasingly become aware of how important narratives, cultural texts, and storytelling are in developing cities, as well as in communicating these plans to a wider public. This new awareness of narrative process is often called the "story turn" of city planning, even though it also affects the work of activists, politicians, and decision-makers on all levels.[8] Within academia, following the "narrative turn" in the social sciences, and the "spatial turn" of the humanities, urban studies is further diversifying toward a systematized interdisciplinarity, while the study of cities to many still appears as the domain of architecture, geography, anthropology, sociology, and the social sciences more generally.[9] However, the field of Literary and Cultural Urban Studies has been gaining traction in recent years. In its transdisciplinary translation of narratological, anthropological, planning, and design methodologies, this new field is able to provide important contributions to urban *and* narrative analysis, methodology, and theory alike. And it might help to address a methodological challenge that arises from the persisting difficulties to account for narrative's stellar career in fields and disciplines other than literature and literary studies.

The central venues for literary and cultural urban studies are the journal *Literary Geographies*, the Association for Literary Urban Studies, as well as Palgrave's book series "Literary Urban Studies."[10] Published since 2015, the

---

8. An early example of scholarship attuned to how stories and storytelling affect and even compete for our interrelated understanding of cities, (urban) sustainability, and democracy is the collection *Story and Sustainability: Planning, Practice, and Possibility for American Cities* (2003), edited by Barbara Eckstein and James A. Throgmorton. The growing awareness of the importance of culture and narrative for the analysis of urban phenomena is also documented in book series such as Architecture/Technology/Culture, edited by Klaus Benesch, Jeffrey Meikle, David Nye, and Miles Orvell, published first by Brill and more recently the University of Pennsylvania Press.

9. We describe the spatio-narrative confluence of the distinctive fields of urban, cultural, and literary analysis in Buchenau and Gurr, "City Scripts." In Buchenau and Gurr's "Textuality," we explore disciplinary oppositions to more effective cross-disciplinary debates between urban research, narratology, and cultural studies.

10. Founded in the same year, the formerly Scandinavia-based Association for Literary Urban Studies by now possesses a thoroughly international membership and puts on frequent meetings, workshops, and conferences. Its members are involved with and publish in Palgrave's new "Literary Urban Studies" book series.

journal *Literary Geographies* accommodates the diversity of a field in which some are interested in "generating maps from quantitative data as a means of correlating genre with geography or charting the lineaments of a narrative trajectory," whereas others are interested in "the nature of the relationship between material and metaphorical spaces" (Alexander 5). Several companions seek to provide an overview of how this field gradually developed into a discipline in its own right, for instance, *The Cambridge Companion to the City in Literature* (2014) edited by Kevin R. McNamara, *The Palgrave Handbook of Literature and the City* (2016) edited by Jeremy Tambling, and *The Routledge Companion to Literary Urban Studies* (2023) edited by Lieven Ameel. Further, Lieven Ameel, Jens Martin Gurr, and Jason Finch have respectively published monographs on literary urban studies.

As Ameel's most recent edited collection highlights, the field of literary urban studies can be subdivided into "classical" and "postclassical" approaches. Classical literary urban studies originated in the second half of the twentieth century. This subfield is dedicated mostly to the canonical texts of urban realism, naturalism, and modernism. For their analysis, literary scholars here turned to the formative thinkers of urban studies and (cultural) geography, such as Henri Lefebvre, Michel de Certeau, Walter Benjamin, or Georg Simmel. A compelling example of such an approach is Gerd Hurm's study *Fragmented Urban Images* (1991) with its chapters on authors such as Stephen Crane, Theodore Dreiser, Upton Sinclair, F. Scott Fitzgerald, John Dos Passos, Richard Wright, Hubert Selby, and Thomas Pynchon.

Meanwhile, postclassical literary urban studies as the more recent section of the field draws on such previous studies and their theoretical concepts but seeks to challenge its blind spots—the prevalence of mostly white and exclusively male authors. Such recent approaches frequently employ postcolonial and intersectional methodologies and are critical of canonicity and highbrow/lowbrow distinctions of their materials, as well as the primacy of certain urban centers over others. As one example, in *The Black Skyscraper: Architecture and the Perception of Race* (2019), Adrienne Brown demonstrates how urban built environments are central to the perception of race, specifically that "the experience and reception of skyscrapers [. . .] mediate the experience and reception of race" (26). Moving from the invention of the skyscraper in the 1880s to the erection of the Empire State Building in 1931, Brown reads canonical texts by W. E. B. Du Bois, Henry James, F. Scott Fitzgerald, and Nella Larsen alongside lesser-known works of pulp, romance, and science fiction, as well as labor histories of steelworkers and office managerial manuals. Thus, Brown's study demonstrates the strengths of postclassical literary urban studies. A cultural studies example for this kind of work is Kyle T. Mays's *City of Dispos-*

sessions: Indigenous Peoples, African Americans, and the Creation of Modern Detroit (2022).

Mays can be said to push postclassical approaches a little further in the direction of urban narratology, since he gathers oral and family histories as well as community documents and archival material for a groundbreaking argument about the histories of race, colonialism, and sovereignty that have shaped Detroit since its beginning. Further, the collection *Literary Second Cities* (2017), edited by Finch, Ameel, and Salmela, turns to literary and cultural productions about previously neglected peripheral or "second cities." This collection targets the "blind spot, in which a small set of alpha cities [such as New York, London, or Paris] with the strongest magnetic effect over whole countries and global areas are often taken to be the types for all cities" (Finch, Ameel, and Salmela 5).

A final important shift in recent literary urban studies is the broadening of the corpus to include nonliterary *pragmatic* texts such as planning documents. Here, recent scholarship has shown the productivity of applying analytical methods developed in literary studies to nonliterary texts (see Ameel, *Narrative Turn*; Buchenau and Gurr, "City Scripts," "Textuality," and "Urban Development;" Gurr).

In addition to international literary and cultural urban studies, our volume positions itself in the field of transnational American studies and urban American studies. Recent edited collections are *Urban Transformations in the U.S.A.: Spaces, Communities, Representations* (2016) edited by Julia Sattler and *The City in American Literature and Culture* (2021) edited by Kevin R. McNamara. In their introductions, both Sattler and McNamara respectively highlight the city's role in American studies and US-American national mythology. Moreover, both quickly move on to the diversity of alternate visions of the US-American city between modernization, urbanization, and immigration, which include ethnic enclaves, dichotomies between the city and its suburbs, as well as anti-urban differentiations between the city and the country. Both volumes call attention to the necessity for a transatlantic perspective in urban American studies. Sattler argues that "America, at least in the European imagination, is a mostly urban nation, home to New York City or Los Angeles. These cities might in fact be exceptions to American urbanity at large, but they are celebrated in their iconicity" (13). Contributing to McNamara's collection, John Carlos Rowe states that "the transnational turn [. . .] is not just a phenomenon of literary studies: transnationalism is the defining social condition of contemporary US urban life in cities across the nation" (137). Our collection offers conceptualizations of how urban narratives "travel" (*sensu* Bal) or are "translated" (*sensu* Tsing) not only between disciplines and professions but also countries, regions, and cities (for a discussion of traveling urban models, see Gurr). Some contributions in our collection explicitly look at the ways in which scripts for urban development and urban interaction emerge from conceptual transfers and translations between the US and Germany, such as the essay by Wood and Gunzenhäuser as well as the essay by Rodewald and Grünzweig. Some essays—Borosch and Buchenau as well as Deckers and Moreno—build on the transatlantic placement and cooperation of their authors. Other essays consider the ways that US-American cities such as Detroit, New York, Chicago, Denver, Cleveland, Iowa City, or Oakland are impacted by increasingly globalized scripts of urbanity. The ways that narration affects and determines these cities' industrial pasts and postindustrial urban futures runs as a common interest through all the contributions.

SUGGESTIONS FOR A TRANSDISCIPLINARY NARRATOLOGY: CONCEPTUALIZING SCRIPTS AND SCRIPTINGS

For any inquiry into the impact of narratives on the construction and perception of actual real-world spaces, Marie-Laure Ryan, Kenneth Foote, and Maoz Azaryahu's *Narrating Space / Spatializing Narrative* (2016) was groundbreaking in its explanation of how objects and things can challenge their observers and users to engage in narrative. Moving forward from a particular urban form that has narrativity (as Ryan, Foote, and Azaryahu argue for maps, for example), there is a need to advance a transdisciplinary narratological methodology that systematically develops notions of "script," "scripting," and "scriptivity" (Bernstein 69, 89) in both narrative theory *and* literary analysis. A "large conceptual leap" has already been made by the work of Ryan, Foote, and Azaryahu. They have moved forward from the traditional realm of literary narratology showing how "roadside markers, memorials, tourist signage, and landscape are types of 'media' for storytelling" (163). From the perspective of urban literary studies, as well as reflecting the ways transdisciplinary narratology has evolved in recent years, this undertaking will necessarily lead to much-needed methodological innovations regarding the materiality, spatiality, and the social and emotional impact of narrativity. This book addresses the "repertoire" of daily activities and impersonations of powerful texts as much as the "archive" of stored texts, conceptual frames, and materials, reading the often-seamless assemblages of "written" and "embodied culture" through a postindustrial urban lens (Taylor 20, 16; see Bernstein). Our use of the script's performative edge, we hope, will offer novel insights into pragmatic storytelling phenomena.

The conceptualization of city scripts promoted here is a decisive step in the direction of a transdisciplinary narratology, since these scripts possess a unique relationship to materiality, mediality, time, space, and people. In their audiences, city scripts seek to inspire an understanding about a specific city itself, just as much as its inhabitants, their shared history, present, and future. Thus, to analyze scripts is to engage with and understand a contentious hermeneutics inscribed in such storytelling: As procedural knowledge, scripts evaluate the past and construct (often conflicting) urban heritages. As self-descriptions, scripts attempt to describe the present-day state of a city. As blueprints, scripts regulate and prescribe possible visions of the future city that can take on utopian but also dystopian qualities.[11] At their best, scripts "imagine viable paths into a better future. At their worst, they unleash anxieties and build scenarios that propel further segregation, conflict and economic disintegration" (Buchenau and Gurr, "Urban Development" 153).

The analysis of scripts as a method offers guidance for urban geographers and urban studies scholars from the social sciences on how to approach both pragmatic/real-world and literary storytelling as much more than alternative forms of documenting and accompanying planning processes and as a means to convince decision-makers or inhabitants of a proposed urban development. But the script is an equally useful analytical category for narratological inquiries in the humanities, since it allows for a context- and agency-sensitive study of everyday and popular fictional and nonfictional storytelling that involves complex media and art environments, features fragmentation and standardization, and develops stark condensations and abbreviations. The notion of the script draws attention to distributed and communal forms of authorship, both abstract and immensely concrete ambitions of mimetic effect and representation, strong forms of intertextuality, elements of serial narration, and generic forms of temporal and spatial collocations.

Addressing scholars and students from literary studies, cultural studies, media studies, (cultural) history, and narratology, the essays of this volume all perceive the emerging field of literary and cultural urban studies as a test site to establish the analysis of scripts as a methodology genuine to this field. There is an interdisciplinary multiplicity in the ways the term script is used. These range from the standardized, highly regulated, occasionally refurbished, "tightly scripted" (Felski 122) forms of writing and thinking often found in academic or political arguments, to the theatrical script premeditating and

---

11. There is also a strong line of research on scripts in cognitive narratology that is outside the scope of this volume. We found Albrecht Koschorke's discussion of the "elementary operations" of narration (15–85) and "sense and non-sense" particularly helpful in this regard (117–20). For the mimetic/performative confluence of urban scripts and scapes, see Mahler.

guiding a performance on stage, in a movie, or in carefully curated spaces.[12] The script has a technological as well as material side to it, as in the scribal and medial inventory used in documented, reusable language production and reception or the technological script of algorithms and code. And, there is an equally prominent psychological and epistemological dimension of the script: This is the gendered, racialized, and class-driven "social script," which favors some ways of knowing over others (Moya 14), while it provides instructions on what behavior is expected in certain situations. Finally, the script has an emotional, relational, and spiritual dimension, ranging from the theological-religious understanding of authoritative scripture (see Buchenau and Gurr, "Urban Development" 146–49) to the "attachments" and "devotion" (Felski 7) called for by the compounds of narratives, media, and poetics that we call scripts. Rita Felski's sense of the liveliness of responses to art is worth quoting here, since we believe that scripts do not differ from art in their dependence on audience involvement: "Works of art [and their many mediations by the literary and social fields in which they exist] invite and enlist us; they draw us down certain perceptual or interpretive paths. They have their own distinctiveness and dignity [and] can affect us in ways we did not imagine or anticipate. [. . .] Artworks must be *activated* to exist" (6–7). Historian Natalia Molina foregrounds the psychological and epistemological as well as the material dimension of the script when she develops the notion of "racial scripts" to describe how the lives of diverse racialized Americans are connected across time and space in the nexus of US-American immigration, racism, and history. She pulls "the lens back so that we can see different racial projects operating at the same time, affecting different groups simultaneously" (Molina 7). Molina shares with our understanding the attention to the historical and narrative contexts of scripts—as well as the alternative counterscripts put forth as challenges by racialized groups themselves—as inseparable from the script itself: "By seeing these processes as *scripts* that can occur over and over, we expand our focus from just the *representations* to include the structural conditions that produced them" (9).

The dimensions of emotion and relation, as well as reason and psyche, play a crucial role for historians Keith Michael Baker and Dan Edelstein. Their collection *Scripting Revolution* (2015) suggests that revolutions of different

---

12. Bernstein uses the terms "script," "scripting" (68), "scriptive" (69), and "scriptivity" (89) in a strictly performative, theatrical sense to argue that "agency, intention, and racial subjectivation co-emerge through everyday physical encounters with the material world" (69). For Bernstein, the term *script* applies to "an evocative primary substance from which actors, directors, and designers build complex, variable performances that occupy real time" (69). Bernstein's emphasis on the conjunction between embodiment and material world is immensely useful for our concern with the temporal dimension of scripting processes. We are grateful to Stephanie Leigh Batiste for this suggestion.

countries and periods are guided by a revolutionary script when revolutionaries interpret the unfolding of past revolutions "as frameworks for political action. Whether they serve as models or counterexamples, they provide the outlines on which revolutionary actors can improvise" (2). In our understanding, scripts can prescribe sequences of events and suggest options for action, precisely because they are frameworks through which social actors develop intertextual modes of reading and interpretation. Conflicts over authorship and interpretation are central to scripts: "Competition to impose a script, or to control a script that has been imposed, is a fundamental fact of politics, though perhaps never more in evidence than in a situation that has been declared revolutionary" (Baker and Edelstein 3). However, such competitions over scripts also occur within the dramaturgy of urban developments.

As cultural imaginings of the city, regardless of whether they occur in planning documents or fictional storytelling, scripts involve a broad set of converging cultural practices. Scripts communicate and negotiate various understandings of the city in close interaction with mass media affordances. Elsewhere, we have argued that scripts may consist of media, figures, and narratives (Buchenau and Gurr, "Urban Development" 146). In other words, they develop stories through different combinations of figural expressions (poetic language and tropes, but also statistics and charts), narrative expositions (related sequence, perspective, plot, or narration), and media affordances (in audiovisual media: camera shots, angles, framing, soundscapes, digital media's options of commentary, art's "distributed agency" [Felski 64], rewatchability, etc.). Scripts mobilize the genre and media knowledge of their audiences, just as much as factual representations and assumed common knowledge. Scripts frequently evolve from collectives that share and contest authorship. They have much in common with popular seriality and its "dispersed" authorship of "a work-net of agencies" that is involved in serial production, distribution, and reception—writers, producers, actors, watchers as much as institutions and technologies (Kelleter, *Serial Agencies* 5–6). Scripts thrive in social media and online environments, and they "create ever more scripts" (Mahler 38).

Scripts are not synonymous with narratives since they rarely have identifiable narrators and often do not seem to be plot-driven. Neither are they synonymous with stories: While sequentiality does matter, temporal *and* spatial lines determine sequences in scripts. And yet, scripts quite reliably invite broadly distributed, sprawling storytelling for the city.

Ryan, Foote, and Azaryahu establish that narratological explorations of "landscape narratives," or any kind of texts with narrative structure occurring in a spatial environment, need to distinguish between such artifacts "being a narrative" and "possessing narrativity" (139). In light of their argument, it seems fair to say that scripts *can* be narratives; they may possess the sequential structure, narrative discourse, and development of plots that we associate with narratives in literature, poetry, or audiovisual media. But scripts do not necessarily *have* to be narratives. However, scripts always do *possess narrativity*, i.e., they "suggest[ ] stories to the mind" (Ryan, Foote, and Azaryahu 139). They may also be described as having narrative potential. This narrativity is key, especially when it is connected with intertextual ties to texts that explicate and flesh out the script. Scripts additionally also have an inclination for serial proliferation—the quality of "constantly bringing in new material and integrating it into what came before" (Kelleter, *Serial Agencies* 29). This cooperation of narrativity, intertextuality, and seriality formally allows scripts to inspire visions of a city's past, present, and future.

For narratologists interested in the power of narrative to evoke "fictional social worlds" and yet to affect and change "the real everyday social worlds" of those who read (Moya 35), the script (along with the psychological concept of the schema that plays a prominent role in Moya's argument) has served as a kind of container or framework for reader comprehension, as well as expressions of agency and experience in texts. Monika Fludernik summarizes that "one can construct basic 'scripts' for tellable stories, and these scripts can be analyzed structurally as incorporating the central notions of intentional action and incidence (extraneous occurrence)" (55). Such an understanding of scripts borders on expressions of storytelling convention and narrative traditions, especially within "realistic" texts but also in fantastical genre fiction: "Our understanding of what is real derives precisely from well-worn clichés of what should happen, has been known to happen, conventionally does happen, reflecting an array of frames and scripts, conventionalized expectations, moral attitudes and commonsense notions of the agentially and psychologically verisimilar" (Fludernik 121).

Indeed, scripts depend on plausibility, experience, and genre conventions. This is not to say that scripts necessarily always contain predictable clichés. Instead, in her work on storytelling in urban planning, literary scholar Barbara Eckstein finds that surprise and the breaking of expectations are what makes the best stories about cities: "Stories that defamiliarize can compel audiences to shift their usual interpretative scale or spatial perspective" (29). Hence, scripts depend on the evocation of conventional frames and storylines (often harnessing a broad spectrum of intertextual and intermedial techniques); they offer substantive repetition and serial storytelling, and yet they also play a critical part in what Rita Felski calls popular and narrative art's "dynamic and agitated force field of action and transformation" (63–64).

In their management of recognizability (Fludernik's "cliché") and surprise (Eckstein's "defamiliarized story"), urban continuity and innovation, scripts in our understanding share important characteristics with the commercially oriented serial narratives that the contributions to *Media of Serial Narrative* (2017) describe as "popular series." Scripts, like popular series, are evolving in an overlap of their production and reception practices, which manifests in a serialized feedback loop: "They can register their reception and involve it in the act of (dispersed) storytelling itself. Series observe their own effects—they watch their audiences watching them" (Kelleter, "Ways" 14). Just like series seeking to be continued, scripts need to incorporate viewer responses in future renditions to be convincing to urban decision-makers and neighbors. And not unlike popular series, city scripts, analytically speaking, are "moving targets" (Kelleter, "Ways" 14) that pose significant methodological challenges to analysts, even if we tackle them with methods expanded in transdisciplinary training. As Frank Kelleter puts it, serialized cultural forms such as these "exist, not so much as structures that can be programmatically designed, but as structures whose designs keep shifting in perpetual interaction with what they set in motion" ("Ways" 14). It is not only the flexible design but also the inclination to expand and sprawl with hardly any control that city scripts share with popular serial narration.

Long-running and collaboratively produced serial narration as well as conflicts of authorization and narrative control can "feed into genre profusion and genre diversification." These conflicts "rende[r] the separating line between producers and fans permeable" (Kelleter, "Ways" 19)—and they might also weaken the dividing line between urban developers and urban dwellers. Such a rapprochement would require both parties to involve themselves in a form of "realistic storytelling [that] invites people not only to lose themselves in the story but also—perhaps even more so—to find themselves there" (Kelleter, *Serial Agencies* 74). But these potentially empowering dynamics of a rapprochement, described by Felski in terms of attunement-turned-attachment and further defined by dialogue and interpretation in the work of Moya, do not seem to work smoothly in commercially oriented serialized and scripted narrative production and reception. As Maria Sulimma has shown in her analyses of "serial genders" and "gendered serialities" (*Gender and Seriality* 1), there is a remarkable "capitalistic flexibility to mix and match various ideological positions in the interest of maintaining them" in and via serialized narration (*Gender and Seriality* 220). Additionally, serial narratives tend to develop fictions of authorship that "often express more about a cultural artifact's reception than its actual production," hence, there is little indication that the kind of serialized narration found in urban scripts can offer enabling identification to its urban recipients/audiences (Sulimma, *Gender and Seriality* 154).

In fact, the frequently absent authors of the urban stories evoked in urban planning, Barbara Eckstein finds, create scepticism and a lack of trust among audiences/urban dwellers: "As a citizen-reader, I too want to be able to identify the authors of the stories planners use and tell so I can assess the bases of their claims [. . . and] comprehend their place in systems of power" (17). Scripts, too, obscure the collective storytelling of which they are the result and may favor more or less convincing author fictions. "Who is the originator of a story about the city that draws on multiple accounts, textual predecessors, and embodied knowledges?" (Sulimma, "Scripting" 2). Hence, to employ scripts as a method is to study "how scribal agency and modes of scripting and deciphering empower legal codes which regulate the underlying obligations and rights of [both] the producers and the users of texts and images" (Buchenau and Gurr, "Urban Development" 151).

While we do not want to oversimplify global urban developments, city scripts often respond to three larger social, economic, and environmental challenges, transformations, or crises of cities in the twenty-first century: (a) the weakening of industries and labor markets, a crisis often addressed in pleas for creativity as a remedy enabling the replacement of previously lost well-paying jobs; (b) the aggravation of social polarization, a crisis most frequently addressed in searches for cultural practices of inclusion, equity, and diversity as measures against the displacement of urban communities; and (c) the deterioration of livability due to climate change and general environmental degradation, a crisis addressed in proposals for resilient or sustainable cities that equally have a strong cultural and literary component. Scripts for these changes are particularly active in transformation cities that are of merely peripheral importance to contemporary expert debates about urban as well as economic growth. These scripts thrive in second cities that have lost their lifeline industries in the second half of the twentieth century as part of structural changes referred to as postindustrialism or deindustrialization.[13]

The first urban challenge that motivates a standardized script of creativity and originality is described by Andreas Reckwitz as the "*structural breach*" between the modern logic of industrialization with its emphasis on standardization and sameness and the postmodern logic of the "*cultural capitalism* and the *economy of singularities*" with its stressing of creativity, culture, and individuality (7). Reckwitz has argued that postindustrial regions are highly unlikely, if not outright unable, to make it in the late modern race for narrative distinction and "singularity." As a sociologist, Reckwitz does not register

---

13. Sherry Lee Linkon proposes the term deindustrialization over postindustrialism or postfordism because the latter terms suggest "that we have moved beyond earlier conditions. The continuing economic and social effects of deindustrialization suggest that we are not yet 'post' anything" (5); instead, deindustrialization possesses a continued "half-life." For the culturalization of the debate about attractive urbanization, see Reckwitz 269–85. For the lessons to be learned from North American legacy cities in the debates on global cities and global urbanization, see Buchenau and Gurr, "Textuality" 138–40.

the distinctions between the broad spectrum of narrativity produced in this scenario of massive transformation. The contributions in this volume, however, amply show that this pessimistic reading of the creative rescripting of postindustrial cities might not be the only appropriate analysis. With their diversifying, aging populations, former Western centers of industrial production—including the coal, steel, and car industries—such as the US-American so-called rust belt cities and the German greater Ruhr region engage in multifarious plans to bolster the urban art scenes and host creative industries as sources of inspiration *and* new labor markets. Art and the creative industries here are charged with the task of rewriting the past, while envisioning a radically different future. "Landscapes once drastically altered by industrialization do not, as one popular story goes, return to the 'rural,' but rather transform into something else altogether" (Sattler 12), creating a particular need for the artifices and the temporal dynamics of contending *creativity scripts*.

A second urban challenge that motivates city scripts is found in the processes of economic, ethnic, racializing stratification, as well as polarization and the dynamics of direct or indirect displacement of urban dwellers who can no longer afford to live in their former neighborhoods. The resultant cultural homogenization has come to be understood as gentrification, but the dynamics involved might also be addressed as scripts of inclusive as well as excluding neighborhoods (*inclusivity / exclusivity scripts*). Ever since urban sociologist Ruth Glass coined the term gentrification in *London: Aspects of Change* (1964), academia and activism have been struggling to understand the host of socioeconomic phenomena associated with the term, including privatization, neoliberal capitalism, and globalization of capital. The seeming promises of gentrification attract those who hope for urban revitalization or renaissance while worrying less about the strengthening of whiteness and upper-middle-class status accompanying the renewal. Within literary urban studies, there is a growing body of scholarship that explores the mutual implications of literature, visions of the inclusive city, and gentrification. So far, Thomas Heise explores the "gentrification plot" of New York City's crime fiction; James Peacock argues against the monolithic construction of a gentrification genre (105); and, for novels set in Berlin, Hanna Henryson demonstrates how the competition of social groups over urban space is a central dimension of gentrification in literary representations.

The third urban crisis or challenge that inspires city scripts is the current ecological crisis: Global warming, loss of biodiversity, and the dramatic overstepping of ecological boundaries and excessive use of natural resources as key issues have all been linked to—especially Western—metropolitan centers and urban lifestyles. Thus, from manuals and handbooks instructing planners in the prevention of urban heat islands all the way to the global role of cities in climate change mitigation, from local "greener city" initiatives to networks such as "ICLEI—Local Governments for Sustainability"—the *sustainability script* (or "sustainability fix," see Jonas) in its numerous variations and subscripts is central to current urban development worldwide. Its abundant manifestations confirm the importance of narratives, medial imaginaries, and figural condensations due to its global prevalence as a *traveling concept* in the sense of Mieke Bal (Buchenau and Gurr, "Urban Development"; Gurr; see also Wilson).

Responding to either one or several of these challenges for cities, the contributions of this book engage with the different kinds of scripts predominant in the storytelling of and about the city, as well as with the entanglements of two or more of these scripts: socially inclusive scripts (Deckers and Moreno; Sattler; Sulimma), sustainable scripts (Haefs and Gurr; Wood and Gunzenhäuser; Throgmorton and Eckstein), and creative scripts (Rodewald and Grünzweig; Deckers and Moreno; Borosch and Buchenau). As further perspectives, several contributions seek to develop concrete aspects of scripts to improve the conceptual grasp of the method. These aspects range from a historiographic grounding and teleological thrust of scripts (Krickl and Wala), their "narrative path dependencies" (Haefs and Gurr), their transhistorical and transregional dynamics of "figural interpretation" (Borosch and Buchenau), their self-descriptive functions (Freitag and Katzenberg), to counterscripts (Deckers and Moreno), redemptive scripts (Ameel), marginal microscripts (Sulimma), and the political and moral "forms and frames" that develop in conjunction with particularly consequential city scripts (Throgmorton and Eckstein).

ABOUT THIS VOLUME

Following this conceptual introduction, three larger sections discuss examples of urban scripting as challenges for a transdisciplinary narratology and further the conceptualization of city scripts. The sections are organized through the kinds of materials under consideration: nonfictional, pragmatic texts or artifacts (Part 1: Urban Spaces); urban poetry and prose (Part 2: Urban Literature); and conceptual and intellectual debates (Part 3: Urban Histories of Ideas). These divisions are by no means absolute. All contributors to this collection approach city scripts from the perspective of literary studies, cultural studies, or urban history.

The first section demonstrates the contribution of the humanities, and especially literary studies and narratology, to previously more social science-oriented, architecture- and geography-minded urban research. Moving from the microscale of concrete urban artforms, facades, and houses to the mesoscale of neighborhood designs, these essays investigate the narrativity of nontextual urban artifacts, figures, plans, buildings, and spaces (and their multimedia effects as well as paratexts). This section explicates the potential of such spatial forms to inspire and direct storytelling.

In this vein, the first chapter by Florian Deckers and Renee Moreno considers artistic urban expressions of dissent and the Black Lives Matter (BLM) movement. Combining the volume's understanding of city scripts with Michel de Certeau's "tactic," Deckers and Moreno approach BLM graffiti and street art as *counterscripts,* that is, as "visual narrative artworks that inscribe themselves into urban space in order to rescribe local and translocal urban tales of belonging, social cohesion, and political action" (28). That these artworks are frequently criminalized examples of urban expression and urban dwelling raises further questions about collective authorship and local as well as transnational audiences of scripts, especially when such artworks are framed as vandalism, illegal political action, or avant-garde beautification propelling a neighborhood's gentrification and desirability.

In the second chapter, Juliane Borosch and Barbara Buchenau also focus on issues of in-/exclusivity, inequality, and place-making in prominent street design, public sculptures, and monuments that rescript past events as prophecies for future urban development. They turn to Detroit's main downtown artery, Woodward Avenue, as a case study of such urban (re-)development and (re-)writing. This chapter examines the original nineteenth-century design of Woodward Avenue as well as today's sculptures, street art, and monuments on the walkable stretch of Woodward Avenue, showing how these objects possess "scriptivity" (Bernstein 89) and embodied forms of "figural narrativity" (Ryan 378). Moving forward from a rereading of Erich Auerbach's foundational work of figural interpretation, this chapter shows how an assemblage of urban figures projects and scripts a place's (official) public story while, simultaneously, redirecting expressions of contested geographic memory. Raising questions concerning the future orientation of public space, commemoration, and representation, such figures are shown to be powerful engines in the cyclical (re-)narration of a city's past, present, and future. Urban figures "contribute to a naturalization of both narrativity and scriptivity. That is, they turn the idea of temporal and spatial supersession, of future-oriented structure and resistance, [. . .] into an everyday conflict of the imagination at work" (66).

If urban figures bear the weight of popular representation of the status quo, new kinds of building styles supposedly represent their communities' ambitions for a better, more sustainable future. The third chapter by Katharina Wood and Randi Gunzenhäuser turns to increasingly popular discourses surrounding tiny house living, minimal urban spaces, and economic "degrowth" as well as "sufficiency" scenario building. The chapter shows how this trend emerged in the US-American mid-nineteenth century, but scripts of sustainable living today feature most prominently in European tiny house settlements. Their analysis of plans and advertisements developed by architectural and engineering firms and taken up by private clients/future inhabitants in The Netherlands, France, Austria, and Germany demonstrates how ecological narration as well as American myths of self-reliance drive these collective experiments in more sustainable urban planning. These buildings function as "cultural narratives that communicate with the outside world about themselves, alongside the larger story of the neighborhood or city that surrounds and frames it" (70).

Current city scripts indeed do frequently take on issues related to sustainability, climate change mitigation and adaptation, and environmentalism generally. In chapter 4, Elisabeth Haefs and Jens Martin Gurr connect their analysis of city scripts for the Albina district of Portland with the notion of "narrative path dependencies" to describe how the combination of different kinds of scripts in planning and administrative documents can create conflicts due to the divergent narrative paths envisioned through a script's specific genre, plot patterns, or tropes. For instance, the inflated expectations that urban planners and politicians place on green infrastructure (such as parks, bike lanes, and urban gardens)—casting them as automatic *builders of community*—seem at odds with the narrative formatting that "create[s] [a] literary equivalent of path dependencies, suggesting or even determining specific outcomes, inclusions, and exclusions" (100) when a city is posited as a sustainable green utopia.

Following these investigations of the scriptings that are associated with the narrativity of planning documents, urban spaces, and built environments, the second section applies the notion of city script to (fictional) literature set in and engaging with cities. Collectively these chapters argue that fictional storytelling promotes individual scripts, which help readers navigate contending stories about actual cities and the changes and challenges that they face. Gentrification looms large in these chapters that also demonstrate how literature contributes to discussions surrounding its causes and effects, as well as the individual and communal experience of living in gentrifying neighborhoods.

Introducing the scripted components in autobiographical prose and poetry from Detroit, in chapter 5, Chris Katzenberg and Kornelia Freitag provide a transition from the first section's concern with the transhistorical and transregional scriptings of and for postindustrial spaces to the second section's interest in translocal dwellings in literature proper. This section maintains the volume's shared attention to the role of storied scripts in urban design and development by explicating the extra-literary powers of narrative agency that postindustrial urban planners seek to harness. "In memoirs that focus on a city [. . .] the presented 'city script' is based on personal experience that is transposed into a stand-in for the community the memoirist lives in. Thereby it is much more provisional, more fragile, and less encompassing than" pragmatic urban plans and spaces (109). Focussing on texts set in and engaging with Detroit, the chapter discusses the Detroit-based "Rust Belt Memoirs" by Jamaal May, Shaun Nethercott, and Marsha Music, showing how these texts "reclaim agency over 'self-narration' as a key aspect of human identity formation" (119).

In the sixth chapter, Julia Sattler continues this interest in Detroit as a hub for a new kind of regional narrative tradition that writes back to the accepted metropolitan centers of literary innovation. This is an engaged kind of literature dedicated to the postindustrial crisis in the US and sensitive to the responses of its urban dwellers, old-time inhabitants, as well as newcomers, oftentimes belligerently fighting with and against the script of postindustrial decline. Sattler explores tensions regarding real estate ownership in *You Don't Have to Live Like This* (2015) by Benjamin Markovits and *The Turner House* (2015) by Angela Flournoy. These novels share the understanding that "any script for the postindustrial city which is to be viable will have to engage with questions of property, ownership, and truly redemptive strategies of land use—beyond their economic dimension" (136). As Detroit-based fictions of ownership demonstrate, due to the intertwined histories between land ownership, race, and class, urban renewal or redevelopment projects of all kinds have become matters of open contestation.

The seventh chapter likewise focuses on current novels and gentrification: Maria Sulimma studies contemporary fiction that does not take the explicit form of gentrification narratives—unlike the novels considered by Sattler—and instead presents stories of gentrification in marginal passages. Drawing on Gerald Prince's notion of "disnarration" and Robyn Warhol's "unnarration," Sulimma argues that such passages function as microscripts because, although they appear marginal, they trigger their reader's understanding of gentrification, consumerism, and positions of gentrifiers and victims of gentrification.

She explores microscripts of gentrification through characters drinking coffee in distinct urban locations such as the upscale café or the bodega.

In chapter 8, Lieven Ameel draws attention to a core scriptural component informing the history of American literature: the fear of declension and the "promise of redemption, of past faults redeemed and of virtue in the world restored" (156). This chapter examines redemptive scripts in city novels. Drawing on a corpus of New York novels, Ameel argues that endeavors toward personal, communal, and national redemption have provided a powerful script over more than a century of writing New York City. These texts are driven forward by "a redemptive plot" and its "desire for the restoration of balance" (158). The fiction he discusses casts "doubts on the transformative benefits of modernization and urbanization. Such fiction expresses a profound uneasiness about what technological, industrial, and social 'elevation' has wrought in terms of moral, spiritual, or societal forms of a fall from grace" (166–67). Finally, the chapter explicates how these literary notions of redemption also inform modes of storytelling in urban planning. These redemptive scriptings are particularly apparent in New York City's comprehensive waterfront plans.

The final section expands the volume's understanding of scripts and especially the notions of city scripts as standardized and serialized responses to urban crises. It additionally brings the shared concern for a transdisciplinary narratology into conversation with intellectual histories and interdisciplinary debates. The chapters explore the relevance of scriptings and scripts in and for broader public discourses and urban development initiatives, offering additional conceptual dimensions and integrating theoretical debates surrounding, for instance, creativity, historicity, and futurity. In chapter 9, Johannes Maria Krickl and Michael Wala move forward from the redemptive scripts for waterfront development discussed by Lieven Ameel, as they analyze the story crafted by Cleveland city officials and citizen stakeholders to move beyond deindustrialization with its toxic 1960s legacy of the repeatedly burning Cuyahoga River. The authors productively use the connection between philosophy of history, cognitive narratology, and semiotics of culture. Historical patterns and scripts fuse in processes of historical sensemaking; the reduction of historical complexities and contingencies affords the persuasiveness of urban development visions. Krickl and Wala identify urban reinvention as a prime field of a strategic urban historiography that they develop from Jörn Rüsen's *Historik* and the semiotic theory of Juri Lotman. Their analysis of how the "Blazing Paddles" initiative is reclaiming the Cuyahoga River shows the usefulness of this new kind of historiographical narratology.

Just as the Cleveland example indicates the limits of sustainable city scripts, proposing strategic irony as a better narrative path toward a postindustrial redemption, there is also growing doubt about the role played by creative city scripts. Although the notion of creativity has become an integral component of urban planning campaigns, there is a strong gentrifying effect in the many initiatives that highlight a ubiquitous group of *creatives* as a desirable demographic for which cities across the globe must compete. In chapter 10, Hanna Rodewald and Walter Grünzweig interrogate this creative city script within a wider theoretical history of culture and creativity. Moving forward from a close reading of Janna Banning's public art installation called "Volunteering for Gentrification," presented in the city of Dortmund in 2019, the authors demonstrate how the creative city theorizing of urban economist Richard Florida has reduced urban creativity to economic functionalism and profitability. Rodewald and Grünzweig situate the script advanced by Florida in dialog with Ralph Waldo Emerson's original understanding of the "creative class" and philosopher John Dewey's noncommodified notion of "creative democracy." The result is an overdue critical intervention into the current discourse of postindustrial renewal and gentrification.

In the final chapter, Barbara Eckstein and James A. Throgmorton reconsider key concepts of their coedited volume *Story and Sustainability* (2003). Attentive to what has changed on the ground as well as in scholarly literature about the interaction between narrative theory and city transformation, they highlight the importance of narrative framing as one of the core functions of city scripts. Following Caroline Levine's work on literary forms, their chapter suggests scripts as an "interpretive means to think differently about the interface of cities, stories, sustainability, and democracy" (217). Eckstein and Throgmorton provide two distinct frames close to their complementary professional experiences: Throgmorton explicates the public frame of city governance and its limited access to long-term scriptings, drawing on his experience of serving as a member of a city council for eight years, during four years of which he was mayor. Eckstein finishes with what she calls "the private frame of the human heart" (217) informed by political developments such as the BLM movement just as much as her experiences as an academic in the humanities and a narratologist who has worked with sustainability researchers for decades.

These personal and professional experiences draw to the forefront many of the themes that earlier contributions of the volume understand as central components of urban scripts: Katzenberg and Freitag's readings of individual memoirs within a larger city, Deckers and Moreno's attention to artistic dissent and communal interpretation, Krickl and Wala's patterned historiographies, just to name a few examples. Altogether, the volume seeks to demonstrate how the future orientation of urban planning, urban activism, urban literature, and urban histories invests in conflicting, complex processes of storytelling that seek to script and thus forge paths into a greener, more inclusive, more creative future. Our readings flesh out a new method for the analysis of the growing importance of storytelling, scriptivity, and narrativity for nonfictional engagements with the agency of the human, nonhuman and more-than-human world. This method respects the explicit redemptive bend of much future-oriented pragmatic narration and opens it to critical analysis. The eleven chapters provide different interpretative strategies to understand the processes through which city scripts come into being, take action, and do things for and toward a specific urban future. *City Scripts* showcases the explanatory power of literary and cultural urban studies, inviting further research on a transdisciplinary narratology of the urban.

WORKS CITED

Alexander, Neal. "On Literary Geography." *Literary Geographies*, vol. 1, no. 1, 2015, pp. 3–6.

Ameel, Lieven. *The Narrative Turn in Urban Planning: Plotting the Helsinki Waterfront*. Routledge, 2021.

———, editor. *The Routledge Companion to Literary Urban Studies*. Routledge, 2023.

Baker, Keith Michael, and Dan Edelstein. "Introduction." *Scripting Revolution: A Historical Approach to the Comparative Study of Revolutions*. Stanford UP, 2015, pp. 1–21.

Bal, Mieke. *Travelling Concepts in the Humanities: A Rough Guide*, edited by Sherry Marx-MacDonald. U of Toronto P, 2002.

Bernstein, Robin. "Dances with Things: Material Culture and the Performance of Race." *Social Text*, vol. 27, no. 4 (101), 2009, pp. 67–94.

Brown, Adrienne R. *The Black Skyscraper: Architecture and the Perception of Race*. Johns Hopkins UP, 2017.

Buchenau, Barbara, and Jens Martin Gurr. "City Scripts: Urban American Studies and the Conjunction of Textual Strategies and Spatial Processes." *Urban Transformations in the U.S.A.: Spaces, Communities, Representations,* edited by Julia Sattler, transcript, 2016, pp. 395–420.

———. "On the Textuality of American Cities and Their Others: A Disputation." *Projecting American Studies: Essays on Theory, Method, and Practice*, edited by Frank Kelleter and Alexander Starre, Winter Universitätsverlag, 2018, pp. 135–52.

———. "'Scripts' in Urban Development: Procedural Knowledge, Self-Description, and Persuasive Blueprint for the Future." *Charting Literary Urban Studies: Texts as Models of and for the City*, by Jens Martin Gurr, Routledge, 2021, pp. 141–63.

Davis, Charles L., II. *Building Character: The Racial Politics of Modern Architectural Style*. U of Pittsburgh P, 2019.

Eckstein, Barbara. "Making Space: Stories in the Practice of Planning." *Story and Sustainability: Planning, Practice, and Possibility for American Cities*, edited by Barbara Eckstein and James A. Throgmorton, MIT Press, 2003, pp. 13–36.

Felski, Rita. *Hooked: Art and Attachment*. U of Chicago P, 2020.

Finch, Jason. *Literary Urban Studies and How to Practice It*. Routledge, 2021.

Finch, Jason, Lieven Ameel, and Markku Salmela. "The Second City in Literary Urban Studies: Methods, Approaches, Key Thematics." *Literary Second Cities*, edited by Jason Finch, Lieven Ameel, and Markku Salmela, Palgrave, 2017, pp. 3–20.

Fludernik, Monika. *Towards a 'Natural' Narratology*. Routledge, 1996.

Gamper, Michael, and Ruth Mayer, editors. *Kurz & knapp: Zur Mediengeschichte kleiner Formen vom 17. Jahrhundert bis zur Gegenwart*. Transcript, 2017.

Glass, Ruth. *London: Aspects of Change*. MacGibbon & Kee, 1964.

Gurr, Jens Martin. *Charting Literary Urban Studies: Texts as Models of and for the City*. Routledge, 2021.

Guterres, António. "Covid-19 in an Urban World." *United Nations*, July 2020, https://www.un.org/en/coronavirus/covid-19-urban-world.

Heise, Thomas. *The Gentrification Plot: New York and the Postindustrial Crime Novel*. Columbia UP, 2021.

Henryson, Hanna. *Gentrifiktionen: Zur Gentrifizierung in deutschsprachigen Berlin-Romanen nach 2000*. Peter Lang, 2021.

Huber, Martin, and Wolf Schmid. *Grundthemen der Literaturwissenschaft: Erzählen*. De Gruyter, 2018, https://doi.org/10.1515/9783110410747.

Hurm, Gerd. *Fragmented Urban Images: The American City in Modern Fiction from Stephen Crane to Thomas Pynchon*. Peter Lang, 1991.

Jonas, Andrew E. G. "Beyond the Urban 'Sustainability Fix': Looking for New Spaces and Discourses of Sustainability in the City." *The Politics of the Urban Sustainability Concept*, edited by David Wilson, Common Ground Publishing, 2015, pp. 117–35.

Kelleter, Frank. "Five Ways of Looking at Popular Seriality." *Media of Serial Narrative*, edited by Frank Kelleter, The Ohio State UP, 2017, pp. 7–34.

———. *Serial Agencies: The Wire and Its Readers*. Zero Books, 2014.

Koschorke, Albrecht. *Fact and Fiction: Elements of a General Theory of Narrative*. 2012. Translated by Joel Golb, De Gruyter, 2018.

Linkon, Sherry Lee. *The Half-Life of Deindustrialization: Working-Class Writing about Economic Restructuring*. U of Michigan P, 2018.

Mahler, Andreas. "City Scripts/City Scapes: On the Intertextuality of Urban Experience." *Exploring the Spatiality of the City across Cultural Texts*, edited by Martin Kindermann and Rebekka Rohleder, Geocriticism and Spatial Literary Studies, Palgrave Macmillan, 2020, pp. 25–43.

Mallach, Alan, and Lavea Brachman. *Regenerating America's Legacy Cities*. Lincoln Institute for Land Policy, 2013.

Mays, Kyle T. *City of Dispossessions: Indigenous Peoples, African Americans, and the Creation of Modern Detroit*. U of Pennsylvania P, 2022.

McNamara, Kevin R. "Introduction." *The City in American Literature and Culture*, edited by Kevin R. McNamara, Cambridge UP, 2021, pp. 1–20.

———, editor. *The Cambridge Companion to the City in Literature*. Cambridge UP, 2014.

Molina, Natalia. *How Race Is Made in America: Immigration, Citizenship, and the Historical Power of Racial Scripts*. U of California P, 2014.

Moya, Paula M. L. *The Social Imperative: Race, Close Reading, and Contemporary Literary Criticism*. Stanford UP, 2016.

Neumann, Tracy. *Remaking the Rust Belt: The Postindustrial Transformation of North America*. U of Pennsylvania P, 2016.

Peacock, James. "Gentrification." *The City in American Literature and Culture*, edited by Kevin R. McNamara, Cambridge UP, 2021, pp. 103–17.

Reckwitz, Andreas. *The Society of Singularities*, translated by Valentine A. Pakis, Polity Press, 2020.

Rowe, John Carlos. "Transnational American Cities: Camilo Mejía's ar Ramadi, Iraq, and Jason Hall's Topeka, Kansas." *The City in American Literature and Culture*, edited by Kevin R. McNamara, Cambridge UP, 2021, pp. 136–50.

Ryan, Marie-Laure. *A New Anatomy of Storyworlds: What Is, What If, As If*. The Ohio State UP, 2022.

Ryan, Marie-Laure, Kenneth Foote, and Maoz Azaryahu. *Narrating Space / Spatializing Narrative: Where Narrative Theory and Geography Meet*. The Ohio State UP, 2016.

Ryberg-Webster, Stephanie, and J. Rosie Tighe. "The Legacies of Legacy Cities." *Legacy Cities: Continuity and Change amid Decline and Revival*, edited by J. Rosie Tighe and Stephanie Ryberg-Webster, U of Pittsburgh P, 2019, pp. 3–19.

Sattler, Julia. "Narratives of Urban Transformation: Reading the Rust Belt in the Ruhr Valley." *Urban Transformations in the U.S.A.: Spaces, Communities, Representations*, edited by Julia Sattler, transcript, 2016, pp. 11–26.

Strohmaier, Alexandra, editor. *Kultur—Wissen—Narration. Perspektiven transdisziplinärer Erzählforschung für die Kulturwissenschaften*. Transcript, 2013.

Sulimma, Maria. *Gender and Seriality: Practices and Politics of Contemporary US Television*. Edinburgh UP, 2021.

———. "Scripting Urbanity through Intertextuality and Consumerism in N. K. Jemisin's *The City We Became*: 'I'm Really Going to Have to Watch Some Better Movies about New York.'" *Critique: Studies in Contemporary Fiction*, vol. 63, no. 5, 2022, pp. 1–16, https://doi.org/10.1080/00111619.2020.1865866.

Tambling, Jeremy, editor. *The Palgrave Handbook of Literature and the City*. Palgrave, 2016.

Taylor, Diana. *The Archive and the Repertoire: Performing Cultural Memory in the Americas*. Duke UP, 2003.

Tsing, Anna Lowenhaupt. *The Mushroom at the End of the World: On the Possibility of Life in Capitalist Ruins*. Princeton UP, 2015.

United Nations. "Coronavirus: Reshape the Urban World to Aid 'Ground Zero' Pandemic Cities." *UN News: Global Perspective Human Stories*, 28 July 2020, https://news.un.org/en/story/2020/07/1069041.

Wilson, David, editor. *The Politics of the Urban Sustainability Concept*. Common Ground Publishing, 2015.

PART 1
URBAN SPACES

CHAPTER 1

Black Lives Matter Graffiti and Creative Forms of Dissent

Two Sites of Counterscripting in Denver, Colorado

FLORIAN DECKERS AND
RENEE M. MORENO

The summer of 2020 was a time of upheaval in the United States. From the presidential campaign between incumbent president Donald Trump and his Democratic opponent Joe Biden to the worldwide COVID-19 pandemic, 2020 was marked by uncertainty, fear, *and* possibility. The pandemic, the denial of its impact by pivotal public as well as religious leaders, and the staggering numbers of deaths only seemed to exacerbate existing economic, social, and health inequities, bringing into even sharper relief systemic injustices that disproportionately affect people of color (see Serwer). The death of George Floyd in Minneapolis, Minnesota, remarkable because it was filmed for the world to see, lasted for an excruciating eight minutes and forty-six seconds while Derek Chauvin's knee bore down on Floyd's neck. Had his murder not been filmed and transmitted globally, maybe 2020 would not have seen the resurgence of the Black Lives Matter (BLM) movement, which garnered nation- and worldwide support. The protest around Floyd's death, however, coalesced into protests of other murders of African Americans throughout the US—Breonna Taylor in Louisville, Kentucky; Ahmaud Arbery in Satilla Shores, Georgia; Rayshard Brooks in Atlanta, Georgia; Elijah McClain in Aurora, Colorado, ad infinitum. For Robin D. G. Kelley the ensuing protests marked a critical juncture: "Black Radical Tradition comes together at 'the crossroads where Black revolt and fascism meet'" (Cunningham n. pag.). In the summer of 2020, BLM successfully ignited massive protests, some of them going on for weeks and months.[1]

Our goal in this contribution is to analyze a small part of the visual and graphic narrative modes of protest that emerged in this context as forms of counterscripting and "scriptivity" discussed in the introduction to this collection. Therefore, we are reading graffiti as visual narrative artworks that inscribe themselves into urban space in order to rescribe local and translocal urban tales of belonging, social cohesion, and political action. We will consider the diverse visual/graphic approaches and aesthetics that are applied as expressions of dissent. Focusing on practices that are essential parts of graffiti and street art culture and their application in BLM protest, we interpret those creative interventions as bottom-up renegotiations of US-American society manifested in what Michel de Certeau describes as "the constructed, written, and prefabricated space through which they move" (34). The illegality of some of these writers' expressions can be connected to de Certeau's concept of the "tactic" (36), which refers to marginalized residents' various forms of interaction with the city. This interaction is rooted in a space of otherness that it thus "must play on and with a terrain imposed on it and organized by the law of a foreign power" (37). Graffiti artists, who refer to themselves as writers since their art is based on diverse forms of writing names and drawing letters in a number of different styles, are experts in navigating and reshaping this terrain. Their process of rewriting the city thus neatly fits the daily urban interaction described by de Certeau. However, we do not only read their work as urban practices. Instead, we interpret these graffiti as manifestations of a counterscript—sharing the bottom-to-top directionality with the "tactic" (37)—that criticizes and even tries to deconstruct police violence in the US. The lens of the script allows us to also consider and meaningfully bring together the artifacts that are produced in this context, the paratexts that accompany them, as well as the interplay of narratives, figures, and medium that they enter when they are read as part of a city script.

The creativity of these artistic practices of BLM activists cannot generate an interdisciplinary scholarly interpretation that is distant or removed from

---

1. The movement initially started in 2013 in the form of a social media hashtag after the acquittal of George Zimmermann, who shot seventeen-year-old Trayvon Martin in February 2012. In the early summer of 2020, however, and to a large degree influenced by the openly racist politics of the forty-fifth president of the United States that had further advanced the divide between large groups of the US-American population, the anger at and frustration with the government and society at large had reached a tipping point. People took to the streets in protest across the US and around the globe. For a detailed history of the Black Lives Matter movement and its roots in the continuous fight against racialized violence, see, among others, Lebron.

the practices and artifacts generated in these *tactical* processes. The undeniable realities lived by African Americans and other people of color in the US still entail systemic racism and the resulting threat to life and limb, creating a situation that is like living under "the law of a foreign power" (de Certeau 37) for so many.[2] Our theoretical work is therefore rooted within an activist tradition in which research is not exclusively but also understood as political action (on scholarly alliances with social movements, see, for example, Sudbury and Okazawa-Rey; Clennon). By linking and dialoguing perspectives, realized within and between both authors of this text—US-American and European, cultural studies and literary studies, educational studies and Latinx studies, scholarly and activist writing—we hope to establish a better understanding of the diverse aesthetics and functionalities of the creative forms of dissent and how they are applied in the process of counterscripting the city of Denver, upon which we focus in this contribution. Our two varied and yet adjuvant perspectives on this particular postindustrial urban setting (Clarke 155–80)—one of intimate knowledge resulting from being born and raised in Denver and the other coming from a different city, country, and even continent—are only one reason why we decided to analyze creative countercultural output in this region. The other lies in the city's long tradition as an important place for social rights movements in the US: Some even consider Denver to be the birthplace of the Chicano Movement in the 1960s, and it is the home of some of its influential figures such as Rodolfo "Corky" Gonzales or Guadalupe Villalobos Briseño.

FIRST SITE: THE ELIJAH McCLAIN MURAL IN THE RIVER NORTH ART DISTRICT

On August 30, 2019, twenty-three-year-old Elijah McClain from Aurora, Colorado, died after an encounter he had with local police six days prior. After being held in a carotid control hold, which has since been banned by Aurora lawmakers, and being sedated with ketamine, he went into cardiac arrest in the ambulance taking him to the hospital. His death found little to no recognition in US mainstream media at the time. Only after the BLM movement gained immense traction about one year later did Elijah McClain's death receive new and broader attention. Still, the death of a person of color at the hands of police too often goes unnoticed by national media or is only mentioned briefly in local news coverage. In their work on grief and mourning,

---

2. For a detailed analysis of the systemic nature of racism, see Lipsitz.

Judith Butler describes the dehumanization that takes place when the death of a member of a marginalized group is excluded from public discourse as follows: "It is not just that a death is poorly marked, but that it is unmarkable. Such a death vanishes, not into explicit discourse, but in the ellipses by which public discourse proceeds" (35). Exactly in these "ellipses of public discourse," artists and activists can intervene with their art(-work). By creating artifacts that memorize a lost loved one within a medium located outside of mainstream media and within a public space, the death of that person is distinctly marked as significant. Ideally, the art can thus transform space into a place of healing, a place that helps family and friends in their process of mourning and that at the same time constitutes a social critique that aims to deconstruct the dehumanizing practices at work. In their analysis of the narrativity of places and in particular street names, Marie-Laure Ryan, Kenneth Foote, and Maoz Azaryahu identify that "the use of place names for commemorative purposes is intended to interweave remembrance into the everyday language of the landscape. Underlying the cultural convention that invests the name with mnemonic function is the premise that speaking or reading the name actuates remembrance" (142). A similar process seems to be at the core of RIP murals that present another form of space-bound commemoration. They, too, shape the urban landscape and facilitate repeated, if not daily, encounters and thus remembrance of a person and their stories.

An example of such an intervention can be found in the mural that was painted by artists Thomas "Detour" Evans, Hiero Veiga, and "TukeOne" in Denver, Colorado, which has a colorful portrait of Elijah McClain as its centerpiece (see fig. 1.1; McCort). McClain is depicted wearing earbuds, listening to music, the same as when he was approached by the police on his way home in the encounter that led to his untimely death. For the portrait the artists used colors reminiscent of sunrise and sunset—yellow, orange, pink, and purple and dark blue—to create contrast. The cherry blossoms that frame Elijah McClain's face on the left symbolize spring, which symbolizes his young age at the time of his death. Further, the flowers embody the fleeting nature of life, which is also emphasized through the depiction of petals being blown away by the wind.[3]

The mural is rooted in the RIP graffiti tradition because it is an obituary that is adapted to the street. Cultural scholar Jack Santino refers to such forms of dealing with loss as "spontaneous shrines" (10), for example, memorial crosses placed on the side of roads where lethal traffic accidents occurred.

---

3. The flowers painted in the background are cherry blossoms as well as what appear to be jasmine and hydrangea blossoms. The arrangement evokes the notion of funerals and shrines, where people lay down flowers for the dead.

FIGURE 1.1. Elijah McClain mural by artists Thomas "Detour" Evans, Hiero Veiga, and "TukeOne" on the wall of a local brewery in the River North Art District in Denver. This picture of the mural is used with kind permission of Thomas Evans.

Along these lines, this type of graffiti differs from other forms of graffiti, not in regard to the techniques that are applied but concerning their function and content. In the forms of graffiti that emerged in the context of hip hop culture in New York City and Philadelphia in the 1970s and 1980s, the writers mainly spray their own moniker in various forms (tags, bombings, larger productions) in numerous places across the city (see, among many, Cooper and Chalfant; Cervantes and Saldaña; George). The more a writer "hits" the walls or trains of the city, the more "fame" he or she will acquire within the peer group (see, for example, Bloch; Felisbret; Gottlieb). For RIP murals the situation is different, however: The writers do not promote their own names but create a place of remembrance usually with a large-scale portrait—in many cases as a monochromatic image—and the name of the deceased at a spot that was a central place during the life of the deceased.

The Elijah McClain mural differs from other, more traditional RIP murals in three key aspects. First, it is not a newly created place of remembrance for friends, family, and the community of the deceased's home neighborhood—which lies in the neighboring city of Aurora and not in Denver's River North art district (short: RiNo) located twelve miles away. Second, RIP murals are usually not painted over quickly or only against significant resistance from the community. Such murals produce a place that serves the function of an altar or shrine for the community, where people can lay down bouquets, light candles, and mourn the untimely death.[4] Due to this, RIP murals are highly revered within the community, and graffiti writers would usually not *cross* them (paint over them). Those sites become spatial manifestations of the community's imaginary, and the community will usually go to great lengths to protect these artworks. The Elijah McClain mural was removed after only about eight weeks, while other RIP murals are usually up for several years or even decades. Apart from the spatial as well as temporal factors, the Elijah McClain mural also differs aesthetically. The regularly applied monochromatic color scheme of portraits in RIP murals appears to be connected to, on the one hand, the usage of black-and-white imagery in printed obituaries and, on the other hand, the insertion of monochrome footage in color films and television series to depict the past in flashbacks (see Turim 15–16).

Elijah McClain's colorful portrait does not adhere to this tradition. Rather, it fits the colorful trademark style of the artist Thomas "Detour" Evans, who painted the mural along with fellow street artists Hiero Veiga and "TukeOne." Further, this aesthetic might be more suitable for the context of the art district, where the Elijah McClain mural was located on the wall of a local craft-beer brewery. The area north of downtown Denver and south of the South Platte River is, according to the city's website, "becoming a hotspot for the artsy types in Denver."[5] Per the curative program of the brewery, the mural was painted over in August of 2020 after only two months.[6] This stands in stark contrast to other RIP murals that usually are painted in the neighborhood, street, or even a specific spot where the mourned person used to live

---

4. For a detailed description of the role of early or untimely death in the community's construction of "spontaneous shrines," see Santino.

5. *Denver's Art Districts*. Visit Denver, https://www.denver.org/things-to-do/arts-culture/art-districts/. Accessed 14 Jan. 2022.

6. On the destruction of the mural and repainting of the brewery wall, see Warwick.

and that, more than most forms of graffiti, have a comparably long half-life. Thus, the mural seems to not fulfill the place-bound function of community building that usually presents an essential function of RIP murals. Due to its specific location in the context of the art district, the mural should also be seen within the logic of city and neighborhood planning as well as that of the brewery's marketing. Unintentionally, the artwork becomes a part of the attempt to generate a space that attracts tourists and shoppers seeking entertainment and leisure. In this vein, a colorful image such as this easily fits into those spaces and does not irritate its recipients too much, despite the more than grave occasion of its creation. It adds to a hip urban atmosphere, within which the political message of Evans, Veiga, and "TukeOne" might however recede into the background or even be lost altogether. In the context of painting on a company's wall with permission, their agenda should not be underestimated. Indeed, there is a danger of losing the sociocritical potential of the naturally political artform by eliminating the illegal appropriation of the urban space that usually is an integral part of this art.

Along these lines, Dumar Brown aka Dumaar Freemaninov, author of *Nov York* (2002), a stream-of-consciousness novel about the life of a young graffiti writer, polemically describes the problem of co-optation and the undermining of countercultural practices through consensual forms of graffiti. His critique of the more mainstream-suitable formations of the artform appears to be too fundamental, however. Brown/Freemaninov illustrates his stance on the tense relationship between political art and marketability as follows:

> the Consensual forms of graffiti, the ones that many can agree on, the pretty stuff, the ironic pieces that make the disillusioned masses giggle. The pretty stencils and the posters and the re-appropriating of pop culture icons to make a message, "Stop Racism!," but in fact say nothing because of the inherent consensuality. The so-called art that actually serves the capitalist captains by prettying up the hood and raises rents and dislocates inhabitants. (Brown/Freemaninov in Schacter xvi)

By dogmatically denying any political agency to the creators of these more consensual varieties of public art, Brown/Freemaninov miss a substantial amount of art that, on the one hand, might be more easily commodified, but that, on the other hand, also reaches a larger audience and seems to evoke fewer hostile reactions. In other words, those consensual forms of graffiti and street art are effective as a part of a rewriting of the urban space that aims to show dissent with the status quo—despite the high danger of being used for commercial purposes.

Still, the Elijah McClain mural constitutes a form of activism and social critique. Directly underneath McClain's name, written in large black and blue letters with blossoms of various flowers in the background, appears a hashtag: #spraytheirnames. As the hashtag suggests, this mural contributes to a larger counterscript that draws attention to police violence and the resulting deaths of people of color by inscribing their names into the city. The two Denver-based artists Thomas 'Detour' Evans and Hiero Veiga, who started the hashtag and the corresponding website, travel the country to collaborate with "black, brown and supporting ally artists to paint murals focused on black and brown victims of police brutality" (spraytheirname.com). They do so out of the urge to "give a voice to individuals who have been shut out, oppressed, and silenced," as they express it on their website. In an interview for dailycamera.com, Evans states that for him, art and activism are always intertwined, and the artists' role is to "try to as much as they can [to] embed truth about current times and what they are exploring." Next to this documenting or archiving task, which can be related to graffiti's function as a societal metadiscourse (see Gottlieb 5), Evans describes his work as centered on "remembering those that have been lost and using it as a healing tool and a way where people can have some therapy" (dailycamera.com). Especially in the context of the BLM movement, the traumatic events that make up its origin, and the history of violence against ethnic minorities in the US, this focus on healing from, with, and for the affected communities appears to be one of the essential functions of this art. In the mural, the words "love" and "respect" (fig. 1) frame McClain's portrait on both sides and reinforce the healing approach of the artists.

In addition to this collaborative initiative of two artists, spectators are also unequivocally encouraged to take action themselves through the use of the hashtag and thereby support the movement via donations that can be made on their website. In this context, the artists' use of the hashtag becomes an urban "tactic" of contestation in de Certeau's sense (36), as well as a means of participating in public discourse from below. Similarly, the Elijah McClain mural was—and its digital remnants still are—not only an RIP mural in the conventional sense but a form of social activism. They communicate agency, and the hashtag constitutes an incentive to intervene in the urban social construct through direct inscription into the city's fabric by adding another layer to the city's text with a spray can. The hashtag asks people to participate in the active construction of the city by creating visible signs of their anger, pain, and frustration. Translated into the form of social media posts, the dissemination of their art and message is reinforced in the digital space. In this remediated form, the image lacks the affective immediacy of the mural itself, but it potentially reaches millions of people all over the world.[7]

The multilayered complexity of the chosen example points to the palimpsest-like structure of public art in general and graffiti in particular. The example's inherent ambiguity is not only evident with regard to its political activism but also to the potential to commodify street art aesthetics and the resulting multitude of possible interpretations and framings. Both resist fixed readings and invite viewers to proceed with a differentiated examination of the art, of her- or himself, and of society in general. As a form of inscription in space, graffiti is characterized by its transience or removability. The process of counterscripting, however, tends to never be complete and always leave traces of what has been there before: While the Elijah McClain mural on the brewery's wall has long been removed, the photos of it and its political message live on in the digital space of social media. This circumstance will become even more apparent in the second example of BLM graffiti that will be analyzed in the following paragraphs.

SECOND SITE: THE EXTENSIVELY TAGGED COLORADO STATE CAPITOL

While the first scrutinized site was closely connected to RIP murals, the second example to be discussed here was painted in the context of BLM protests at the Colorado State Capitol in Denver. This site is connected to a very different subgenre within the art form of graffiti, namely tagging. This art is oftentimes considered to be "unaesthetic" or just plain "ugly" by many residents of the city. Nonetheless, tagging tends to adhere to the same logic and aesthetics of other forms of graffiti and is meant to enhance the aesthetic appearance of their medium. Indeed tagging, or in other words, the writing of a moniker with a marker or a spray can in subway cars or around the city, was the predecessor of more elaborate forms of graffiti such as throw-ups, bombings, larger productions, up to whole-cars or even whole-trains (see Felisbret). Those first tags were not as refined—they did not possess the almost calligraphic aesthetics that tagging would eventually acquire. Rather, the focus of these early

---

7. The usage of digital means such as websites and social media has been described for female writers by Latinx Feminist Performance Studies scholar Jessica Nydia Pabón-Colón. She labels those digital activities by artists "digital ups" (25). This term appears equally applicable for the dissemination of art in other contexts, or, in other words, the "getting up" in the digital spaces in general.

artists was on visual representation through quantity, or in other words, getting "up" in their neighborhood, borough, or even all parts of the city (see Bloch). Out of this competition, however, more elaborate styles developed as another way of getting recognition besides pure quantity.

Writing about the various styles and different modes of graffiti and street art, from those widely considered to be aesthetically pleasing like murals or poster-collages, to those oftentimes categorized as vandalism such as tags or throw-ups, anthropologist and curator Rafael Schacter claims that "these illicit artefacts are both decorative and adjunctive[;] they are accessories to a primary surface, forms of embellishment upon an ancillary plane, and hence objects with a fundamental ornamental status" (26). This analysis would apply to the majority of graffiti created in cities around the globe. Although the aesthetics of tagging, for example, might not be understandable or pleasing for every urban dweller, graffiti writers evaluate the mastery or lack thereof in tags as in any other artistic style. Indeed, a *good* tagging style is understood as the basis for a graffiti writer's art by most practitioners.[8]

This ornamental function that Schacter describes, or in other words, a beautification or adornment of the medium and thus of the urban space, is not the intended effect of the BLM tags to be considered here. Neither is it the advancement of the art as a modern form of urban calligraphy that is at the core of these graffiti. In the case of the tagging of the Colorado State Capitol in Denver by BLM supporters in the summer of 2020, the contrary is the case, as we will show in the following paragraphs. The motivation is not the promotion of an individual's (alter-)ego and their art, but about visibility in a political sense and a clearly defined political message. Thus, the few tags of a writer's name are by far outnumbered by political slogans and abbreviations thereof, as well as the names of victims of police violence such as Trayvon Martin, Michael Brown, Freddie Gray, Corey Jones, Eric Garner, George Floyd, Breonna Taylor, and local youth Elijah McClain, whose hometown of Aurora lies only about ten miles away from the Colorado State Capitol. By writing their names, activists carry out a counterscript that simultaneously criticizes police violence, generates a community among people of color who suffer from this racialized brutality, and commemorates its victims. The written names of the victims evoke the narratives of their deaths in the shortest and thus quickest way possible. Ryan, Foote, and Azaryahu identify a similar narrative condensation in commemorative street names as "a 'title' of a story that stands for and encapsulates a life story of a person or an account of an

---

8. For a detailed description of the relevance of tagging in graffiti, see, for example, the documentary *Infamy* (2005) directed by Doug Pray, which features great artists such as SABER, CLAW, or EARSNOT.

event. In this capacity they weave history and memory into spatial and social practices of everyday life" (143). What the tags accomplish is to achieve such inscriptions without having to wait to be sanctioned by officials. "A city-text has many authors over time—such as successive municipal committees and councils in charge of naming streets but also chiefs of police and national authorities involved in approving names" (Ryan, Foote, and Azaryahu146). Tagging the victims' names, on the other hand, offers an immediate possibility to inscribe their narratives into the urban space and, in Ryan, Foote, and Azaryahu's terms, to become active as an author of the city-text.

Most of the additional tags painted on the Capitol are commonly known abbreviations, such as BLM, ACAB, or FTP.[9] Another tag that has been painted frequently and might not be as easily decipherable is F12. The "12" in this abbreviation plays with ambiguity; however, it is often interpreted as a code for either the police or the Drug Enforcement Administration. In other interpretations, the "12" has been connected to a legal jury in a court case, which in a so-called *petit jury* consists of twelve jurors. Regardless of the exact reference, it is clearly a sign of the rejection of the government in its current form, no matter if it is the executive or the jurisdictive branch of it. Next to those abbreviations, there are also tagged political slogans calling to "Decolonize Denver" or "Defund DPD"—to cut the budget of the local police department—all tying into the overarching theme against police violence and racial discrimination.

Those political tags should be understood as "social and political commentary" (Gottlieb 5) in the historical context of police violence toward people of color in the United States of America. Historian Robin D. G. Kelley illuminates the history of the hostile relationship between the US and its population of Black and Indigenous People of Color (BIPOC), which was intensified even further by the loss of jobs in postindustrial cities and the federal government's "war on drugs" that fed the prison-industrial-complex at the cost of young Black and Brown men and their families. As a result of this war, US police forces became more and more militarized, as Kelley states, including "high-powered police helicopters, patrolmen in riot gear, and even small tanks armed with battering rams [that] became part of the urban landscape in the early 1980s" (48). Kelley goes further back in time by tracing the racialized attacks of white hegemony against people of color to its origin that has "been historically rooted in a colonial encounter" (24). With a detailed description of the seemingly endless violence toward African American, Latinx, and Native American people throughout the last two and a half centuries, Kelley

---

9. ACAB is an acronym for *All Cops Are Bastards*, FTP for *Fuck the Police*.

underlines the systemic nature of this oppression.[10] Historian Khalil Gibran Muhammad shines a light on yet another facet of systemic oppression. In *The Condemnation of Blackness: Race, Crime and the Making of Modern Urban America* (2011), he analyzes how "ideas of racial inferiority and crime became fastened to African Americans by contrast to ideas of class and crime that shaped views of European immigrants and working-class whites" (6). Those hegemonic discourses construct Blackness as criminal by default, while criminal behavior of white people is justified by their economic circumstances.

Within this framework and history of racialized marginalization, the tags of BLM supporters do not constitute a form of urban calligraphy but a clear political message of dissent. A message that is underlined and enforced by its specific aesthetic properties and in this functionality differs from other forms of tagging. As we argue, their aesthetics consciously break with mainstream conventions and try to disrupt hegemonic norms, not only but also on an aesthetic level. Their destructive visual properties correspond with the success of the counterscript of making society aware of the persistent racialized systemic violence. Although this polarizing aesthetic also results in dismissive reactions, the conscious breaking of aesthetic convention and property law parallels the violent realities experienced by (parts of) the BIPOC community and seems to offer an adequate means of expression. Thus, these tags are not meant to ornament the Capitol building and by doing so support the order that it represents. The contrary is the case; they pose a means of deconstruction of the monument and of the oppressive system that it embodies to many people living in the US. Designed by Elijah E. Myers and built from white granite in the 1890s, the Colorado State Capitol is situated slightly higher than the rest of downtown Denver. Its elevated position underlines the representative and symbolic quality of the monument, and, as anthropologist Lisa Maya Knauer and historian Daniel J. Walkowitz point out, the political stakes are high in the fight over representation and what kind of history is told by monuments such as the State Capitol in Colorado:

> [This] can be seen in struggles over the representation of the nation in its monuments, museums, and other public history sites where the various interested parties cannot agree on what the proper tone or the overarching narrative should be. (2)

The messages written in spray paint contrast with the white stone of the monument and clearly communicate the group's antagonism toward systemic

---

10. On discourses trying to naturalize systemic racism by disguising it as individual acts, see Lipsitz.

racism and police violence. Like on a palimpsest, the words that have been written on the Capitol can be removed—but the symbolic action along with stains of the paint will probably remain not only in the porous stone of the monumental building but also in the minds of the people in Denver.[11]

In accordance with the aforementioned, the extensive tagging of this monument can be read as a clear sign of the contestation of the system it represents and a claiming of the space for the group. The tags create a particular aesthetic grounded in dissent by applying destructive force and ostensibly unaesthetic creative production. However, this anti-aesthetic appearance is neither the result of accident, coincidence, nor a lack of ability that results in a design that many may consider ugly or even repulsive.[12] Rather, we argue that this particular style becomes a suitable vehicle for the deconstruction of signs of coloniality and the manifestations of hegemonic power in the form of monuments. Through being ostensibly *ugly,* the crude writing affectively conveys the pain and anger stirred by decades of experiencing violence and abuse. On a textual level, these tags condense this anger into slogans and insults that, on a physical level, deface the monument underneath and the hegemony it represents. At the same time, the application of this style serves as an active renegotiation of established aesthetics and thus a refusal of Eurocentric norms passed down in, for example, art, architecture, education, and literary canons in the US. The multiplicity of graffiti/tags with their palimpsestic layering of different styles, colors, and words thus creates a new aesthetic that embodies a visual canon of different and dissenting voices.

Following Michel de Certeau's observation of bottom-up practices, the tags on the Colorado state Capitol by BLM activists mark the temporal (re-)appropriation of an urban space by its residents. Danish psychologist Cecilia Schøler Nielsen describes tagging as a social practice that is "seen almost everywhere and function[s] as a way of claiming a space, an object, or an area" (304). In direct antagonism to this social function, numerous

---

11. Along these lines, the monument had already been an important site of protest during the time of the Chicano Civil Rights Movement or *El Movimiento.* In 1969 a joined rally of participants of a Chicano/a Youth Conference and activists connected to César Chávez's United Farm Workers Union demonstrated on the Capitol's steps, took down the US-American flag, and replaced it with a Mexican flag. A visually explicit form of protest and contestation that can be compared to the monument's tagging by BLM supporters in the summer of 2020.

12. The tagging of the State Capitol by BLM supporters can be read as an anti-aesthetic approach to art: It presents a clear refusal of an artificial separation of life and art in Nietzsche's sense, who argued against art that revolves around the aesthetic object and its consumption in a state of disinterested pleasure and described art's affective connection to life as its central characteristic (see Wall 73). While for Nietzsche this affect automatically entails a beautification of life, Heidegger stresses that art's affect is not limited to beauty and the satisfaction it provides but that art can also evoke feelings of dislike and rejection (Wall 81). Exactly this affective property seems to be a crucial part of the polarizing tags on the State Capitol.

attempts are made in public discourse to frame this sort of graffiti as violent and responsible for the decline of urban neighborhoods, as, for example, in the broken windows theory by the social scientists James Q. Wilson and George L. Kelling (1982)—developments that seem to correlate with disinvestment by the state and/or the municipality and not with some layers of spray paint.[13] Yet, the severe penalties that are still placed on painting graffiti demonstrate the longevity with which even false theories can affect urban planning, policing policies, and legislation. Moreover, they also highlight the struggle for the sovereignty of interpretation over public space, as well as the level of admission or prevention of dissenting voices in a society. This is not an attempt to conceal the fact that graffiti can be a destructive practice as well, for example, by scratching windows on busses, subway, and trains or by extensive tagging, as in the case of the Colorado State Capitol. Nevertheless, it is not a practice that is violent toward people or one that encourages criminal activities as has been collocated in the discourse on graffiti and tagging in the past. Especially in the context of the BLM movement, it should be read as a form of nonviolent protest. The only people who are at risk are the ones who risk their own well-being by expressing their dissent through this medium (see Bloch).

CONCLUSION

After looking at two distinct sites of BLM graffiti in Denver, a wide range of aesthetics as well as functionalities become apparent, which despite their diversity seem to have the same goal of rewriting US-American society to achieve equal rights for people of color and the end of race-based police violence. From consensual mural productions that adorn the walls of the city's art districts to the symbolic deconstruction of a state monument by means of extensive tagging, the aesthetics applied in expressing dissent appear to be no less ambiguous than other forms of art. As manifestations of activism and protest, these different graffiti fluctuate between poles of consensus and agonism, beautification and destruction, as well as between being easily commodified and being instantly rejected by the public for being too polarizing. Despite this polarizing nature and the occasionally conscious breaking of not only aesthetic norms but also property laws, their condemnation by parts of the media as well as the general public seems to be a superficial and rash judgment. Instead, it seems sensible to interpret them as creative tools with which

---

13. Wilson and Kelling's debatable theory inspired New York's "zero tolerance" approach to policing. For the history of the broken windows theory, see Ansfield. For a discussion of its effects on debates in New York, see Heise (esp. 42–43).

dissent can be affectively communicated from a marginalized position—or, as de Certeau describes it, from the "space of the other" (37).

This creative expression takes place in a medium that through its availability as well as its grounding in public space seems to be more democratic than many others. The use of unsanctioned art in public space as a means of community-building and placemaking is directly related to the inaccessibility of other types of media for a large part of the inhabitants of urban spaces of neglect. In the context of the construction of a *hip* company image situated in a city's flourishing art district, however, the commodification of the art by city or company can result in a depoliticization of the residents' "tactic" (De Certeau 36) to (re)claim their neighborhood through graffiti. Companies try to create a progressive image of themselves by claiming to be an ally of a particular social movement, such as the BLM movement, or just try to create a "cool" and "authentic" place for their customers, thus hollowing out the practice of resistance while following a purely economic agenda.

Apart from the dangers of being co-opted by companies or through a city's plan to transform a neighborhood, the different varieties of graffiti that we visited at the two sites in Denver try to fulfill different functions as well. While Thomas "Detour" Evans and his colleagues beautify the city with their RIP mural for Elijah McClain, the tagging of the state Capitol follows a much more confrontational approach: It seems to be a direct inscription of frustration and anger into the city that is emphasized by its aesthetical characteristics. However, both instances present forms of graffiti, in the broadest sense of the term, and they both are united in the same counterscript that is a critique of systemic racism manifested in police violence—a function that they share, unfazed by their aesthetic variance. This circumstance fits Michel de Certeau's description of the tactical practices produced by the residents of the city that can be, as he states, "poetic as well as warlike" (xix). Along these lines, we read the graffiti created by supporters of the BLM movement as simultaneously creative and disruptive as well as beautifying society and at war with parts of it.

WORKS CITED

Ansfield, Bench. "The Broken Windows of the Bronx: Putting the Theory in Its Place." *American Quarterly*, vol. 72, no. 1. March 2020, pp. 103–27.

Bloch, Stefano. *Going All City: Struggle and Survival in LA's Graffiti Subculture*. U of Chicago P, 2019.

Brown, Dumar. *Nov York*. Xlibris, 2002.

Butler, Judith. *Precarious Life: The Powers of Mourning and Violence*. Verso, 2004.

Cervantes, Marco Antonio, and Lilliana Patricia Saldaña. "Hip Hop and *Nueva Canción* as Decolonial Pedagogies of Epistemic Justice." *Decolonization: Indigeneity, Education & Society*, vol. 4, no. 1, 2015, pp. 84–108.

Clarke, Susan E. "The New Politics in a Postindustrial City: Intersecting Policies in Denver." *Urban Neighborhoods in a New Era: Revitalization Politics in the Postindustrial City*, edited by Clarence N. Stone and Robert P. Stoker, U of Chicago P, 2015, pp. 155–80.

Clennon, Ornette D. *Black Scholarly Activism between the Academy and Grassroots*. Palgrave, 2018.

Cooper, Martha, and Henry Chalfant. *Subway Art*. Holt, Rinehart and Winston, 1984.

Cunningham, Vinson. "The Future of L.A. Is Here: Robin D. G. Kelley's Radical Imagination Shows Us the Way." *Los Angeles Times*, 17 Mar. 2021, https://www.latimes.com/lifestyle/image/story/2021-03-17/robin-dg-kelley-black-marxism-protests-la-politics.

De Certeau, Michel. *The Practice of Everyday Life*. Translated by Steven Randall, U of California P, 1984.

Felisbret, Eric. *Graffiti New York*. Abrams, 2009.

George, Nelson. *Hip Hop America*. Penguin Books, 1998.

Gottlieb, Lisa. *Graffiti Art Styles: A Classification System and Theoretical Analysis*. McFarland, 2008.

Heise, Thomas. *The Gentrification Plot: New York and the Postindustrial Crime Novel*. Columbia UP, 2021.

Kelley, Robin D. G. "'Slangin' Rocks . . . Palestinian Style': Dispatches from the Occupied Zones of North America." *Police Brutality: An Anthology*, edited by Jill Nelson, Norton, 2000, pp. 21–59.

Knauer, Lisa Maya, and Daniel J. Walkowitz. "Introduction: Memory, Race, and the Nation in Public Space." *Contested Histories in Public Space: Memory, Race, and Nation*, edited by Daniel. J. Walkowitz and Lisa Maya Knauer, Duke UP, 2009, pp. 1–27.

Lebron, Christopher J. *The Making of Black Lives Matter: A Brief History of an Idea*. Oxford UP, 2017.

Lipsitz, George. "The Logic of 'Illogical' Opposition: Tools and Tactics for Tough Times." *Antiracism Inc.: Why the Way We Talk about Racial Justice Matters*, edited by Felice Blake, Paula Ioanide, and Alison Reed, Punctum Books, 2019, pp. 273–93.

McCort, Kalene. "Muralist Thomas 'Detour' Evans Brings Activism, Emotionally Charged Artistry to New Heights." *Boulder Daily Camera*, 29 Aug. 2020, https://thedairy.org/muralist-thomas-detour-evans-brings-activism-emotionally-charged-artistry-to-new-heights/.

Muhammad, Khalil Gibran. *The Condemnation of Blackness: Race, Crime, and the Making of Modern Urban America*. Harvard UP, 2010.

Nielsen, Cecilia Schøler. "The Democratic Potential of Artistic Expression in Public Space: Street Art and Graffiti as Rebellious Acts." *Street Art of Resistance*, edited by Sarah H. Awad and Brady Wagoner, Palgrave, 2017, pp. 301–23.

Pabón-Colón, Jessica Nydia. *Graffiti Grrlz: Performing Feminism in the Hip Hop Diaspora*. New York UP, 2018.

Pray, Doug, director. *Infamy*. https://www.youtube.com/watch?v=po_hM9oTgD4. Accessed 1 Mar. 2021.

Ryan, Marie-Laure, Kenneth Foote, and Maoz Azaryahu. *Narrating Space / Spatializing Narrative: Where Narrative Theory and Geography Meet*. The Ohio State UP, 2016.

Santino, Jack. "Performative Commemoratives: Spontaneous Shrines and the Public Memorialization of Death." *Spontaneous Shrines and the Public Memorialization of Death,* edited by Jack Santino, Palgrave, 2006, pp. 5–15.

Schacter, Rafael. *Ornament and Order: Graffiti, Street Art and the Parergon.* Ashgate, 2014.

Serwer, Adam. "The Coronavirus Was an Emergency until Trump Found Out Who Was Dying." *The Atlantic,* 8 May 2020, https://www.theatlantic.com/ideas/archive/2020/05/americas-racial-contract-showing/611389/.

Spray Their Name. Arts Collective #spraytheirname. *Behance,* https://www.behance.net/gallery/107401679/Spray-Their-Name.

Sudbury, Julia, and Margo Okazawa-Rey. *Activist Scholarship: Antiracism, Feminism, and Social Change.* Routledge, 2009.

Turim, Maureen. *Flashbacks in Film: Memory and History.* 1989. Routledge, 2013.

Wall, Tobias. *Das unmögliche Museum: Zum Verhältnis von Kunst und Kunstmuseen der Gegenwart.* Transcript, 2015.

Warwick, Ben. "Epic Brewing's Elijah McClain Mural Repainted as Part of Regular Art Rotation." *CBSN Denver,* 31 Aug. 2020, https://www.cbsnews.com/colorado/news/elijah-mcclain-mural-epic-brewing-art-rotation/.

Wilson, James Q., and George L. Kelling. "Broken Windows: The Police and Neighborhood Safety." *The Atlantic,* March 1982, https://www.theatlantic.com/magazine/archive/1982/03/broken-windows/304465/.

CHAPTER 2

Walking Down Woodward

(Re)Telling a City's Stories through Urban Figures

JULIANE BOROSCH AND
BARBARA BUCHENAU

Etching out, renovating, revolutionizing, revolting, and recreating: Stories told about Detroit's Woodward Avenue are stories of radical spatial, temporal, and social transformation. These stories activate the makeover "narrativity" (Ryan) and the "scriptive" materiality (Bernstein 69) that is the everyday fare of any major city, whose inhabitants use structural elements of narrative as well as scriptive props to project and generate "attachment" (Felski), "belonging" (Bieger), and ethical engagement (Phelan) in contexts of complex sociohistorical, spatial, and economic change and displacement.[1] Storytelling on and about Woodward is an interesting example of community-based figural

---

1. For the narrativity of urban structures, see Ryan, Foote, and Azaryahu 139. For the "scriptivity" (Bernstein 89) of a material object serving as prop that "forces a person into an awareness of the self in material relation to the thing," see Bernstein 69–70. Bernstein emphasizes how "scriptive things" encourage a merging of acts of writing/reading with performative acts in space and physical matter. We are grateful to Stephanie Leigh Batiste for bringing Bernstein to our attention. For storytelling as a form of "attachment" driven by interpretation as a means to craft relationships and to build connections otherwise missing, see Felski 121–63. The agencies involved in storytelling as a technique of "belonging" are the subject of Bieger's argument. The figural and rhetorical dimension of an ethical engagement of both the audience the storyteller/artist has in mind and the narratees addressed are discussed by Phelan.

formation. This everyday narrativity and engagement with scriptive matter differs from narrative fiction in that it actively calls on its *readers* to *intellectually, emotionally, and bodily respond* to "the fact that the future is a space of yet unrealized potentiality" (Bode and Dietrich 1). The power of narrativity in textures such as poetry, historiography, philosophy, and, by implication, urban infrastructure was theorized by Marie-Laure Ryan as early as 1992. When Ryan defined "figural narrativity" as the process by which "the reader extracts characters and events out of images through a process of individuation and temporalization" (378), she circumscribes the specific (self-)explanatory activities of an urban walker. Ryan adds that "the figural plot must be subjected to an allegorical reading in which characters and events become again bearers of conceptual values" (378). This figural dimension of both storytelling activities and urban walking are the topics of this chapter. It will explore very concrete and effective acts of identification, interpretation, and formation that revitalize a spatial and temporal hermeneutics of the *figura* that has not been brought to rest with Erich Auerbach's discussion of Christian mimetic world-making.

We will put this hypothesis of scriptive urban *figurae* and figural narrativity to the test on downtown Detroit's most prominent street. Throughout its history, Woodward Avenue has been read as a space of potentiality inviting realization, especially by those who felt empowered by the prophetic thrust of the urban figures of and on Woodward. The avenue today is the most important one of the five main roads segmenting the large downtown of Detroit. Beyond its condensed pedestrian point of departure at the waterfront of the Detroit River, it is a crucial part of Michigan State's trunkline highway system and a prominent witness to the massive transformations that occur along its twenty-seven-mile north-to-south course. It is "one of America's most iconic roads," as Michigan-based reporter Jessica Shepherd has said. As such it is not only a *sujet* for serial remediation and a *fabula* for a broad array of stories. It is also a *persona* in transcultural figuration, most prominently known for its role in abrogating the social, political, and economic functions of the Saginaw Trail, an early modern road utilizing a precolonial Anishinaabe path (see Pielack). Woodward Avenue also superseded several subsequent infrastructures for social interaction—trails and roads built by the many Indigenous, French, British, Dutch, and other colonial actors in the region. Today, it is held accountable for its figural promises of colonial, industrial, and neoindustrial expansion (see Kickert).

ON THE PROMISES OF FIGURAL WALKING

This chapter takes seriously the idea that—for the urban walker—a street has and produces narrativity.[2] In order to contribute to the volume's goal of developing a methodology for the analysis of urban scripts—strategic forms of placemaking that try to prompt, prescribe, and narrate possible futures without abandoning popular concerns with the status quo—we here set out to test the imaginative impact of figures. Figures, as we want to understand them, are compounds that yank together, conjoin, and connect (a) a concrete urban instantiation—for example, an artwork, a map, or a sign; (b) a persona—sometimes alive, mostly historical, but often simply invented; and (c) frequently also a *figura*. The *figura* recalls Erich Auerbach's observations concerning the interpretive bridging of unrelated people, events, and regimes across time and space (see Auerbach in Auerbach, Porter, and Newman 96). This futurity-driven bridging is enabled whenever comparative interpretations understand one historical moment as a fulfillment of an ostensible promise made by an earlier historical moment, thus turning both events into ideas that develop a life of their own beyond the framework of the original occurrence. From a dual—close-up and long-distance—perspective we offer to take our readers along on a figurative walk down the very short walkable section of Woodward Avenue, a stretch of less than a quarter of a mile. One of us, Juliane Borosch, has taken this walk innumerable times during her work as a visiting scholar at Wayne State University in 2021 and 2022. Juliane's literal urban walking was part of her fieldwork, which enabled the "observant participation" (Wacquant 2) in several Detroit-based developments of climate-friendly historic preservations directed by Diane van Buren and Ernest Zachary. Another one of us, Barbara Buchenau, has taken these walks only via (pre)mediation and textual exposure. Barbara's armchair urban walking is part of her work on literary, imaginative, and political figurations of historical, spatial, and social conflicts in colonial and present-day North America.

Readers will soon realize that walking as an urban practice takes less effort and certainly less time than writing and reading about it. This temporal

---

2. For the topos and figure of the urban walker, the influential accounts in Benjamin's *Arcades Project* (416–55, 516–26) or de Certeau's chapter on "Walking in the City" (91–110) come to mind. In his history of the postmodern displacement of walking as a daily necessity, regional historian Joseph A. Amato addresses walking as "a language having its own vernacular, dialects and idioms" (4); it is arguably a form of "talking" (4) that is particularly relevant in discussions of urban transformations. "Walking has continued to be a focus in urban restoration. Increasingly it is understood that the walker makes and becomes the city he or she walks. It is conceded that walking plays an indispensable role in restoring neighborhoods, luring tourists and shoppers, designing beautiful streets, and adding vitality to an entire city. It is also understood that walking cannot be politically willed or conjured by planning" (Amato 273).

extension of a dense geographical space is another dimension of the collusions between the fixed and the temporary nature of the city that take shape in urban figures—material and immaterial (see Autry and Walkowitz 1). In his influential chapter "Walking in the City," Michel de Certeau states that "pedestrian movements form one of these 'real systems whose existence in fact makes up the city'" (97). This transformative urban practice is heightened when walking readers and scholarly analysts write about their experiences. Their "operations of walking on can be traced on city maps in such a way as to transcribe their paths (here well-trodden, there very faint)" (de Certeau 97). Note, for instance, how Leslie Pielack's description transcribes Indigenous into national place, while also transcribing space into time:

> The Saginaw Trail was the key to gaining access to Michigan's wild country and all it had to offer. It was so significant to the settlement patterns and economic foundation of our state that it could be said that the Saginaw Trail built Michigan and was the most important reason that Detroit became the Motor City and, ultimately, the global center of the auto industry. (17)

The trail-turned-street once was a convenient starting point for European-American exploration. With the changed name and claim to the land, Woodward Avenue turned into "the invisible parts of the 'Indianized' landscape and the lingering legacies" (Jarzombek n. pag.). Soon enough new walkers used this road as Detroit became a gateway to the West. Especially after the Erie Canal was opened in 1825, thousands came through Detroit and walked along the Saginaw Trail/Woodward Avenue. The material conditions of and on Woodward Avenue changed with the development and growth of the settlement, and along the way, walking down Woodward first became a choice, then a peril in times of increased infrastructural focus on cars. Today, it is turning back into a place of increasing walkability—at least for a quarter of a mile.

Conrad Kickert's study of Detroit's planning history and his insights into the present-day "rebirth" (269) of downtown Detroit inspire the key question this chapter will explore: Why does walking on and talking about Woodward so easily spark, even demand, a strong sense of futurity, of possibility and indeterminacy? Offering to record and analyze our concrete, but certainly not representative, transatlantic story-based urban experience, the argument draws attention to the hermeneutic and interpretive process that allows walkers to be readers, performers, and meaning-makers, who place urban figures in ever new relation to each other and themselves. These are figural interpretations produced by active *readers* and *actors* of and in the environment. Urban meaning makers engage with this potentially "*multi-linear*" setting (Bode and

Dietrich 17) as readers would do with *Future Narratives* (1). In walking, they understand public sculptures, plazas, and artwork as figures, or "nodes" (xvii) as literary theorist Christoph Bode and Rainer Dietrich would have it, that "contain [stage, present, act out] situations that allow for more than one continuation" (2). As Bode might argue, how we "enter situations that fork into different branches and actually *experience* that 'what happens next' may well depend upon us, upon our decisions, our actions, our values and motivations" (Bode and Dietrich 1). And yet walking, observing, and being "observant" (2) in the sense of Loïc Wacquant's immersive urban research must also be rooted in the past and immersed in the present moment. Walking links the narrative future to selectively activated senses of past stories. This interlinking is an activity that draws attention to the walkers' engagement with urban figures that promise to redeem and deliver exemplary prophecies of the past. It is, in fact, a politically consequential art of yanking together distinctive moments in time and space, as Erich Auerbach might have seen it.

Writing "Figura" in Istanbul in 1938, Erich Auerbach was the first to describe the transhistorical and transcultural, interreligious powers of figural interpretation. Although his concern was with late Antiquity and medieval literature, his understanding of the image-word compounds described in the hermeneutic procedure of the *figura* can improve our understanding of urban figuration and its visionary, future-oriented energies. What he identified as the most basic interpretive activity of the ancient Church Fathers—an act of visually and verbally interweaving historical personas to build a shared history and establish viable connections between distinct sociopolitical settings—did not stop once the mutual interdependence between Old and New Testament that had been forged through figural interpretation became widely accepted. Instead, the ancient tradition of prefiguration, fulfillment, and refiguration described in Auerbach's "figura," also known as religious typology, proved to have been vastly effective in colonial and early national North American writings as well. Especially colonial writers such as Mary Rowlandson, John Williams, and the Jesuit missionaries, but also Indigenous and African American Enlightenment writers, as well as the writers of the American Renaissance turned to figural interpretation in efforts to make sense of their own standing in a world undergoing radical transformations. In the old Northwest of the continent, of which Detroit was one of the most important intercolonial, interreligious centers, typological thinking and figural interpretation revitalized into religious readings and performances of the history of settler colonization (Bercovitch 147–67; Buchenau 179–81).

In Detroit's public history, this heritage of figural interpretation is quickly spotted in the very insistence that a major road such as Woodward Avenue fulfills the best promises of the local Indigenous societies of earlier centuries (see Pielack). Located in Detroit's downtown central business district, today's Woodward Avenue was planned as a replacement for the Saginaw Trail, a heavily traveled road allowing travel inland through the wetlands from the banks of the Detroit River. This figural etching out, overwriting, and colonization of a major Indigenous route establishes Woodward Avenue as Saginaw's legal successor—despite the force employed in its displacement. Its designer was Judge Augustus B. Woodward (1774–1827), the first Chief Justice of the Territory of Michigan (established in 1805), a man deeply involved in creating and implementing the legal protocols for the wresting of power from the many Indigenous, imperial, and early national competitors for the control over the land west of the thirteen states that had ratified the Constitution. Woodward arrived in Detroit right after a fire had destroyed the settlement in 1805, and it was one of his first tasks to develop the plan for rebuilding Detroit that would suit his "astronomical interest and observations of star movements" (Pielack 33) but also more concrete ideas for city planning. His city plan was never fully implemented but survived as a story of future possibilities. It features a number of "interlocking hexagons that created angular lots of various sizes. These were intersected by wide streets that radiated outward from the riverfront and theoretically into the far distance" (Pielack 33–34). An instance of European-style baroque town planning, it establishes a series of focal points that emphasize the new powers of the republic, but equally recall the "highly expressive sensibility" and "emotional theatricality" of eighteenth-century European demonstrations of power (Cohen and Szabo 2).

Visible in Conrad Kickert's map (see fig. 2.1), the layout of the modern city only partially includes this design. And yet, Leslie Pielack's language choice underscores an urgent sense of futurity: "In Woodward's ambitious vision, all roads led from Detroit as the center of the territorial universe" (36–37). The future city to be developed from the plan was conceived as a center and nodal point located at the intersection of at least three imperial peripheries: British America, the expanding United States, and "Indian Country" or "Indian Territory," as it was called since the Royal Proclamation of 1763. Detroit's growing function as a gateway for people seeking liberation from countless shades of nineteenth-century and twentieth-century bondage and slavery reverberates only ever so vaguely in Pielack's use of frontier imagery,

> a wide street that *led northwest away* from the river and into the forest [. . .]. This major street [. . .] bisected the new city plan and was the center of activity. Its planned width—120 feet—befuddled many, who saw it as a waste of perfectly good property lots. [. . .] [Its] predominance foreshadowed its importance to come, and its outer reaches into the forest would *lead to a great future* for Michigan. (34, emphasis added)

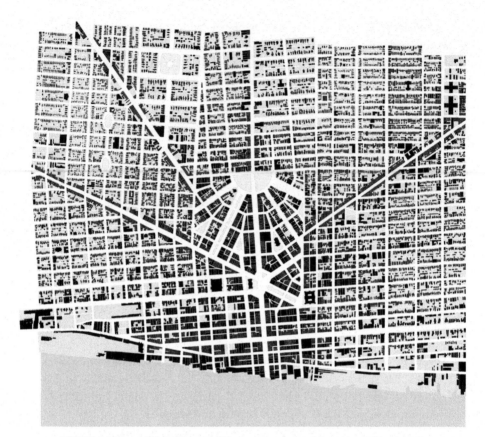

FIGURE 2.1. Conrad Kickert's map of the 1911 remnants of Augustus B. Woodward's design, adapted from figure 2.5 in Conrad Kickert, *Dream City: Creation, Destruction and Reinvention in Downtown Detroit*. © 2019 The MIT Press, p. 49, with the kind permission of the author and copyright holder and MIT Press.

Space and time are yanked together in this description of a plan never fully realized and in its physical existence, if not its ideational content, lost to later generations. Pielack's language builds a bridge for a figuration that Auerbach would call "a historically real prophecy": Woodward's Detroit becomes the shadow of later dispensations for its readers centuries after the initial design (78).[3] Woodward did name the street that superseded the Saginaw Trail after

---

3. The *figura* as a historically real prophecy observed by Auerbach interlinks two events in history that are both real, yet unconnected to each other: "The prophetic figure is a material historical fact and is fulfilled by material historical facts" (Auerbach in Auerbach, Porter, and Newman 80). Yet the linkage between these events is usually rather flimsy: "Shadowy similarities in the structure of events or in the circumstances that accompany them are often enough to make the figura recognizable" (79).

himself, Woodward Avenue. The second main thoroughfare along the river was named after his idol and then president Thomas Jefferson.[4] As Derek Alderman points out, "place naming represents a means of claiming the landscape, materially and symbolically, and using its power to privilege one world view over another" ("Place" 199). The place claimed was an important part of the infrastructure built by Anishinaabe, Potowatomi, Ottawa, and other Indigenous communities in the region. But after the partial realization of the plan, it was Woodward rather than any Native name that became the "sign of a space and provide[d] symbolic reference to the underlying logic maintained within it" (Hickey 1). After this rewriting by urban planning, there might be much less of a chance to remember Detroit's past as a commons for multiple Indigenous and colonial interest groups. Woodward's cartographic design for Detroit's future was barely put into action, and yet it endures in conversations and cartographic images of downtown Detroit's layout until today (Kickert 11–19, 74).

ON WALKING FOR PROPHECIES

Our walk starts where Woodward Avenue relates to the radial design once envisioned: Walking away from Campus Martius toward Hart Plaza on the riverfront will provide several encounters with urban figures (see fig. 2.2).

These figures are strategic embodiments of a place's—official or authorized—public story; simultaneously, they are expressions of contested geographic memory that invite further examinations of the layering, (re)writing, and performing of urban scripts, symbolized and embodied by these figures. Scripts, in this case, refer to strategic and embodied urban place-making activities that interweave narrative—the meaning-making activity that brings a variety of events and people into a coherent order—with matching medial frames and figurative extensions. In other words, these figural components of paradigmatic urban scripts invite the urban dwellers to attach their active sense of a concrete place to an abstracted mode of temporal and spatial thinking about its past, present, and future. The figural dimension of the script thus provides both material embodiment and ideational bridging of temporal and spatial differences and divides. Multifaceted urban figures, including statues,

---

4. "While belonging to master-narratives of national and local history, each commemorative street name is also a 'title' of a story that stands for and encapsulates a life story of a person or an account of an event. In this capacity they weave history and memory into spatial and social practices of everyday life. The commemorative function assigned to street names predominates in the naming process, when eligibility for commemoration and the placing of the commemoration in urban space reign supreme" (Ryan, Foote, and Azaryahu 143).

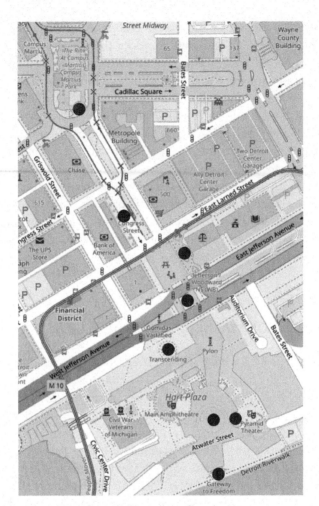

FIGURE 2.2. Walking among figural sculptures on Woodward Avenue, downtown Detroit, 2021. Map data © OpenStreetMap (ODbL).

monuments, streets, or squares, invite questions concerning the use of public space. Finally, these urban figures are also key agents in processes of cyclical (re)negotiation of narratives that ostensibly address a place's past, even as they are geared toward the future. The figures on Woodward invite the walker to turn their locations into "storied places," a move which, according to Virginia Reinburg, "highlights the collaborative process of creating significant places by means of story [. . .] over time and across space" (1–2).

Campus Martius is one such "storied place"; it condenses time and space. The nexus point of the Woodward Plan of 1805, the former militia gathering ground later became a public square and was "envisioned to be the central focus point of the city's activities" (Poremba 12), thus revitalizing the core ideas of baroque town planning. At the beginning of the Civil War, Michigan troops gathered on Campus Martius before moving south. After the war, Campus Martius was hence the location of a publicly funded war memorial as a form of instant commemoration, inviting stories of attachment and belonging. The *Michigan Soldiers' and Sailors' Monument* is one of the oldest Detroit monuments with its unveiling dating back to a ceremony attended by twenty-five thousand people in 1872 (see Lees). The idea for a monument had already taken shape during the war, thus seeking to render this moment in time sacred via instant commemoration (see Assmann). As the Michigan Historical Society points out,

> support for the monument extended to the community at large. While the war dragged on, community and fraternal organizations held pledge drives and bake sales to finance the project. Rev. George Taylor, a Methodist minister, organized an appeal to Michigan schoolchildren for contributions, with each donor being given a certificate of appreciation. (Vachon 16)

The monument by Randolf Rogers, the neoclassical sculptor of the *Columbus Doors* at the US Capitol (1855–61) and four prominent Civil War memorials, consists of

> a four-tiered, four-sided structure with gradual setbacks. On the first level are four bronze screaming eagles, a symbol of military strength and later, during the 20th century, the insignia of the Army's 101st Airborne Division. The second level features four male figures, each representing a branch of the 19th-century military: Infantry, Artillery, Calvary [sic], and Navy. Each was instrumental in the Union victory. While the figures on the second tier symbolize the agent of war, the third level depicts four female characters [added in 1881] that personify its spoils: Victory, Union, Emancipation, and History. On the monument's pinnacle is a 10-foot-high female figure holding a shield and sword. She is modeled after a Native-American woman and metaphorically represents Michigan. Between the second and third tiers are bas-relief figures of President Lincoln, Generals Sherman and Grant, and Admiral Farragut. (Vachon 17)

Prominently displayed on Campus Martius, this landmark with its *figurae* for "Victory, Union, Emancipation, and History" was at the center of many public gatherings, political rallies, and events until the 1950s. At that time Detroit had become a car-centric city, and Campus Martius lost its central role in civic life when much of the space gave way to streets and many activities started to move closer to the riverfront or into the suburbs. The monument's placement on a small traffic island on a major street led to a loss of status and frequentation.

Campus Martius was the starting point of the current downtown revitalization efforts that led to Detroit's frequently being dubbed "the comeback city." As political scientist Peter Eisinger explains,

> [the] face of the downtown began to change in 2003 when Compuware, a large software company headquartered in a Detroit suburb, moved its main office and 4,000 employees to a newly constructed office building in the Campus Martius area of the central business district. Spurred by this development, Detroit 300 Conservancy, a nonprofit subsidiary of the business organization Downtown Detroit Partnership, raised $20 million to create a multiuse park and central gathering place at Compuware's doorstep, and then donated it to the city. (111)

After its degradation to a traffic circle, Campus Martius is a pedestrian-friendly public square once more today. Investments by wealthy individuals such as Dan Gilbert, who "has been by far the dominant force in reshaping the downtown" (Eisinger 111) rang in an era of downtown investment and revitalization initiatives. With the Q-Line, the streetcar is back, reintroduced as part of Dan Gilbert's downtown renewal efforts, seeking to reduce automobility and thus to realize once more the potentialities of walkability within the Woodward Avenue area. Yet, a car-centered city such as Detroit still puts most pedestrians at high risk. The lack of pedestrian-friendly infrastructure is matched by the searing question of who walks by choice and who has to walk because they have no (financial) access to other forms of mobility.

In 1963 the Walk to Freedom spoke to the complex nodes offered by the multilinear *figurae* of the monument. Organized by the Detroit Council on Human Rights (DCHR), the Walk to Freedom was the largest civil rights demonstration in the US up to that day, with 125,000 people in attendance. Martin Luther King Jr. addressed the crowd in words that foreshadowed his famous "I Have a Dream" speech a few months later. A racially integrated coalition lead the march. It included the mayor of Detroit and the president of the United Automobile Workers, as well as prominent civil rights leaders such as the Reverend C. L. Franklin, who was the main organizer of the march. This consequential march is not materially memorialized on Woodward Avenue today, even though the Walk to Freedom symbolizes a historic moment that opened the possibility of Detroit "becoming the place where black America would leave behind the legacy of slavery and Jim Crow and become full partners

FIGURE 2.3. Hubert Massey's *Power to the People* (2020). Photo by Juliane Borosch, July 4, 2021.

in the prosperity of industrial America" (Fishman 34). A sense of unrealized potentiality marked the Walk to Freedom, reminding its commemorators that walking "assumes a powerful symbolic role as a means of protest and develops an enhanced potential to evoke alternative worlds and experiences" (Amato 18). This symbolism addresses us in early 2022 as we walk further down Woodward (see fig. 2.3). As part of the Juneteenth celebrations in downtown Detroit and as part of the racial justice fights and campaigns of the summer of 2020, a "microscript" of this struggle was painted onto the southbound side of Woodward Avenue between Larned and Congress (see Sulimma in chapter 7 of this collection).

Commissioned by the city, designed by Detroit-based public artist Hubert Massey, and painted onto the street by students and youth activists, the so-called street mural reads "POWER TO THE PEOPLE" (Gray). "POWER" is written in white except for the "O," which is a black circle with a red fist in it. In the wake of protests against white abuse of power and police brutality, the color of the word can stand as criticism of this prevailing system, while the black "O" encircles and embraces the fist of radical political activism used in the Black Power movement and other civil rights protests around the world, which can here serve as a challenge to these power structures. According to

Hubert Massey, the fist, color-coded in red, represents the lives lost to police violence (see Stitt). The words "TO THE" are written in black surrounded by a white frame, leaving them with a background in the color of the pavement. The framing of these two words underscores directionality: the transfer of "power" to someone else (i.e., "people") that allows for a change of the status quo, signaling social movement.[5] "PEOPLE" then is written in all white. Aside from an effective contrast to the gray pavement, the color here can be interpreted as an empty canvas, a unifying, inclusionary statement that signals "power to *all* people," just as the color white is created when mixing all the colors of the rainbow. This message is highlighted by the slogan chosen for the street mural: "Power to the People" is a social and racial justice chant used by the Civil Rights Movement, the Black Panther Party, and South African anti-Apartheid activism, but also labor activists in Britain and anti–Vietnam War student activists, among others.

The street mural follows a general trend of the summer of 2020, when activists as well as officials took to the streets and created hundreds of Black Lives Matter (BLM) pavement murals in cities across the US, most prominently in downtown Washington, DC, leading up to the White House. This practice was soon criticized by members of the BLM movement as merely performative and happening instead of concrete judicial or governmental action (possibly also as a co-optation of the movement; see Mask). "*Performative* can also refer to words that," as Deidre Mask writes with reference to the philosopher J. L. Austin, "don't just speak but act" (n. pag.). Indeed, as we have seen with Woodward and the settler-colonialist appropriation of the Saginaw Trail, naming a place is claiming a space. Although the durability of this kind of public art is limited, its ability to claim space is immediate and visible—especially compared to a tedious, official renaming process. Centrally located pavement murals proclaiming "POWER TO THE PEOPLE" or "BLACK LIVES MATTER" support the "scaling of memory" (Alderman, "Street Names" 163) to prioritize civil rights causes. Geographer Derek H. Alderman defines the "scaling of memory" as "a socially contested process of determining the geographic extent to which [something or someone] should be memorialized" ("Street Names" 163). Since the transient street murals are prominently placed in the hearts of cities, broad distribution in the media and in public history—and thus refigured survival even after destruction—is guaranteed. Given the size and placement of *Power to the People,* this pavement mural can only be experienced in its entirety from an aerial view. Ongoing traffic hides parts of the writing, and the direction of car traffic means that the

---

5. For graffiti, murals, and street art in general, see chapter 1 by Deckers and Moreno in this collection.

FIGURE 2.4. Marshall Fredericks's *The Spirit of Detroit* (1958). Photo by Juliane Borosch, July 4, 2021.

slogan can only be read backward, piece by piece from inside a vehicle. True to the message, however, the street mural empowers the individual walkers who can walk against the direction of traffic and thus read the message. Walking is an oppositional practice on Woodward in more than one sense: "Landscapes are thus inscribed not just through physical marks [. . .] but through a social engagement that serves to anchor people in place" (David and Wilson 6).

Walking down Woodward Avenue past Larned Street, we fittingly step onto a temporary installation in urban space turned permanent through public negotiation: Spirit Plaza. The plaza is named after *The Spirit of Detroit*, Michigan-based Marshall Fredericks's emblematic formation of the iconic statue, epigrammatic inscription, and seals serving as lemmata (see fig. 2.4). Cast in Oslo, Norway, and erected on Woodward Avenue in 1958, the statue is a large bronze sculpture of a near-naked man sitting cross-legged and holding up a stereotypical nuclear family in his right hand and a gilded globe radiating beams in his left. The plaque in front reveals this statue as a *figura* in the sense of "'shape' and 'form,' which is now a *praefiguratio*"—obscurely hinting at "something that will happen in the future" (Auerbach in Auerbach, Porter, and Newman 90). The plaque reads: "The artist expresses the concept that God, through the spirit of man, is manifested in the family, the noblest human relationship." The sculpture's globe cites the Woodward Plan as its own *figura*.

The emblematic setting of the sculpture intensifies this sequence of *figurae*: Behind the sculpture, a wall holds as a lemma the seal of Wayne County, also designed by Fredericks in the spirit of Christian figural interpretation.

Even though Wayne County was founded as the sixth county of the Northwest territory in 1796, it was still without a seal at the time of Fredericks's work on the emblematic ensemble. Fredericks designed the seal in 1955, figuratively representing "the signing of the peace treaty between Chief Pontiac (Ottawa) and Brig. General Anthony Wayne in 1796. [. . .] The treaty opened the land to be settled into what is now the city of Detroit. Included on the medallion are the phrases 'Seal of the County of Wayne Michigan 1796,' 'We Produce,' 'We Defend,' 'Freedom of Man' and 'In God We Trust'" (Fredericks). Obliterated is the immense death toll of the 1794 Ohio Battle of Fallen Timbers in which the army led by General Wayne destroyed the Northwestern Indian Confederacy / United Indian Nations, effectively ending Indigenous resistance to the encroachment by British and American settlers in the Great Lakes region. This seal visually and verbally reframes the colonial and imperial history of the region by using post-Christian figural interpretation to signify a peaceful transition of power in the spirit of liberty and military production.

The second seal or lemma on the wall guarding the sculpture is the seal of Detroit. Its Latin inscriptions commemorate the Detroit fire of 1805 (and hence the Woodward Plan)—"Speramus Meliora / We hope for better things" and "Resurget Cineribus / It will rise from the ashes." These words are attributed to Father Gabriel Richard, a contemporary of Augustus B. Woodward, who was commissioned to missionize and serve as pastor in Detroit in 1798. He later became the delegate of the Michigan Territory, sponsoring the rollout of settler colonialism in and beyond the territory (1823–27). The wall finally features a biblical quote as the epigram of the emblematic figural ensemble: "Now the lord is that spirit and where the spirit of the lord is, there is liberty" from 2 Corinthians 3:17. The ensemble calls on the walkers/readers to employ figural interpretation throughout their attempts at engaging with the scene on their very own terms. Iconic sculpture, lemmata, and epigram are "scriptive" (Bernstein 69) in that they invite walkers to inscribe themselves into space and time like the represented *figurae*, adopting the role and the legal authority of those whose figural depiction promises an effective transfer of power. Urban interpreters of the scene can project the threats as well as the promises and prophecies of a set of unrelated historical events into the future, thereby establishing a sequence of providential history in the making.

The figurative interpellations of the statue and its emblematic setting have been embraced by generations of Detroiters until today. Numerous transient and more permanent urban practices have produced a symbol of the city and a symbol of community: Many city logos use adaptations and simulations of the sculpture. *The bronze man* is frequently dressed up in the jerseys of local sports teams or used in other occasions of community spirit. Most recently the Spirit was masked up and dressed in colors honoring the essential workers during the COVID-19 pandemic. A pop-up square, set up in front of the statue on the last block of Woodward Avenue before the riverfront in the summer of 2017, was "designed to serve as the 'civic plaza' of Detroit," as the space in front of the statue was understood to be a "natural gathering place" (City of Detroit) for citizens. The newly pedestrianized piece of Woodward Avenue turned it into a permanent fixture to become "the first public space in the city designed for all citizens to get together, get involved, learn about local initiatives and enjoy civic, culinary and cultural attractions that highlight the many Detroit voices and a unique identity" (City of Detroit). Despite this unifying message, the square is not an uncontested space with the city council only narrowly and in a second attempt deciding to make the plaza permanent amid protests by drivers for closing down one of the city's main crossings. The fact that Spirit Plaza now has a permanent status and that infrastructural improvements have been made to this public square shows that placemaking practices and unspectacular everyday popularity can produce material manifestations in urban space.

South of Spirit Plaza, at the intersection of Woodward Avenue and Jefferson Avenue, we pass the former site of a whipping post erected shortly after the Woodward Plan had been put into partial action. This post was removed in 1831, the year of the arrival of the first fugitive slaves in Detroit, six years before the state constitution would ban slavery. The post is commemorated by a 1926 plaque currently only available in the digital collections of the Detroit Public Library.[6] Right then and there we are "struck" by the "fist" of Joe Louis (2001), a piece by the Los Angeles–based Mexican American sculptor Robert Graham (see fig. 2.5).

The sculpture designed by Robert Graham in Venice, California, celebrates the fist of the prominent Black boxing champion Joe Louis (1914–81) who was knocked out by German boxer Max Schmeling in 1936, but who won against him in less than three minutes in 1938. These two battles reflect at least three simultaneous struggles: the radically racialized status of African American athletes in the transatlantic as well as the national public sphere in the 1930s, the growing tension between the US and national-socialist Germany, and the

---

6. The inscription on this anonymous roaring-twenties plaque erases all traces of the local struggle over bondage and slavery in Detroit. It reads: "This tablet marks the site of Detroit's only whipping post. Detroit's first and only whipping post was erected in Woodward Avenue near this location in 1818 to rid the town of petty thieves and vagabonds. The last two culprits to be punished were flogged by the sheriff in 1830, and shortly afterward the whipping post was removed, the law legalizing its use was repealed on March 4, 1831. Presented to the city of Detroit in the month of September, 1926."

FIGURE 2.5. Robert Graham's *Monument to Joe Louis* (1986), with David Barr and Sergio De Giusti's *Transcending* (2003) in the background. Photo by Juliane Borosch, July 4, 2021.

weakening position of German immigrants in pre-WWII Detroit. The sculpture itself looks back at this historical event and projects its energies forward to ensuing decades of fighting against racial injustice in and beyond Detroit. It can be read as a fulfillment of the conflicted potentialities offered by the figurative (visual) language of the monument at Campus Martius, the street mural, and the 1926 plaque commemorating the whipping post.

HOW TO REWRITE THE FUTURE

By now we have reached the riverfront, walking toward a fixture at the end of Woodward Avenue, Hart Plaza. It is named after prominent Detroiter and late Senator Philip A. Hart (1912–76) and located roughly on the first landing spot of colonial settlers in 1701. This concrete plaza designed by famous New York–based Japanese American sculptor Isamu Noguchi was created during a 1970s redesign of the riverfront, which saw the adding of land roughly the width of the square to the bank of the Detroit River. As the plaza was built on one of the first and main contact zones between the city and the world and between the water and the land, building a civic center at the place had long been discussed. Hart Plaza has room for about forty thousand people and is the site of different festivals and public events. Next to amphitheaters and access to the river and a cruise ship terminal, this square today hosts an array of urban figures.

Hart Plaza is the location of the Horace E. Dodge and Son Memorial Fountain designed by Isamu Noguchi in 1978. The futuristic fountain consists of two stainless steel beams that hold up a circle. It also includes water and light features. Not unsurprisingly the Motor City that rose to power as an industrial city pays tribute at this central location to the industrial magnates that contributed to the city's rapid rise and epic fall. While funded by the Dodge family, the prominent placement on the square and within the city expresses an official appreciation of Dodge's work and a "scaling of memory" by the city council that leaves little room for widely publicized performative contestations (Alderman, "Street Names" 163). There is also a Ford Motor Company historical marker featured on Hart Plaza. In 2013, during the height of Detroit's postindustrial crisis, including the city's filing for Chapter 9 bankruptcy, the plaza and especially the fountain were vandalized conspicuously, yet the central message still is that Dodge and Ford are Detroit's foundational figures much like Woodward and the abstract military figures on Campus Martius that foreshadowed them.

A number of sculptures were added to Hart Plaza in the context of Detroit's tricentennial celebrations in 2001. This collocation of prominent urban figures is in line with what Aleida Assmann calls the "canonization of one's own present" (21, our translation) and can ideally help to readjust the representation of memory. *Transcending*, the largest figure on the plaza beside the fountain, is a workers' rights and achievements memorial. It was added to the plaza in 2003, counterpoising the prominent memorials to the Dodge and Ford industrial magnates.

> "Transcending," as [the Detroit-based sculptors David Barr and Sergio De Giusti] named their plan, was to rise 63 feet above street level in the form of two stainless steel arcs, geared on the inside to reflect Detroit's industrial might, and open at the top to symbolize labor's unfinished work. At night, the gap would be lit as a reminder of the energy of working people. A spiral walkway at the base would lead visitors to seven granite boulders, split in half with the polished inside faces holding bronze reliefs telling labor's story. Embedded in the walkway would be milestones telling labor's achievements for the public good. A raised dais, intended as a speaker's stand, would include quotations from prominent activists for labor rights and social justice. Beneath the dais would be a time capsule holding letters, badges,

newspapers, and other labor mementos of the first years of the 21st Century. ("Labor's Legacy" 1)

Transcending complements and augments the ambition of the *Soldiers' and Sailors' Monument* and especially *The Spirit of Detroit* to serve as an immersive emblematic space in which the urban spectators/readers/walkers may cast themselves into the providential shoes provided by the respective sculptures and their visual and verbal imagery. It is much more reverenced than an already overgrown statue on the plaza, unveiled as well as part of Detroit's tricentennial jubilee. *The Landing of Cadillac* (see fig. 2.6) includes a sculpture by the California-based sculptor William Kieffer of Antoine Laumet de la Mothe, Sieur de Cadillac, the founder of Fort Pontchartrain du Détroit (1701), the earliest colonial version of Detroit. This sculpture commissioned by the French American Chamber of Commerce was unveiled in 2001, depicting Cadillac stepping onto land and planting the French Fleur de Lys flag.[7]

Two decades later, it is poorly maintained, absent from remediations and Detroit documentaries—clearly not a public figure sparking the realization of potentialities. Hart Plaza lacks figures of Indigenous Detroit agents. As part of 2020's public reckoning of the colonizing messages that many monumental urban figures are sending, a group of Indigenous female activists used media-relayed performance to "[fight] the spirits" of the space of the colonial figures by reclaiming the location of a removed bust of Christopher Columbus just off Woodward Avenue (Allaire). On Independence Day a Blueberry Moon Ceremony in Campus Martius Park celebrated interconnectedness. The Cadillac statue, however, does not seem to script comparable refigurations because it lacks the palimpsestic energies and the prophetic bend visible in many of the sculptures discussed. Cadillac's character and its design are presented in the frame of timeless and contemporary French American interactions, avoiding both memories of colonial destruction and promises of future fulfillments.

As we reach the very end of Woodward Avenue, looking south, gazing at the Canadian side of the Detroit riverfront, we encounter a final figural manifestation of downtown Detroit's powerful selective memory. At the waterfront, in full sight of its Canadian twin on the other side of the Detroit River,

---

7. A rather abstruse inscription on the plaque provides no historical background for Cadillac's role among Indigenous people, whereas his founding activities are sketched on a bilingual historical marker. The monolingual inscription gives as much credit to Cadillac as to a motley group of contemporary sponsors: "Antoine de la Mothe Cadillac, 1658–1730, Founder of the City of Detroit, Dedicated July 24, 2001. In commemoration of the tricentennial of his arrival. Sculptors William Kieffer and Ann Feeley. A gift to the people of the French-American Chamber of Commerce Auto Chassis International—Burelle Dessault Systemes—Delmia—Faurecia Hutchinson Jean-Pierre Kemper—Bruno Marko—Sescoi Sofanou—Valeo Arcadis Giffels—; Barton Malo Detroit Recreation Department."

FIGURE 2.6. William Kieffer and Ann Feeley's *Antoine de la Mothe Cadillac* (2001). Photo by Juliane Borosch, July 4, 2021.

stands *Gateway to Freedom: International Memorial to the Underground Railroad* by Denver-based Ed Dwight (see fig. 2.7), the first African American astronaut trainee.

This densely woven emblematic ensemble juxtaposes inscriptions, icons, and sculpture in a manner not unlike *The Spirit of Detroit*. It depicts a sculptural group of eight enslaved people and an Underground Railroad conductor pointing toward Canada, the place of potential liberation.[8] Added to Hart

---

8. The inscription informs visitors that

> until Emancipation, Detroit and the Detroit River community served as the gateway to freedom for thousands of African American people escaping enslavement. Detroit was one of the largest terminals of the Underground Railroad, a network of abolitionists aiding enslaved people seeking freedom. Detroit's Underground Railroad code name was Midnight. At first, Michigan was a destination for freedom seekers, but Canada became a safer sanctuary after slavery was abolished there in 1834. With passage of the Fugitive Slave Act in 1850, many runaways left their homes in Detroit and crossed the river to Canada to remain free. Some returned after Emancipation in 1863. [. . .] The successful operation of Detroit's Underground Railroad was due to the effort and cooperation of diverse groups of people, including people of African descent, Whites, and North American Indians. This legacy of freedom is a vital part of Detroit and its history. ("Contemporary Monuments").

FIGURE 2.7. Ed Dwight's *Gateway to Freedom: International Memorial to the Underground Railroad* (2001). Photo by Juliane Borosch, July 4, 2021.

Plaza in 2001, this ensemble memorializes Detroit as the endpoint of the Underground Railroad and stepping stone to post-slavery life. This composite urban figure at the limen between the water and the land as much as between two settler-colonial states memorializes the history of hardship and perseverance of Black people in the US and in North America, recalling and refiguring the personification of "Emancipation" in the *Soldiers' and Sailors' Monument* at Campus Martius. *Gateway* reframes the city's role in this history in images and words, thereby creating living ideas, best condensed in the plaque that speaks of a "legacy of freedom as a vital part of Detroit and its history."

The emblematic monument thus casts a providential light on the early republic, which assumes a healing function for the economically increasingly hard times of its own construction. When Detroit served as a frontier town and during a transition phase to statehood, Detroit was home to slaveholders. Many fugitives in Detroit could not be safe from being taken captive and resold into slavery ("Mapping Slavery"). And even today, emancipation is never real enough. While these stories (much like the history of Indigenous Detroit) do not feature prominently in the artistic memorialization on the part of Woodward Avenue we traversed as walkers, they can always come in by the interpretive acts that are sparked by the urban figurations. The memorial to the Underground Railroad in Detroit, for instance, presents a powerful reimagination of the history of civil rights in the light of the best hopes for a better future. It is a refigurative reckoning in Detroit's civic square in the center of the city. This monument has "scriptivity"—folding "dramatic narrative and movement through space" into one another (Bernstein 89), offering attachment, belonging, and ethical engagement to its readers/walkers. *Gateway* also offers to hold its observers in the bonds of the prophetic, forward-looking sway of the *figurae* of its individual characters.

CONCLUSION

The place now called Detroit has been many things in its long history: vital access point to water, starting point for ventures into the peninsula, trading post, utopian idea, fortified settlement, agrarian land, industrial boomtown, site of the Fordist revolution, union town, place of racial conflict and cooperation, the arsenal of democracy, Motown, boiling point of racial injustice, the city in ruins, "the comeback city," "the city and the neighborhoods," still the most segregated city in the US—the list goes on. At the turn of the twentieth century already, one Detroiter remarked that "every 25 years the city is entirely built anew" (qtd. in Kickert 36). Downtown Detroit is not only the ground where this material change takes place. It can be seen as a symbol of the city's transformation throughout time, revealing the city to be both a fixed and a transitory space, a product and a practice in time and place. The city changed from small settlement to big city and downtown, from center of urban life to place of representation, consumption, and experience at the cost of the surrounding neighborhoods. Throughout these transitions, it was Woodward Avenue, the original main street of Detroit, that remained its central *figura* and fixture promising redemption.

Writing down our encounters with more-or-less permanent urban figures and fixtures on Woodward Avenue in these pages, we have immersed ourselves as transient, even transmedial, walking and talking figures on Woodward Avenue, becoming part of the compound of figures, narratives, and media that script the ongoing reimagining of Detroit. In light of this spatial and narrative immersion, we come to a set of tentative conclusions. First, these figures have both narrativity and scriptivity in ways that challenge their counterparts on and off the street to speak to them and to talk about them in order to develop a sense of place, agency, and time. Second, because of this possessive rather than active relationship to narrative and script, these figures just as the walkers looking at them, functionally speaking, are not so much protagonists, but rather minor characters in the larger story of the city. The figures on Woodward are sequentialized parts of a redemptive city script that engages eclectic understandings of the past to spell out a persuasive blueprint for the future. While they appear to be fixtures, they might be replaced by new figures over time. Third, precisely in this potential of being etched out, these figures work and function as *figurae* in the sense described by Auerbach: They anticipate and promise future fulfillment; and this fulfillment includes the replacement by some future *figurae*. The urban figures discussed in this chapter script a future-oriented, forward thrust of urban development that seeks replacement and deauthorization of past figureheads more than a fair transition of power or a reckoning with the past. Because of their ability to bridge time and space, these figures are the driving force behind the future orientation of Detroit's postindustrial script. Finally, these figures contribute to a naturalization of both narrativity and scriptivity. That is, they turn the idea of temporal and spatial supersession, of future-oriented structure and resistance, of focalization, replacement, and delegitimization—core elements of the narrative and scriptive reformulation of a speaker's sense perceptions—into an everyday conflict of the imagination at work.

WORKS CITED

Alderman, Derek H. "Place, Naming and the Interpretation of Cultural Landscapes." *The Ashgate Research Companion to Heritage and Identity*, edited by Brian Graham and Peter Howard, Ashgate, 2008, pp. 195–213.

———. "Street Names and the Scaling of Memory: The Politics of Commemorating Martin Luther King, Jr. within the African American Community." *Area*, vol. 35, no. 2, 2003, pp. 163–73.

Allaire, Christian. "Over the Fourth of July, These Indigenous Women Healed Colonized Spaces." *Vogue*, 6 July 2020, https://www.vogue.com/article/indigenous-women-heal-colonized-spaces-detroit.

Amato, Joseph A. *On Foot: A History of Walking*. New York UP, 2004.

Anonymous. "Plaque Marking Site of Detroit's Only Whipping Post." Resource ID bh009345. Burton Historical Collection, Detroit Public Library, Digital Collections, https://digitalcollections.detroitpubliclibrary.org/islandora/object/islandora%3A145178. Accessed 7 Feb. 2022.

Assmann, Aleida. "Geschichte findet Stadt." *Kommunikation—Gedächtnis—Raum*, edited by Moritz Csáky and Christoph Leitgeb, transcript, 2015, pp. 13–28.

Auerbach, Erich, James I. Porter, and Jane O. Newman. *Time, History, and Literature: Selected Essays of Erich Auerbach*. Princeton UP, 2013.

Autry, Robyn, and Daniel J. Walkowitz. "Editors' Introduction: Undoing the Flaneur." *Walkers, Voyeurs, and the Politics of Urban Space*, special issue of *Radical History Review*, vol. 114, Duke UP, 2012, pp. 1–5.

Benjamin, Walter. *The Arcades Project.* Translated by Howard Eiland and Kevin McLaughlin, Belknap Press, 2002.

Bercovitch, Sacvan. *The Rites of Assent: Transformations in the Symbolic Construction of America.* Routledge, 1993.

Bernstein, Robin. "Dances with Things: Material Culture and the Performance of Race." *Social Text,* vol. 27, no. 4 (101), 2009, pp. 67–94.

Bieger, Laura. *Belonging and Narrative: A Theory of the American Novel.* Transcript, 2018.

Bode, Christoph, and Rainer Dietrich. *Future Narratives: Theory, Poetics, and Media-Historical Moment.* De Gruyter, 2013.

Buchenau, Barbara. "Prefiguring CanAmerica? White Man's Indians and Religious Typology in New England and New France." *Transnational American Studies,* edited by Udo J. Hebel, Winter Universitätsverlag, 2012, pp. 165–82.

City of Detroit. "Spirit Plaza. The People's Plaza!" https://detroitmi.gov/departments/parks-recreation/spirit-plaza. Accessed 3 Sept. 2020.

Cohen, Gary B., and Franz A. J. Szabo. "Introduction. Embodiments of Power: Building Baroque Cities in Austria and Europe." *Embodiments of Power: Building Baroque Cities in Europe,* edited by Gary B. Cohen and Franz A. J. Szabo, Berghahn Books, 2008, pp. 1–8, https://doi.org/10.1515/9780857450500-004.

"Contemporary Monuments to the Slave Past," https://www.slaverymonuments.org/items/show/1170. Accessed 7 Feb. 2022.

David, Bruno, and Meredith Wilson. "Introduction." *Inscribed Landscapes: Marking and Making Place,* edited by Bruno David and Meredith Wilson, U of Hawai'i P, 2002, pp. 1–9.

De Certeau, Michel. *The Practice of Everyday Life.* Translated by Steven Rendall, U of California P, 1984.

Eisinger, Peter. "Detroit Futures: Can the City Be Reimagined?" *City & Community,* vol. 14, no. 2, 2015, pp. 106–17.

Felski, Rita. *Hooked: Art and Attachment.* U of Chicago P, 2020.

Fishman, Robert. "Detroit and the Acceleration of History." *Log,* no. 37, 2016, pp. 32–48, http://www.jstor.org/stable/26324715.

Fredericks, Marshall M. "Sketch for 'Seal of Wayne County, Michigan,' c. 1955. Description." *Marshall M. Fredericks Sculpture Museum,* Digital Archives and Objects Collection, 1995, https://omeka.svsu.edu/items/show/7605.

Gray, Kathleen. "'Power to the People': Detroit Students Preserve This Moment in Paint." *New York Times,* 18 June 2020, https://www.nytimes.com/2020/06/18/us/politics/detroit-protests-mural.html.

Hickey, Andrew T. *Cities of Signs: Learning the Logic of Urban Spaces.* Peter Lang Publishing, 2012.

Jarzombek, Mark. "The 'Indianized' Landscape of Massachusetts." *Places Journal,* February 2021, https://placesjournal.org/article/the-indianized-landscape-of-massachusetts.

Kickert, Conrad. *Dream City: Creation, Destruction, and Reinvention in Downtown Detroit.* MIT Press, 2019.

"Labor's Legacy. A Landmark for Detroit." *The Michigan Labor Legacy Project, Inc.,* August 2005, http://mlhs.wayne.edu/files/050821_LaborsLegacy.pdf.

Lees, James A. "The Soldiers' and Sailors' Monument." *Michigan History Magazine,* September/October 1999, pp. 7–14.

"Mapping Slavery in Detroit." *University of Michigan Undergraduate Research Opportunity Program (UROP),* 2014, http://mappingdetroitslavery.com/.

Mask, Deirdre. "The Black Lives Matter Movement Is Being Written into the Streetscape." *The Atlantic,* 22 July 2020, https://www.theatlantic.com/ideas/archive/2020/07/street-naming-more-performative-gesture/614416/.

Phelan, James. *Living to Tell about It: A Rhetoric and Ethics of Character Narration.* Cornell UP, 2005.

Pielack, Leslie K. *The Saginaw Trail: From Native American Path to Woodward Avenue.* History Press, 2018.

Poremba, David Lee. "Detroit's Field of Mars: Campus Martius." *Michigan History Magazine,* September/October 1999, pp. 12–13.

Reinburg, Virginia. *Storied Places: Pilgrim Shrines, Nature, and History in Early Modern France.* Cambridge UP, 2019.

Ryan, Marie-Laure. "The Modes of Narrativity and Their Visual Metaphors." *Style,* vol. 26, no. 3, 1992, pp. 368–87.

Ryan, Marie-Laure, Kenneth Foote, and Maoz Azaryahu. *Narrating Space / Spatializing Narrative: Where Narrative Theory and Geography Meet.* The Ohio State UP, 2016.

Shepherd, Jessica. "Detroit's Woodward Avenue Is One of America's Most Iconic Roads." *MLive,* 6 Apr. 2018, https://www.mlive.com/entertainment/erry-2018/04/57da31c03d/woodward_avenue_detroit.html.

Stitt, Chanel. "'Power to the People' Mural Painted on Woodward Avenue in Downtown Detroit." *Detroit Free Press,* 18 June 2020, https://eu.freep.com/story/news/local/michigan/detroit/2020/06/18/power-to-the-people-detroit-woodward-mural/3212918001/.

Vachon, Paul. "Detroit's Soldiers & Sailors Monument." *HSM Chronicle,* 2012. Library of Congress, LC-D4-7336, Historical Society of Michigan, pp. 16–18.

Wacquant, Loïc. "For a Sociology of Flesh and Blood." *Qualitative Sociology,* vol. 38, no. 1, 2015, pp. 1–11.

CHAPTER 3

Tiny Architecture and Narrative

Scripting Minimal Urban Living Spaces

KATHARINA WOOD AND
RANDI GUNZENHÄUSER

> The reduction of living space per capita is one of the most urgent tasks of our society in the struggle for a sustainable future. The reduction in living space contributes to the fact that a whole series of other sufficiency aspects can come into play. A prerequisite for feasibility, however, is that the potential user is able to recognize very concrete advantages for himself despite the decision of spatial self-restraint.
> —Arne Steffen, "Chance auf Umsetzbarkeit"

Tiny houses are trending in Europe and North America as one possible answer to the challenge of building during the global increase of anthropogenic climate change.[1] Tiny-building projects follow diverse *city scripts* or *city narratives,* which we will analyze exemplarily with respect to four tiny-living projects in Europe situated in Rotterdam (NL), Poissy (F), Gutenstein (A), and Dortmund-Sölde (D). The narratives employed reflect the aims and interests of different parties involved in their creation, such as engineers, architects, city planners, municipalities, politicians, and citizens. Our hypothesis is that buildings are not only constructed physically but also narratively. We ask what kinds of narratives or scripts of the sustainable and degrowth city can be found in the context of our examples.

First, we will discuss the connection between architecture, narrative, and narrativity. Then we explore the narrative contexts of contemporary green-

---

1. All German texts were translated by the authors. For an English language discussion of "material sufficiency" as a transition toward more frugal lifestyle habits and an endorsement of degrowth as "a planned economic contraction" of overgrown economies on the path to a steady-state or zero-growth economy, see Alexander and Gleeson (54). The architectural journalist Klaus Englert describes the historical context of small-scale approaches among others in his monograph *Wie wir wohnen werden: Die Entwicklung der Wohnung und die Architektur von morgen* (2020).

building practices in Western Europe, concentrating on different aspects of sufficiency such as minimized land use per capita, flexible use of space across time, serial and modular ways of construction, less resource consumption, healthy and sustainable building material, efficient energy use, and others. Lastly, we will compare the building projects' narrative conceptualizations to their practical construction and underlying scripts of sustainability.

ARCHITECTURE, LANGUAGE, AND NARRATIVE

The exploration of narratives surrounding the building of houses serves as a starting point to outline how far buildings can be analyzed through the lens of literary and cultural studies. How can architecture be related to concepts and terminologies of cultural studies such as narrative, language, and media?

Every building bears cultural meanings specifically related to its time and place, functions, ownership, and many other aspects, including its sustainability. Compared to literary texts, architectural texts often less consciously express meaning, as Frishman pointedly phrases it:

> All human landscapes are embedded with cultural meaning. And since we rarely consider our constructions as evidence of our priorities, beliefs and behaviors, the testimonies our landscapes offer are more honest than many of the things we intentionally present. Our built environment, in other words, is a kind of societal autobiography, writ large. (Frishman, n. pag.)

Within this "societal autobiography," buildings can be read as cultural narratives that communicate with the outside world about themselves, alongside the larger story of the neighborhood or city that surrounds and frames it. Buildings also draw from their historical context, the history of their architectural and technical makeup, their design history and technological history, as well as the history of building laws, technical norms, and aesthetics.

In his introduction to the anthology *The Routledge Companion on Architecture, Literature and the City* (2018), Jonathan Charley describes these narrative aspects of buildings themselves, as found in space, by comparing them to the function of architecture in literature:

> We can clearly talk about the construction and representation of architecture in literary narratives. But we can also talk about the narrative content of architecture. All buildings, whether a garden shed or a cathedral[,] have functional and programmatic stories that are inscribed in plan, form and

spatial organisation. [. . .] Read thoroughly from cover to cover and wall to wall, architectural narratives, like their literary counterparts can speak of many things—ideology and power, history and geography, order and control, discipline and punishment, love and desire, birth and death. (2–3)

From Charley's perspective, architecture (as the manipulation of space and materials) always possesses narrative content. He further writes that "both architects and novelists in this sense are jugglers of space, time and narrative" (3). For him, all texts are part of historical ideological developments in their structures and patterns: "The modernist use of abstraction, collage, and narrative fragmentation to represent the dynamic pulse and accelerated space-time reality of the revolutionary modern city" is also represented in the city's buildings and architecture (3). Parallel to this modernist context, we are examining today's architectural texts for postmodernist discourses about the space-time reality of the sustainable and degrowth city.

In *The Words between the Spaces: Buildings and Language* (2002) architect Thomas Markus and linguist Deborah Cameron depict a building's design process as communication-oriented: Architects are in constant dialogue with engineers, contractors, and fellow architects (1). In their analysis, the authors argue that "the language used to speak and write about the built environment plays a significant role in shaping that environment, and our responses to it" (2). As researchers, Markus and Cameron "try to show that reflecting systematically on language can yield insight into the buildings we have now, and the ones we may create in [the] future" (2).

They explain that "a productive metaphor compares architecture to grammar rather than literature, suggesting that buildings, like sentences, are constructed by combining a set of formal elements according to a set of formal rules" (4). Accordingly, Markus and Cameron raise the question "Do buildings communicate directly, in their own semiotic codes?" and come to the conclusion:

Buildings, it seems, do not explain themselves. While something like the contrast between light and dark in a Gothic cathedral may be apprehended directly, the *significance* of that contrast is not apprehended directly. Rather it is apprehended with the assistance of language, in the primary and literal sense of that term. (7)

Markus and Cameron describe the relationship between architecture and language as interactive rather than analogous. For their analysis, they choose to focus mainly on writing or speech about architecture as social practices:

"*Both* buildings and language are irreducibly social phenomena, so that any illuminating analysis of them must locate them in the larger social world" (9). Our approach follows a similar logic, laying emphasis on the social, economic, and ecological scripts of buildings.

In *Architecture and Narrative* (2009), Sophia Psarra additionally contemplates the relationship between architecture, narrative, and the larger construction of space and cultural meaning:

> Narrative enters architecture in many ways, from the conceptual "messages" it is made to stand for to the illustration of a design through models, drawings and other representational forms. This aspect of architectural expression, what the design speaks of, is relevant to narrative as representation. It concerns the semantic meanings of buildings and places, and the contribution of architecture to the expression of social and cultural messages. (2)

Psarra stresses that buildings and places function as signs across diverse media and are thus working on different cultural levels, from macro- to microlevels, from large social discourses to individual identity building.

In line with Lieven Ameel, we argue that buildings do not present "fully-fledged narratives," but contain *narrativity* (25) and thus should be defined as opening up to larger medial contexts and connections, inspiring narrative responses across space and time. Ameel bases his argument on the interdisciplinary definition of *narrativity* by literary and geographic scholars in *Narrating Space/Spatializing Narrative* (Ryan, Foote, and Azaryahu). Buildings do not explain themselves to a general audience, who (in contrast to expert audiences) is not familiar with their manifold architectural and historical codes, but they can be explained through the use of oral or written text, through large frame narratives as well as small, identity-building microscripts that are told about them. Ameel writes that "a building, or a built environment, does not tell a story, unless the term 'story' is used figuratively" (25).

Besides their narrativity as seen in conjunction with words, buildings contain aspects of scripts based on other media. Digital maps, floor plans, and guidance systems, as well as tables of materials used to activate different kinds of procedural knowledge, come together in a building. Each room, from the entrance hall across the living room, bedrooms, and bathrooms to gyms and storage spaces, activates knowledge about its functions. At the same time, buildings are accompanied by media such as brochures, videos, photographs, web pages, planning documents, or certification texts—microscripts that happen at the individual level of single-building projects in contrast to macrolevel scripts that operate at a larger scale.

Generally, an individual building participates in processes of prescription, inscription, and description on a macro- and microlevel. Building codes act in prescriptive ways, embedding specific standards into the building's construction. Construction concepts such as the *Passivhaus-Standard* ("passive house standard" resulting in ultra-low-energy buildings) or *Niedrigstenergiehaus-Standard* ("nearly zero energy building" standard) are defined by highly energy-efficient criteria. First, for certification, each building standard prescribes a standard of construction and performance that must be achieved. Second, a building inscribes itself into its urban context, within which it serves specific cultural, social, and economic functions. Finally, a house entails a self-description, which is always accompanied by medial frame narratives that reflect on current ideas and values serving as blueprints for the future.

LIVING SMALL: A HISTORICAL PERSPECTIVE

Living small has an extensive past reaching back to the beginning of human history. In the past thousands of years, most people around the world used to survive under cramped living conditions with little privacy. Geographer Krista Evans traces North American forms of small housing back to the frontier log cabin, bungalow, cottage, shotgun house, and camp ("Integrating" 35). In German architectural history, there are many forms of more recent small-living situations such as large *Mietskasernen* (tenement houses or rookeries) with small apartments for large families who took on extra boarders, but also *Ledigenheime* (homes for single workers) and boarding houses (see Schmid, Eberle, and Hugentobler). In the Ruhr area, *Zechensiedlungen* (colliery settlements) were built for miners and their families during the nineteenth and twentieth centuries. Even today, public housing provides small apartments for low-income residents—often without providing communal green or social spaces. Historically, living small stands for poor living conditions.

Small living has also been thriving among people who were mobile, such as nomads or circus members but also immigrants and settlers who took their families across continents. Through the popularization of the automobile and the evolution of assembly-line production, a new type of housing emerged in the United States and Europe: the *mobile home,* also referred to as "manufactured housing" (Evans, "Integrating" 36). Culminating in times of depression, mobile homes were inhabited by the poor, which led to a condescending view of their homes by the middle class. Today, trailer parks tell the story of cheap holidays at best, of poverty and squalor at worst.

Small wonder that specifications in German development plans (*Bebauungspläne*) and zoning laws in the US make it difficult for small, tiny, and mobile houses to find room among existing permanent residences. Changing this situation is one main concern of people in the tiny-house movement. Tiny houses are becoming a trend among diverse groups of people in North America and Europe and have been popularized through TV shows such as *Tiny House Nation* (FYI/A&E/National Geographic, 2014–present) as well as through social media platforms.

When the self-proclaimed tiny-house movement, which had originated in the United States, came to Europe, it brought along many a story. The US-American tiny-house movement has been inspired by, among other narratives, the nineteenth-century works of Transcendentalists such as Henry David Thoreau and Ralph Waldo Emerson (see Anson). In *Walden; or, Life in the Woods* (1854), Thoreau criticizes the affluence and luxury of his time and tells the story of his simple life in the cabin he built on Walden Pond. The tale about his immersion into nature still inspires many tiny-house occupants and can easily be integrated into more recent tales promoting minimalist lifestyles and the credo that "less is more" (Ford and Gomez-Lanier 394).

People with limited financial means view tiny houses as an opportunity for homeownership. And owning one's home remains an essential part not only of the American Dream but also of European dreams. Today's shortage of affordable urban housing has increased the interest in small houses. Living tiny, of course, is not always sustainable, although it generally has a smaller carbon footprint than its larger counterparts. Yet, the free-standing tiny house has many of the disadvantages all free-standing buildings for one or only a few families share. How then, can tiny living become fully environmentally friendly and follow the logics and narratives of sufficiency?

SUFFICIENCY: HOW TO MAKE IT FEASIBLE

Sufficiency narratives are inspired by ideas of the degrowth movement that criticizes the neoliberal primacy of economic growth. Degrowth and sufficiency have practical implications for spatial planning as Benedikt Schmid, Christian Schulz, and Sabine Weck point out. Many efforts at sufficiency are organized at the level of civil society by individuals and groups interested in creating spaces of change and model projects that exist outside of the logics of increasing capital accumulation. Schmid, Schulz, and Weck call these projects *Reallabore* (living labs) and *Möglichkeitsräume* (spaces of possibility), spaces for experimenting with new communal ways of life and thus helping to create communities for the future. The narratives of degrowth and sufficiency can, for example, be connected to the concept of the sharing economy, where resources such as tools or machines are shared and used communally. This saves resources and is cheaper than individually owning objects. On a different scale, tiny-house building projects can be turned into living labs in order to test practices of sufficiency and do further research.

In their recommendations for the German Environmental Agency (*Umweltbundesamt*) from 2018, Carina Zell-Ziegler and Hannah Förster from the German Öko-Institut confirm that when developing governmental strategies for sufficiency, the most important factor is to negotiate every step with those who actually put sufficiency into action. In order to convince people, new narratives—scripts—have to be found. The scripts aim to translate necessary technical steps toward sufficiency into vivid images that help everybody understand how one can eventually profit from them (5). The Öko-Institut writes:

> Communication in this context is not an end in itself, but serves to improve understanding of sufficiency, reduce prevailing reservations and obstacles, and create acceptance for sufficiency. The latter should be understood and worked on as a design task. In addition, efforts should be made to communicate sufficiency strategies positively, for example with the help of their co-benefits. (Zell-Ziegler and Förster 35)

The authors insist on the necessity of translating the technical term *sufficiency* into the contexts of everyday life and personal-identity categories. Like many other researchers, they consider scripting—as a form of communication that comes in many medial guises—as absolutely necessary for inducing changes in planning and constructing the sufficient buildings we urgently need today.

MODEL PROJECTS IN EUROPEAN CITIES

Our analysis of the following model projects focuses on their narrative and practical construction and on how they are influenced by scripts of the degrowth and resilient city; on the other hand, we explore how they themselves are supposed to act as potentially redemptive microscripts (see Sulimma in chapter 7 and Ameel in chapter 8 of this volume). We concentrate on the project websites and the narratives brought forth by planners and architects who translate their professional engagement into larger social terms in stories told through and about the building. Planners frame the buildings

FIGURE 3.1. An explosion drawing of the Didden Village.
© MVRDV, used with the kind permission of MVRDV.

with narratives that are in turn used by journalists, private builders, and government officials.

Nowadays one can find examples for many different combinations of sustainable practices and their respective scripts and narratives. We will introduce and analyze four recent projects illustrating different combinations of small and sufficient strategies contributing to greener cities. The first example will take us to the Netherlands, where avant-garde builders have been thinking about small-housing solutions since de Stijl Modernism, which still inspires architects today.

In 2006 Winy Maas and his team from the internationally active architectural firm MVRDV in Rotterdam constructed modular rooftop tiny-house extensions in their city. The three small buildings of "Didden Village" added to the flat roof of the Didden family's house are painted a widely visible bright blue (see fig. 3.1). Both name and color already refer to small-town living in nature, close to the blue sky. At the same time, the position on a historical, privately owned building in the middle of Rotterdam opens up the possibilities of privileged, comfortable urban living—all you have to do is go downstairs and immerse yourself into city life. MVRDV's homepage underlines these aspects:

> Situated on top of an existing historical building and atelier, the bedrooms are conceived as separate houses, optimizing the privacy of every member of the family. The houses are distributed in such a way that a series of plazas, streets and alleys appear as a mini-village on top of the building, a kind of heaven for its inhabitants. ("Didden Village")

The phrasing "heaven for its inhabitants" constructs Didden Village as an upscale redemptive project for inhabitants who spatially and socially reside on top of the city, apart from everybody else.

The architects' webpage refers not so much to the economically privileged circumstances of the Diddens who built a whole tiny-house village for themselves; the architects don't use images of futuristic skyscraper settings with luxury penthouses. Rather they construct a socially romantic script that reminds us of Jacques Tati's comedy *Mon Oncle* (1958) whose old-fashioned, poor title character lives on top of a very old house, overlooking the quaint old part of town. The film's bicycling uncle, too, is a very private person but he keeps aloof from the cool modernist bungalow his nephew lives in, a bungalow representing not only modernist aesthetics but also the car-centered postwar spending economy that he doesn't want to be part of. This reference to small-town and artistic nineteenth-century living is strong in the comments about Didden Village; it supports the story of a redemptive lifestyle of convinced minimalists and individualists rather than capitalists.

The plan of Didden Village on MVRDV's homepage, which is not a detailed explosion drawing for professional architects but a simplified version for laypeople, shows only the rough layers of the built as well as planted elements of the construction (fig. 3.1). It abstracts from the technical details and stresses the simplicity of the extension. Maas, an internationally known experimental architect, conceives of the small buildings as spaces for testing how city roofs can be used for extensions without sealing up any additional land: "The addition can be seen as a prototype for the further densification of the existing city. It adds a roof life to the city. It explores the costs for the beams, infrastructure, and extra finishes, and it ultimately aims to be lower in cost than the equivalent ground price for the building" (MVRDV, "Didden Village"). For Maas, the project is part of a larger vision of building for times of degrowth and climate change, a "living lab" and a "space of possibility" in the words of Schmid, Schulz, and Weck. These real-life small buildings serve as a research project, testing technical, economic, and ecological motifs and narratives. They are not about future high-rise buildings, but about the prolongation of an old building's life span by adding one *small* story to the existing roofline and thus adjusting it to its inhabitants' twenty-first-century requirements. In this sense, a high-end project like Didden Village can open up green possibilities for the future: "We planted trees and can install water reservoirs," the Dutch architect points out in an interview for *Arte Magazine* (Idris and Schneider). The project thus extends the original urban family house by three bedrooms which, along with two trees breaking up and greening the formerly sealed roof space, not only add village charm to the city surroundings but also offer the possibility for additional rainwater infiltration. Hiring a famous architectural firm resulted in a first-class densification project: three small cubes with traditional gable roofs, made from extremely light materials—mostly wood—to make the construction statically safe and to show off modernist architectural principles in their typical simple forms and primary colors, red (for the door frames), yellow (for the outdoor accessories), and blue (Englert 119).

Klaus Englert sums up MVRDV's accomplishments: "In this sense, the blue village on the roofs of Rotterdam is a contribution to the housing policy debates that could ease the housing shortage in our cities" and insists that this solution is, in fact, cheaper than building an addition on extra ground, which does not exist in this part of Rotterdam (119–20). He tells a story of redensification and its potential to lessen the urban-housing crisis. Just like the Diddens, wealthy builders all over the world are ready to invest in such a costly individualistic green future. Roderick Rauert, managing director of LBBW Immobilien Capital GmbH, foregrounds the willingness of private upper-middle-class residents to even profit from "sharing" culture and "collaborative consumption" (26). But as we will see next, nowadays, not only well-to-do citizens profit from these sufficiency measures and sustainability scripts.

Like other industrialized countries including the Netherlands, France has a history of apartment blocks with practically identical floor plans also resulting from avantgarde theories—some of them huge "machines for living," a term coined by Le Corbusier in the 1920s, when he synthesized prefabrication, flexibility, and minimalism. In 2016 in the town of Poissy, the architects Béatrice Vivien and Laurent Pillaud from the office Virtuel Architecture in Paris added more than extra stories to an existing apartment ensemble that was erected in 1957 for workers of the Simca car factory. They also combined cost-saving modular construction of prefabricated concrete slabs with a new aesthetic and new technologies in a densification project. Thus, they upgraded the existing *Plattenbauten* (modularized apartment blocks) aesthetically as well as technically by adding the comfort of healthy materials, insulation, and balconies.

By placing thirty-three additional tiny houses onto the previously block-shaped slabs of concrete, the architects created additional space on existing roofs (see fig. 3.2). The modular construction shortened the time of production and installation and allowed the residents of the original parts of the building to remain in their apartments during construction (see Idris and Schneider). This state-of-the-art, user-friendly approach to building is stressed in a video on the firm's webpage; it shows the positioning of the modules onto the roofs in fast-forward mode, as if by magic. For this quick and easy solution, the architects have further perfected the modernist idea of modular prefabrication: They assembled each of the small extensions in the factory according to its individual plan and measurements before cranes put each on top of the original buildings and complimented them with the readymade roofs. Thus, repetitive design is optimized with the highest modular flexibility and individual comfort. On its homepage, Virtuel Architecture describes its aims:

> Our projects respond to strong social and environmental issues. The HQE approach [Haute Qualité Environnementale, a standard for green building in France] is a citizen's one; it seems to us inescapable. The reflection on the high environmental quality [. . .] influences the organization of the plan, supposes innovative materials, implies intelligent techniques. The investment, particularly in time, which is linked to an environmentally friendly approach is "profitable." (Idris and Schneider)

Virtuel Architecture thus sticks to the narrative of the three-pillar model of sustainability that, first, considers social aspects by putting human beings in the center of their plans, second, follows the sustainable HQE standard while, third, also actively pursuing an economic agenda.

Comparable to MVRDV, Virtuel Architecture answers to modernist building practices by adding today's technology. "Innovative materials" and "intelligent techniques" securing the static stability of the enlarged house as well as the concern for the priorities of the inhabitants prove the office's efficient approach. When the architects insist on "profitability" and "quantifiable savings," they fulfill a prerequisite for the feasibility of sufficiency practices exemplified in the above excerpt from Arne Steffen's criteria of sufficiency, namely that everybody involved should be "able to recognize very concrete advantages for themselves despite the decision of spatial self-restraint" (Steffen 8). The enlarged apartments gain extra space that is, for the first time in the apartment blocks' history, insulated according to the French green-building standard. Consequently, the additions with their new technologies improve the whole building. So, for the tenants of the enlarged apartments, for the other residents, for the lessor, and, last but not least, for future generations, these

FIGURE 3.2. 33 Logements à Poissy. The extension of existing working-class apartment blocks with thirty-three small-living spaces. © Virtuel architecture, used with kind permission of the copyright owners.

investments are "profitable." Above all, this script aspires to not be a story of gentrification; the residents of the rental apartments stay the same before and after the extensions.

Moving forward from two static densification projects, we turn to "Wohnwagon," a modular, individual tiny-house structure that adds self-sufficiency and the possibility of lower-income homeownership without sealing up additional ground (see fig. 3.3). In 2017 the architectural journalist Claudia Siegele describes the Austrian mobile tiny-living entity:

> Young start-up entrepreneurs have developed a mobile housing unit that is completely self-sufficient thanks to a [. . . photovoltaic] system, wood-burning stove, and water circulation system with green sewage treatment plant. The "caravans" are joined from natural raw materials and regional materials. Depending on their size and equipment, they can also be used as offices or hotel rooms. (48)

The journalist narrates the caravan not as an architectural achievement, but rather as a return to primeval living, an autonomous housing space with

FIGURE 3.3. A prototypical Wohnwagon. © Wohnwagon GmbH, used with kind permission of the copyright owners.

state-of-the-art efficiency and consistent solutions. One price to pay for this self-sufficiency is the occupants' constant awareness of limited energy reserves, or, in other words, their awareness of sufficiency as a leading principle of their lives. The start-up's homepage promises buyers that they will "be natural, self-determined, independent" and "inspired by nature" ("Wohnwagon"). After all, the mobile home is built from all-natural materials such as wood and clay, its insulation material is wool.

This wholesome impression is reinforced by pictures of the mobile home standing alone on an open field, under trees, or surrounded by mountains (see fig. 3.3). Headlines such as "Paths to Self-Sufficiency" on the Wohnwagon website and its *Autarkieblog* discuss the tiny house in terms reminiscent of Thoreau's dream of the simple, independent life close to nature. Whereas the individualized examples given here can be rather costly, the Wohnwagon can also become a less expensive do-it-yourself project. Accordingly, the projects range from pricey investments to cheaper do-it-yourself versions of independent living, all under one small roof. And besides being used as a *datcha*, a hotel, office, or studio space, the Wohnwagon can be an inspiration for communal projects among small-living fans of all ages, even providing solutions for generational living. Generational living is part of the degrowth-city script; it means flexible building solutions with more rooms for growing family situations and fewer rooms for families becoming smaller. But let us look at a different tiny-living project in Dortmund-Sölde, which adds even more communal dimensions to tiny living.

The city campaign for tiny living in Dortmund-Sölde follows the sustainable-city script (Stadt Dortmund, nordwärts, and Bund Deutscher Baumeister). As this chapter is prepared for publication, the model project is still in its planning stage and building will not start before 2023. A research project accompanying the planning and building process of the tiny village was wished for by many to gain experiences for the future. It would have been another exemplary lab script as advertised by Schmid, Schulz, and Weck.

Dortmund's model project stresses the relative affordability in comparison to larger housing; the webpage argues that the "need for action on the housing market is immense" and "new ideas for living that are quick and affordable are necessary" (Stadt Dortmund, nordwärts, and Bund Deutscher Baumeister). The model project promising redemption from the housing crisis does not challenge the spatially nonsufficient idea of the *Einfamilienhaus* (single-family home), but the single tiny houses will be grouped in clusters that share spaces such as tool and bike sheds or piazzas and thus participate in a narrative of close communal living. At the same time, the Sölde project incorporates a *Wohnprojekt* (multiparty housing project) with a modular structure that can respond to generational changes.

Adding to the space-consuming logic that undermines the sustainability of this model project, Sölde is set in a suburban area on the outskirts of the city of Dortmund, which will increase the area's sealed-off space. Nevertheless, one can argue that tiny houses consume less resources and especially less concrete than regular houses—after all, the production of concrete is highly carbon-intensive and depends on the scarce resource of sand. Some prospective tiny-house builders in Sölde also emphasize their wish to build with wood and use sustainable insulation materials such as straw or wood fiber.[2] The Sölde website by the city of Dortmund and other collaborators builds on the sustainability narrative that "small houses present an environmentally-friendly alternative to regular houses," although savings are relativized by the individual houses' large exterior surface (Stadt Dortmund, nordwärts, and Bund Deutscher Baumeister).

---

2. Due to Katharina Wood's privilege of interning with the Öko-Zentrum NRW, she was able to participate and take notes in planning meetings for the tiny village with the prospective building groups. In those organizational meetings, future builders presented their ideas and aspirations.

The narrative of the circular economy is also a popular argument within the tiny-house movement in general and in Sölde in particular. Within the circular economy, not only the production costs but the entire life cycle of a product is evaluated, and all products used for building are supposed to be reused, reusable, or recyclable. This sufficiency model of ecological circulation is often termed the "cradle-to-cradle" principle, which aspires to run against capitalist principles (Cui 22). Tiny-house inhabitants in Sölde are influenced by diverse sufficiency narratives. For some, living small entails approaches to conscious consumption and strategies of reducing waste. Since tiny houses only have a limited capacity to store waste, there always is a pragmatic necessity to reduce it. The website celebrates "Wasteland rebel" Shia Su, who lives with her partner in a 30m² flat in Cologne and pursues a zero-waste lifestyle. She is presented as an inspiration for tiny living in Sölde (Stadt Dortmund, "Lebensqualität auf 30 qm").

Narratively, the official campaign advertises the idea of "small house. large life." This tale resonates with sociologist Tracey Harris's observation that tiny-house occupants tend to spend less money and yet perceive their lives as more "meaningful" and "fulfilling" (Harris; see Ingram 640)—a redemptive dream of living small starts to replace economic aspects central to the former American Dream.

The reasons for moving into tiny houses vary widely, ranging from values like freedom and minimalism to the wish to be close to nature and live more environmentally friendly to affordability or preventing homelessness (see Evans, "Tackling Homelessness"). The minimal narrative insinuates that small houses award their inhabitants with more free time, less cleaning, and a larger quality of life. The Sölde website refers to overflowing possessions as "ballast" from which one should free oneself. It raises the questions: "How much time and money do I really want to invest in a house on a day-to-day basis?" or "How much space do I need to live?" These are very urgent questions on a planet where especially Western lifestyles are depleting resources at an unprecedented pace. These limitations are also narratively packaged on the website, which argues against the "massive consumption of resources and land" despite its own adherence to single family homes and the suburb. The project website includes environmentally friendly approaches to building, including scripts of anticonsumerism, individual freedom, a future-oriented community life, and affordability; builders show tendencies to organize themselves according to the triple-bottom-line of sustainability. Here, tiny living has proved to be a very flexible concept. The most diverse and sometimes contradictory narratives are connected to any of the prospective builders' personal and personalized tiny-house plans.

CONCLUSION

This chapter shows that tiny architecture follows innumerous narratives, among them ancient cultural discourses from different parts of the world, romantic ideals of a self-sufficient life close to nature, modernist and postmodernist plans for redemptive city architecture, historical and recent scripts of urban densification, the traditional dream of home ownership, stories testifying to a contemporary awareness of living in times of climate change, plots of sustainability and sufficiency, scripts of degrowth and the sustainable city, as well as many others. The mix of stories across digital platforms proves to be dense and so does a complex system like the three-pillar model of sustainability, which is often reiterated, emphasizing the ecological, social, and economic benefits of projects—but always differently. For future research, it will remain important to read the narrative texts alongside the scripts of architectural and technical construction in order to assess this diversity, its congruencies, and its discrepancies. An additional analysis of the narratives used across architectural projects further illuminates the inescapable complexity of understanding greenness and sustainability by the different parties involved in building processes.

WORKS CITED

Alexander, Samuel, and Brendan Gleeson. "Collective Sufficiency: Degrowth as a Political Project." *Post-Capitalist Futures: Paradigms, Politics, and Prospects*, edited by Samuel Alexander, Sangeetha Chandrashekeran, and Brandon Gleeson, Palgrave Macmillan, 2022, pp. 53–64, https://doi.org/10.1007/978-981-16-6530-1_5.

Ameel, Lieven. *The Narrative Turn in Urban Planning: Plotting the Helsinki Waterfront*. Routledge, 2021.

Anson, April. "'The World is My Backyard': Romanticization, Thoreauvian Rhetoric, and Constructive Confrontation in the Tiny House Movement." *Research in Urban Sociology*, vol. 14, 2014, pp. 289–314.

Charley, Jonathan, editor. *The Routledge Companion on Architecture, Literature and the City*. Routledge, 2018.

Cui, Mengmeng. "Key Concepts and Terminology." *An Introduction to Circular Economy*, edited by Lerwen Liu and Seeram Ramakrishna, Springer, 2021, pp. 17–34.

Englert, Klaus. *Wie wir wohnen werden. Die Entwicklung der Wohnung und die Architektur von morgen*. 2nd ed. Reclam, 2021.

Evans, Krista. "Integrating Tiny and Small Homes into the Urban Landscape: History, Land Use Barriers and Potential Solutions." *Journal of Geography and Regional Planning*, vol. 11, no. 3, 2018, pp. 34–45.

———. "Tackling Homelessness with Tiny Houses: An Inventory of Tiny House Villages in the United States." *The Professional Geographer,* vol. 72, no. 3, 2020, pp. 360–70.

Ford, Jasmine, and Lilia Gomez-Lanier. "Are Tiny Homes Here to Stay? A Review of Literature on the Tiny House Movement." *Family and Consumer Sciences Research Journal,* vol. 45, no. 4, 2017, pp. 394–405.

Frishman, Richard. "Hidden in Plain Sight: The Ghosts of Segregation." *New York Times,* 30 Nov. 2020.

Harris, Tracey. *The Tiny House Movement: Challenging Our Consumer Culture.* Lexington Books, 2018.

Idris, Jana, and Jamin Schneider. "Eins aufs Dach." *Arte Magazin,* June 2020, https://www.arte-magazin.de/eins-aufs-dach/.

Ingram, Daniel J. "Tracey Harris, The Tiny House Movement: Challenging Our Consumer Culture." *Human Ecology,* vol. 48, no. 5, 2020, pp. 639–40.

Markus, Thomas A., and Deborah Cameron. *The Words between the Spaces: Buildings and Language.* Routledge, 2002.

MVRDV [Architectural Office]. "Didden Village." *MVRDV.nl,* https://www.mvrdv.nl/projects/132/didden-village. Accessed 18 Mar. 2021.

———. "Example House." *MVRDV.nl,* https://api.mvrdv.boerdamdns.nl/media/uploads/project/132/120.jpg?width=1920. Accessed 30 Nov. 2022.

Psarra, Sophia. *Architecture and Narrative: The Formation of Space and Cultural Meaning.* Routledge, 2009.

Rauert, Roderick. "Nach dem Prinzip des Teilens: Apartmenthaus 'Friends' in München." *Deutsche Bauzeitung. Tagungsband zum 2. DB-Suffizienz-Kongress 13. Oktober 2015,* 2015, pp. 26–29.

Ryan, Marie-Laure, Kenneth Foote, and Maoz Azaryahu. *Narrating Space / Spatializing Narrative: Where Narrative Theory and Geography Meet.* The Ohio State UP, 2016.

Schmid, Benedikt, Christian Schulz, and Sabine Weck. "Keimzellen für die Transformation. Postwachstum und Raumentwicklung." *Politische Ökologie,* vol. 38, no. 160, 2020, pp. 19–26.

Schmid, Susanne, Dietmar Eberle, and Margrit Hugentobler, editors. *Eine Geschichte des gemeinschaftlichen Wohnens: Modelle des Zusammenlebens.* Birkhäuser, 2019.

Siegele, Claudia. "Autark und mobil. Der 'Wohnwagon': Mobile Kleinstwohneinheit." *Deutsche Bauzeitung,* vol. 6, 2017, pp. 48–51.

Stadt Dortmund. "Lebensqualität auf 30 qm." https://www.kleinehaeuserdortmund.de/2019/08/28/shia-su/. Accessed 17 Mar. 2021.

Stadt Dortmund, nordwärts, and Bund Deutscher Baumeister, Architekten. "Kleine Häuser Dortmund Webpage." https://www.kleinehaeuserdortmund.de/. Accessed 30 Mar. 2021.

Steffen, Arne. "Chance auf Umsetzbarkeit: Zehn Kriterien der Suffizienz im Wohnen." *Deutsche Bauzeitung. Tagungsband zum 2. DB-Suffizienz-Kongress 13. Oktober 2015,* 2015, pp. 8–11.

Umweltbundesamt. "Energieverbrauch nach Energieträgern und Sektoren." https://www.umweltbundesamt.de/daten/energie/energieverbrauch-nach-energietraegern-sektoren. Accessed 18 Mar. 2021.

Virtuel Architecture [Architectural Office]. "Extension sur les toits de 33 logements et réhabilitation de 216 logements à Poissy." *Virtuel.fr,* http://www.virtuel.fr/extension-sur-les-toits-de-33-logements. Accessed 18 Mar. 2021.

———. Logements á Poissy. http://www.virtuel.fr/wp-content/uploads/1810_Villogia_Poissy_Aero_Porcher_09-1295x863.jpeg. Accessed 30 Nov. 2022.

Wohnwagon GmbH. "Wohnwagon." https://wohnwagon.at. Accessed 18 Mar. 2021.

Zell-Ziegler, Carina, and Hannah Förster. *Mit Suffizienz mehr Klimaschutz modellieren: Relevanz von Suffizienz in der Modellierung, Übersicht über die aktuelle Modellierungspraxis und Ableitung methodischer Empfehlungen,* edited by Umweltbundesamt, EVUPLAN des Bundesministerium für Wirtschaft und Energie, Texte 55, 2018.

CHAPTER 4

Narrative Path Dependencies in Sustainable and Inclusive Urban Planning

Portland's Albina Neighborhoods

ELISABETH HAEFS AND
JENS MARTIN GURR

This contribution examines *narrative path dependencies* in the context of urban planning (for a tentative account, see Gurr 125–40): While path dependencies in urban planning point to an irreversible planning decision with long-term impacts on urban environment, *narrative path dependencies* are "activated" when the narratives invariably contained in planning discourses (implicitly or explicitly) rely heavily on specific genres, plot patterns, or tropes (see Ameel). Depending on the context of the planning project, the genre or the tropes suggested in the plan or in the discourses surrounding it thus invoke specific plot trajectories and predetermine future developments. City scripts, as "assemblages of figural expression [. . .], of narrative exposition [. . .], and of media presentation" (Buchenau and Gurr 6) frequently create path dependencies, while the combination of *different* city scripts often produces conflicts and contradictions. This essay highlights this phenomenon specifically in urban planning that seeks to combine sustainability and social inclusiveness: The scripts of sustainability and inclusivity discussed here do not always function harmoniously in combination and sometimes conjure up contradicting narrative patterns.

The case study we use to illustrate this phenomenon is Portland, Oregon—frequently hailed as a "world-renowned sustainability mecca" (Goodling, Green, and McClintock 4)[1]—and particularly its Albina district, a collection of neighborhoods (see Gibson). Here, too, a central issue is the extent to which *sustainability* and *privilege* are connected. More specifically, the conflict in Albina revolves around the question to what extent strategies of urban revitalization and urban renewal—in Portland, these are closely associated with *green* amenities for a sustainability-minded clientele—inevitably bring about processes of gentrification. Does sustainability for some inherently mean exclusion for others—in other words, can one tell a story of urban renewal without having to gloss over processes of gentrification? After the Albina discussion, we draw on recent work in planning theory and literary urban studies to propose the notion of *narrative path dependencies* and discuss the potentially conflicting scripts of sustainable and of socially inclusive urban development.

All in all, by discussing the interplay between urban development strategies and their accompanying imaginaries and narratives—conceptually as well as in our Portland case study—this contribution seeks to explore what narratology and urban planning can learn from each other.

THE SUSTAINABILITY SCRIPT, THE INCLUSIVE SCRIPT, AND THE CLASH BETWEEN "URBAN RENEWAL" AND "GENTRIFICATION"

In urban planning, green space is frequently posited as a good to be saved, or, simultaneously, as a savior of declining and unhealthy cities, thus rendering green or ecologically sustainable planning a morally imbued enterprise. As the sociologist Hillary Angelo explains, the "'green as good' formula has become ubiquitous in urban planning [. . .]. Today, urban greening is understood to be a global policy trend, used by transportation planners, architects, locavores, activists, and city governments to make urban environments more hospitable and more sustainable" (646). Charged with such implications, the idea of the sustainable city functions as a script to be followed by the actors tasked with urban development. In this context, Jonas argues that sustainability is a trope used for redevelopment: "Sustainability plays a part in representing urban change as both desirable and necessary: it is a trope to be mobilised selectively in the service of redevelopment—after all, who would want to argue that unsustainable urban development is a good thing?" (Jonas 120). The narrative framework surrounding ecological sustainability often conceals aspects

---

1. For Portland's "green exceptionalism" (Goodling, Green, and McClintock 19) and its long-standing role in pioneering innovative strategies of sustainable urban development since the 1970s, see also Gottdiener and Budd 149.

of *social* sustainability, because "sustainability has also helped to script a language of urban development from which the voices and everyday struggles for survival on the part of poorer and minority communities are excluded" (Jonas 121; for a compelling account of the intersections between narrative and sustainability, see also Eckstein and Throgmorton and the contributions in James and Morel).[2]

Though many urban development projects gloss over the contradiction between economic, ecological, and social dimensions of urban development, these contradictions have more clearly come into focus in recent years. In their discussion of one of these conflicts, Wachsmuth, Cohen, and Angelo describe the phenomenon of "environmental gentrification:"

> As districts become greener, they become more desirable and expensive. The premiums placed on neighborhood amenities—such as walkability, public transport and the proximity of parks, farmers' markets and "greenways" such as hiking trails and bike paths—by residents who can afford to pursue them raise the cost of living. (Wachsmuth, Cohen, and Angelo 392)

In contrast to the sustainability script, development in the name of the inclusive city normally aims at spatial, social, and economic inclusion (see Armendaris 13), as well as access and participation. Like sustainability, it can induce similar effects of coating injustices, but given its focus, these effects are less likely to occur than the *greenwashing* that often accompanies sustainable development efforts. The inclusive city script works with less corporate and institutional support and is therefore a minor force in global urban development compared to sustainable, creative, and smart city development.

The redevelopment of urban areas in the service of sustainability, hinted at by Jonas (120), is of central concern for our study. The bulk of Portland's planning efforts appears to be directed at remaining a "standard bearer of sustainability" (Goodling, Green, and McClintock 18). A policy that is central to Portland's reputation in this regard is the city's Urban Growth Boundary (UGB), installed in the late 1970s to curb urban sprawl and to enable condensed urban development. The controversy central to our interest in the potential conflicts between sustainable and socially inclusive urban development with their specific narratives and imaginaries also centers on the question whether the UGB, by limiting space for development, leads to increased

---

2. Our analysis of the impact of planning narratives on the physical spaces and experiences in Albina would at first sight fall into the category of econarratological investigation (see James). However, as our work closes in on urban planning texts rather than works of literature, it is still different from what is commonly considered a subject of econarratology.

real estate prices inside the city. The answers are by no means as clear as one might think.

By contributing to the city's reputation, the UGB also plays a role in attracting "investment capital and more affluent residents" (Goodling, Green, and McClintock 13). Moreover, the image of Portland as an ecologically inclined, quirky hipster paradise has famously even entered popular culture, as it is crucial to the TV series *Portlandia* (IFC, 2011–18), a series that has been criticized for predominantly representing privileged, mostly white urbanites and their health- and sustainability-oriented lifestyle while largely ignoring the role of African Americans in Portland.

Portland's overall "sustainability fix" (Goodling, Green, and McClintock 3) forms the backbone of so-called urban renewal and revitalization efforts, which are usually aimed at increasing urban "livability" with a strong focus on economic growth. In the course of Portland's urban development strategies, the city has seen various waves of investment and disinvestment in different neighborhoods (see Goodling, Green, and McClintock), which have frequently been accompanied by conflicting accounts of revitalization and gentrification. Generally, urban renewal can contribute "to sustainable development through the recycling of derelict land and buildings, reducing demand for peripheral development and facilitating the development of more compact cities" (Couch and Dennemann 137–38). However, it seems that in the case of Portland's Albina district, the city's reputation for sustainability was used as a pretext to implement urban renewal for economic development. It is specifically in Albina that sustainable planning in the name of "urban renewal" and catering to ecologically minded, affluent residents has been a major driver of gentrification (see Goodling, Green, and McClintock 14, 19).

PLOTTING PORTLAND'S ALBINA NEIGHBORHOODS

Our discussion focuses on the 1993 "Albina Community Plan" (ACP), which dramatically shaped developments in the Albina district for almost two decades. The plan aimed at "beautifying the district's streets and sidewalks, developing several of its over 2,000 vacant lots, and providing loans for storefront improvements along a handful of dilapidated historic business corridors" (Goodling, Green, and McClintock 13).[3] We argue that the "urban renewal"

---

3. It was only in 2017 that Prosper Portland, the former Development Commission, released a plan that officially addressed the toll that the displacement largely driven by the Albina Community Plan (ACP) took on the Albina community. However, even the 2017 plan does not properly acknowledge that the process that changed Albina could be described as *gentrification*, because the term only marginally appears in the glossary (Prosper Portland 4, 17).

proposed by the ACP signifies gentrification. In the terminology established in this collection, one might say that the ACP formulates a script for the overall gentrification of Albina: "This current round of displacements was very explicitly catalyzed and designed by the [ACP] [. . .] with a long lead-up of public admonishments about the state of Albina and the requisite flag-waving for 'urban renewal'" (Hern 8–9). "Urban renewal," "revitalization," "livability," and "prosperity" come to function as stand-in keywords that, from a different perspective, signify gentrification and exclusion. We will contrast the urban development scripts resulting in gentrification—by way of an ostensibly "redemptive," prosperous rebirth plot induced by the ACP—with the entirely different story told by former Albina residents, which rather resembles the plot of a tragedy (Ameel, chapter 8 in this volume). Elements of classical tragedy are also expressed in the inevitable fate of the antigentrifier's dilemma, "the problem that an awareness of one's own privileged position and even activism against gentrification may not be enough to avoid supporting the process by one's mere presence as someone able to pay higher rents" (Gurr 122).

While ecological sustainability is rather a sidenote in the ACP and not an end in itself, it is invoked in the demand for an attractive "Pattern of Green" (Bureau 22, see 85–87). The keywords "urban renewal" and "revitalization" are central concepts of this plan, which has marked the beginning of the "'improvement' in Albina" and "has spelled the dislocation of thousands of African Americans" (Goodling, Green, and McClintock 19).[4] Fittingly, in their analysis of Portland's uneven development, Goodling, Green, and McClintock ask "why the urban core of this paragon of sustainability has become more White and affluent, while its outer eastside has become more diverse and poor" (3). Therefore, while in Portland's overall planning, sustainability seems to clash with social inclusion, the ACP—on a smaller scale—also appears to have induced a clash between economically prosperous urban renewal, on the one hand, and affordability and inclusion, on the other. The conflict between ecologically sustainable and inclusive development is vividly described by John Washington of the North/Northeast Business Association (NNEBA): "I knew Black people were fucked as soon as I saw the bike lanes. That's when we knew Black people weren't welcome here anymore" (qtd. in Hern 10).

In some descriptions, the Albina community resembles a *theater* of gentrification, with displacement as a show: The treatment Albina received by urban planners "*set the stage* for developers to profitably inject Albina with capital, and create the necessary conditions for the displacement of lower-income households and residents of color from inner-core neighborhoods to

---

4. Census data prepared by Portland State University show that in 1990, roughly 23,724 African Americans lived in Albina. By 2020 this number had halved to 11,845. In the same time, the overall population of Albina increased from 77,195 to 94,650 residents (Jaquiss).

East Portland" (Goodling, Green, and McClintock 19, emphasis added). Similarly, Hern speaks of "the combination of historical segregation, community trauma, and ongoing neighborhood disinvestment that *set the stage* for its gentrification" (Hern 6, emphasis added). Hence, gentrification, although it is a highly complex process, can appear deliberate and scripted, therefore emphasizing the sense of a virtually deterministic development logic set in motion by specific plot choices in urban planning. This notion of a scripted theater of gentrification further suggests that scripts as conceptualized in this volume not only have the potential to galvanize citizens into collective action for their neighborhood or their city, but that scripts can also cause or at least reinforce divisive, agonistic, and potentially violent development logics.

Revitalization and urban renewal, on the one hand, and gentrification, on the other hand, though they may refer to the same phenomenon, tell very different stories, actualize very different associations, and suggest very different plots. The familiar planning tales of urban renewal and revitalization invoke a *redemptive rebirth* plot: This pattern seems to mirror what happens in the ACP, as the plan's opening statement by Portland's then mayor, Vera Katz, already outlines that the plan seeks to protect "what is unique to each of these neighborhoods and provides a blueprint for revitalizing areas that have suffered decline" (Bureau n. pag.). The plan recounts this story of "decline" and "disinvestment" (Bureau 2, 35, 65) and promises that the ACP will "combat [. . .] disinvestment and dilapidation" (Bureau 1). The strong drive of this familiar story creates an automatism that overshadows the negative effects of renewal, which is also due to a primary identification with the ostensibly heroic planning commission. Correspondingly, the sense of agency is situated with the planning commission rather than with the neighborhoods and the residents.

Therefore, the rebirth plot of "urban renewal" induces sympathy with the city itself as the protagonist,[5] which becomes a *savior* of the Albina community, while the district, in terms of character stereotypes, is a marginalized outsider left behind by development elsewhere.[6] This story partly coincides

---

5. For the pervasive understanding of the city as protagonist or character, see Ameel 39, 94.

6. While there is limited space for historical background in this chapter, it is important to note that the state of Oregon has been founded "on the notion of creating a racist white utopia" (Imarisha). The history of segregation and housing discrimination faced by African Americans is particularly evident in Portland, where a racist "code of ethics" and redlining prevented mortgage lending and homeownership for many Albina residents (Goodling, Green, and McClintock 10); however, these dynamics are not exclusive to Portland, as they "followed a script playing out in cities across the country" (10). As Karen Gibson puts it, in "Portland, the Black community was destabilized by a systematic process of private sector disinvestment and public sector neglect" (Gibson 6).

with what Ameel calls the *Bildungsroman* plot in urban planning: If urban development narratives are formulated in terms of growth, agency, identity formation, the finding of a proper voice, or attainment of potential, then these are the generic terms of the *Bildungsroman* especially of the late eighteenth and nineteenth centuries as the narrative of emergent self-confidence, self-realization, and agency.[7] In the case of the ACP, Ameel's observation of the center being the character with agency who absorbs the peripheries (96) seems fitting, even though Albina is located close to the city's core. Moreover, the "ideological baggage" (Ameel 5; see also White 1–42) that comes with generic plots is evident in this case: The *Bildungsroman* "envisioned a wholesome individual in harmony with a wholesome society, a vision that was reflected in enlightenment visions of a harmonious spatial environment that could lead to a well-educated citizen able to maximize his or her contribution to society" (Ameel 96). This approach would then imply that Albina needs to be "educated" or even "tamed" in order for it to become a valuable member of the city society, and following the rebirth plot of urban renewal, Albina would then be *reborn* into the larger city fold.

With the prosperous redevelopment induced by the plan so strongly represented, concerns about affordability are relegated to the sidelines: "The Planning Commission and City Council felt that further concentration of low-income households in the Albina Community should be avoided, and that affordability and density issues should be revisited as the area stabilizes" (Bureau 9). This means that affordability is not as important as the welcome gentrification of the area. The choice of the verb is revealing in this case: To read that the council "felt" a certain way about this decision, which impacted countless livelihoods, in hindsight seems condescending. The same applies to the following task formulated in the plan: "Revisit the housing affordability issue in the Albina Community neighborhoods in 10 to 15 years after the Albina Community neighborhoods have stabilized" (Bureau 54). Affordability and social inclusion here again become a side note, implicitly turning the people who depend on them (a large part of the former Albina community) into secondary characters without agency. The direction the Planning Commission wants to take becomes clear, as does the nature of the urban renewal envisaged here: "Aggressively market the Albina Community to investors, developers, business owners, workers, households, and tourists" (Bureau 39).

---

7. These, however, clash with the more recent generic development of the *Bildungsroman*, which frequently no longer follows such optimistic patterns but rather stages abortive attempts at rising from poverty or tells stories of racism and glass ceilings preventing the attainment of agency (for the clash between the *Bildungsroman* emplotment of urban plans with the development of the *Bildungsroman* as a literary genre, see also Ameel 101).

The narrative path taken here suggests an unvarnished welcome to gentrification and the ensuing displacement of the people who will not be able to afford the renewal of the area. Using the word "aggressively," moreover, is unusual in a planning document. While it is often maintained that displacement from Albina was not intentional (Swart, "NorthEast"; Goodling, Green, and McClintock 16), the consequences of suggested plots in planning here appear as inevitable. There is no proof that the narrative trajectories invoked by the ACP are to blame for Albina's gentrification, but it is likely that they strongly contributed to it. This is clearly implied, for instance, when the plan argues that "Albina's public image has improved as the area has been broadly recognized for its historic importance. Its wealth of quality structures of historic value has helped to attract interest" (Bureau 14). In urban development parlance from an investor's perspective, "wealth of quality structures of historic value" had, even by 1993, long been the globally comprehensible euphemism for *gentrifiable housing stock*.

If displacement is the outcome of both the rebirth (renewal/revitalization) and the tragedy (gentrification) plot, these two plots denote the same phenomenon.[8] The development logic invoked and set in motion by the ACP therefore inevitably conjures displacement and posits it as a necessary side effect to ensure renewal. In Cornelius Swart's Albina documentary "NorthEast Passage: The Inner City and the American Dream" (2017),[9] Stan Amy, entrepreneur and philanthropist, provocatively says: "Call it gentrification, call it revitalization. Obviously, there's an implicit point of view in both ways of stating it" (Swart, "NorthEast"). This statement sums up how the same phenomenon is emplotted in two very different narratives with different implied protagonists. Fred Stewart, an African American Realtor also interviewed by Swart states that it is "not too late to make the next gentrification cycle better" ("Priced Out"). This statement is quite revealing because it is the rare exception: "Gentrification" is almost invariably used to talk about the problem of pricing out, while "renewal" or "revitalization" is normally used as the positive term. In this case, gentrification is directly addressed as what happened during the renewal and what is likely to happen again.

The *success story* of Albina becomes a tragedy when it is told from a different perspective: Swart's two-part documentary follows an African American

---

8. For the question of whether gentrification without displacement is possible, see National Low Income Housing Coalition. For an exploration of the "gentrification plot" in crime fiction, see Heise.

9. The first part of the documentary was filmed when gentrification in Albina was already happening, presumably enforced by the ACP. The second part of the documentary is called "Priced Out: Gentrification in Portland."

resident from Albina, Nikki Williams, and her struggle against the changes in her neighborhood. At first, she welcomes gentrification because the situation in the disinvested Albina has become unbearable for her, but in the second part of the documentary, she sees what urban renewal has brought to her door, and she eventually leaves Portland: "And see, [. . .] when I hear the [. . .] new folks moving in and 'oh blah blah' [. . .], it's like, y'all here 'cause you get beer every ten feet and [. . .] can go to New Seasons and buy a $15 organic apple, but [. . .] this is real heartbreaking." Moreover, Williams's daughter adds that she "did not think it would become so bad that [her] mom would be leaving" ("Priced Out"). Apart from a tragedy, this reads like one of the urban narratives described by Throgmorton, namely the "city of ghosts," which contains "a narrative of memory, of loss, [. . .] of neighborhoods being destroyed by urban renewal" (Throgmorton 143–44).

Although tragedy seems obviously encoded in the displacement of Albina residents, the classical tragedy plot, which requires the inevitable downfall of a flawed character, also appears in the gentrifiers themselves: Swart describes himself as a "gentrifier," as an involuntary agent in the process he critically seeks to document. This antigentrifier's dilemma neatly fits the definition of the flawed tragic hero: Although in this case they do not experience their own downfall, but contribute to someone else's displacement and downfall, both the privileged antigentrifier and the tragic hero unwittingly contribute to bringing about the catastrophe they are trying to prevent. Still, the apparent inevitability and the seemingly abstract and virtually automatic process of gentrification, depending on whether gentrification is seen as driven by the demand of an incoming middle class, or by the supply through investors, developers, and real estate agents (for an overview of the debate, see Zapatka and Beck), lends itself to being emplotted as a tragedy.

As a result, the virtually inevitable development logic invoked by both the rebirth plot and the tragedy plot seem powerful in their ability to *naturalize* processes in urban development and make them seem unavoidable, even necessary. This dynamic within the ACP also corresponds with Koschorke's notion of narratives as "formatting templates": In certain situations, reality adapts to the narrative because such narratives strongly suggest certain outcomes and preclude others. The "diagnosis" made by the plan can thus become a "screenplay" (Koschorke 197) of the events that are supposed to unfold in the neighborhoods: This is quite precisely what, in the terminology of our research group, we call a *script*.

The general familiarity of people (planners, residents, incoming residents) with such scripts and basic plots is certainly a factor that contributes to the narrative drive of planning documents like the ACP. The desired trajectories of development, as determined in the ACP, are therefore strongly influenced by narrative. This approach also demonstrates how the (narrative) closure provided by the ACP—a fully *renewed* district—creates new planning problems, namely displacement and the concentration of low-income housing and residents in other parts of the city—in this case, in East Portland (see Goodling, Green, and McClintock 3).

At present, developments in Albina continue, and it remains to be seen whether the plan released by Prosper Portland in 2017 will result in long-term changes that benefit the already displaced community members. Additionally, the successful community-led nonprofit Albina Vision Trust, founded in 2017, is a countermovement that challenges decades of disinvestment, subsequent renewal, and gentrification, by "transforming what exists today into a socially and economically inclusive community of residents, businesses, artists, makers, and visitors" (Albina Vision Trust). The accompanying "Albina Vision Community Investment Plan" for Lower Albina will apparently be a key to this endeavor. In the end, it remains to be seen whether the 2020 Black Lives Matter protests that unfolded across the globe, but especially prominently in Portland, will echo in the years to come and will positively impact future inclusive urban development.

NARRATIVE PATH DEPENDENCIES

Building on our discussion of how the scripted revitalization of Albina set the district on a path of gentrification, and drawing on path dependency research in economics and planning research, on classic narratological research as well as on recent narratological research on planning texts in literary urban studies (for a compelling recent account, see Ameel), we advance the notion of *narrative path dependencies*.[10] Though here exemplified for planning texts, we nonetheless propose *narrative path dependencies* as a more widely relevant concept in literary studies. Path dependencies in general are defined as developments in which a situation or decision to a large extent predetermines the future course of a system, so that decisions at one point in time might severely limit the range of options for future decision-makers. Most research on path dependencies has focused on technology management and standardization in markets with a need for a systemic fit of different components, in which decisions for one system or the other creates technological lock-ins. A widely debated example is the QWERTY keyboard: Originally the result of technical limita-

---

10. Our sections titled "Narrative Path Dependencies" and "Conclusion" reuse a number of formulations from Gurr 125–40.

tions in mechanical typewriters that no longer apply to modern keyboards, where other arrangements of keys would be ergonomically superior and more efficient, QWERTY has nonetheless remained the standard, not least because of the time-consuming need to retrain billions of users for a new typing system (see David, "Clio"). Another notorious example is the issue of rail track gauges, arguably the clearest case of path dependency and technological lock-in: Although wider gauges would be technically superior, it is easy to see that the incompatibility of new tracks and trains with the already installed rail system makes a switch to wider gauges practically impossible. More recently, path dependencies have been more widely discussed in urban planning and urban development (see Hein and Schubert), not least in the field of urban mobility. As a case in point, many postwar European cities as well as much twentieth-century planning in North American cities planned cities around individual automotive mobility at a time when environmental degradation, climate change, or geopolitical considerations with regard to fossil fuel dependencies were not an issue.

Arguing that the notion of path dependency is one that literary studies and more specifically narratology may adapt from urban planning in order to better understand real-world consequences of plot patterns, tropes, interpretive schemata, or scripts, we draw on a number of scholars who have proposed a closer look at narratives and discourses in explaining path-dependencies (see esp. Herrmann). To be sure, the concern in these discussions has primarily been with how narrative accounts *retrospectively* make developments appear path dependent.[11] In this vein, David, as one of the scholars most consistently engaged in path dependence research, has argued that "the tragic form of narrative" that makes a course of action seem "foreordained" clashes with "the stories that economic historians typically wish to tell" ("Path Dependence" 94). In a related vein, Garud, Kumaraswamy, and Karnøe have engaged with the way in which narrative accounts of (allegedly) path-dependent developments foreground the agency (or lack thereof) of key players in these processes. However, the creation of de facto path dependencies through generic choices, plot patterns, and narrative schemata in urban-planning discourses—and hence the more narrowly narratological concerns central to our endeavor here—have only recently begun to be studied (see Ameel in chapter 8 of this volume for the most far-reaching account so far).[12]

---

11. For the related narratological concern with serial narration and its need to work within the confines of previous narrative instalments, see Kelleter.

12. For the seemingly unchangeable notion of "past narratives" and the contrasting notion of "future narratives," which inherently suggest openness because they foreground "nodes" as points of decision between alternative paths, see Bode and Dietrich, especially 1–3.

Given the importance of narrative perspective and the centrality of a protagonist to the perception of a story, which Alex Woloch has rightly drawn attention to,[13] a key question in understanding *narrative path dependencies* in planning documents is to ask who—individual residents, the collective of a neighborhood, the city as a whole, the city administration, a group of developers or planners, the gentrifiers, the victims of gentrification—is cast as the protagonist and thus receives the bulk of the "limited, and unevenly distributed amount of narrative attention" (Woloch 177; see also 2, 14, and throughout). Conversely, who—given the overwhelming identification with the protagonist—is relegated to the periphery of textual (and readerly) attention? With whom are addressees of planning narratives *not* invited to identify? In order to better understand the ideological implications of planning narratives, the tradition of research following Hayden White's classic *Metahistory* (1973) is important: In producing narrative accounts of past developments—and this surely also applies to narrative representations of anticipated futures—White argues, there are only four basic plots available: comedy, tragedy, romance, and satire. The choice of a plot structure, moreover, also implies the choice of a figure of speech and thought—White analogizes them with the established tropes of metaphor, metonymy, synecdoche, and irony—and carries an implicit ideology, a way of seeing the world. One does not need to accept fully White's complex and sometimes quite schematic, though highly suggestive account of the elective affinities between these basic plots, key figures of speech, and ideological implications to see just how loaded with meaning such plot choices are. Research on narratives in urban planning and urban literary studies has similarly pointed out both the very limited number of basic plots commonly encountered in planning texts *and* the way in which they frequently function in profoundly literary ways, calling up epic, comedic, tragic, or melodramatic plot patterns and narrative conventions (for a more detailed discussion, see Ameel; Buchenau and Gurr). In this vein (but without exploring their generic implications), Throgmorton speaks of "at least five broad narratives [that] are commonly told about urban areas in America" (142) and mentions (1) "the city as a site of opportunity and excitement"; (2) "the city as a nightmare"; (3) "the city as a site of injustice, oppression, and exclusion (but also hope)"; (4) "the environmentalists' interpretation [in which] the city is a site of activities that are rapidly eroding the ecological base upon which those activities are founded"; and (5) "the city of ghosts. This offers a narrative of memory, of loss, of small towns drying up and blowing away, [. . .] of

---

13. To be sure, Woloch has also shown—for narrative generally, though with a focus on the realist novel—that attention is by no means focused on the protagonist only (40 passim).

neighborhoods being destroyed by urban renewal [or] being eviscerated by deindustrialization" (143–44). Though this inventory of narratives is hardly complete, it is clear that each of these patterns suggests different outcomes, inclusions, and exclusions. Similarly, Ameel has pointed out that narratives in planning

> are structured according to a limited set of narrative forms and strategies that are well established in literary fiction and in narrative studies: metaphor (such as the city as body), genre (such as the *Bildungsroman*), and the protagonist's development within the broader outlines of a narrative plot. All three of these narrative forms have implications for assessing the planning narratives discussed here. Metaphorization may underscore the implied logical, "natural," or necessary nature of a chosen course of action. (6)

As for genres, plot patterns, narrative templates, and metaphors in planning narratives and their ideological implications, they "come with some ideological baggage that is hard to cast aside" (Ameel 5). Finally, and in keeping with our above discussion of how attributing the role of protagonist in planning narratives serves to direct interest and, conversely, to deflect attention or to gloss over concomitant developments, Ameel argues that plans suggesting "the integration of a marginalized character into the natural urban fold of the city centre" (94) can helpfully be read as following a *Bildungsroman* pattern and that, in such narratives, "agency does not belong to the peripheries, but, rather, to the centre that absorbs them" (96).

In sum, and as exemplified in our case study from Portland, we suggest that what literary studies, and more specifically narratology, can learn from urban planning is more systematically to think in terms of path dependencies and, in taking seriously the notion of *narrative path dependencies,* to consider more systematically the ideological implications of specific narrative patterns and the inclusions, exclusions, and dénouements they imply, suggest, or even predetermine.

CONCLUSION

For the type of contextual analysis of planning documents here exemplified for the case of Portland's Albina district, the notion of *narrative path dependency* may be fruitful: While *path dependency* is a common concept in planning, it is conceptually surprisingly close to the analysis of narrative templates in literary studies, where the choice of specific plot patterns suggests or even predetermines certain outcomes. Even if we eschew the simplistic version of linguistic determinism now largely refuted as being untenable, the surprisingly limited number of plot patterns, narrative templates, and cognitive models available in, for instance, the formulation of urban development, should not be underestimated in their function as "formatting templates" (*sensu* Koschorke) for urban developments: Which *dénouements*, lock-ins, inclusions, and exclusions are suggested or even imposed by the plot patterns associated with different genres or by established patterns of narrative sense-making? How do they thus create the literary equivalent of path dependencies, suggesting or even determining specific outcomes, inclusions, and exclusions? Here, an awareness of the extent to which cognitive models and their emplotment open up or foreclose, suggest, or deter from different possible developments may be conducive to more sensitive or circumspect planning and planning communication. Similarly, the notion of path dependencies as they are studied in urban planning and other fields may be helpful to literary scholars in thinking about the functions and effects of narratives.

WORKS CITED

Albina Vision Trust. "About," https://albinavision.org/about/. Accessed 24 Mar. 2021.

Ameel, Lieven. *The Narrative Turn in Urban Planning: Plotting the Helsinki Waterfront*. Routledge, 2021.

Angelo, Hillary. "The Greening Imaginary: Urbanized Nature in Germany's Ruhr Region." *Theory and Society*, vol. 48, no. 5, 2019, pp. 645–69.

Armendaris, Fernando. "World—Inclusive Cities Approach Paper (English)." 2015, http://documents.worldbank.org/curated/en/402451468169453117/World-Inclusive-cities-approach-paper.

Bode, Christoph, and Rainer Dietrich. *Future Narratives: Theory, Poetics, and Media-Historical Moment*. De Gruyter, 2013.

Buchenau, Barbara, and Jens Martin Gurr. "'Scripts' in Urban Development: Procedural Knowledge, Self-Description and Persuasive Blueprint for the Future." *Charting Literary Urban Studies: Texts as Models of and for the City*, by Jens Martin Gurr, Routledge, 2021, pp. 141–63.

Bureau of Planning Portland, Oregon. "Adopted Albina Community Plan." *City of Portland, Oregon*, 1993, https://scholarsbank.uoregon.edu/xmlui/bitstream/handle/1794/6186/Albina_Community_Plan.pdf.

Couch, Chris, and Annekatrin Dennemann. "Urban Regeneration and Sustainable Development in Britain: The Example of the Liverpool Ropewalks Partnership." *Cities*, vol. 17, no. 2, 2000, pp. 137–47.

David, Paul A. "Clio and the Economics of QWERTY." *American Economic Review*, vol. 75, no. 2, 1985, pp. 332–37.

———. "Path Dependence: A Foundational Concept for Historical Social Science." *Cliometrica: Journal of Historical Economics and Econometric History*, vol. 1, no. 2, 2007, pp. 91–114.

Eckstein, Barbara, and James A. Throgmorton, editors. *Story and Sustainability: Planning, Practice, and Possibility for American Cities*. MIT Press, 2003.

Garud, Raghu, Arun Kumaraswamy, and Peter Karnøe. "Path Dependence or Path Creation?" *Journal of Management Studies*, vol. 47, no. 4, 2010, pp. 760–74.

Gibson, Karen J. "Bleeding Albina: A History of Community Disinvestment, 1940–2000." *Transforming Anthropology*, vol. 15, no. 1, 2007, pp. 3–25.

Goodling, Erin, Jamaal Green, and Nathan McClintock. "Uneven Development of the Sustainable City: Shifting Capital in Portland, Oregon." *Urban Studies and Planning Faculty Publications and Presentations*, paper 107, 2015, pp. 1–27, https://pdxscholar.library.pdx.edu/usp_fac/107.

Gottdiener, Mark, and Leslie Budd. *Key Concepts in Urban Studies*. SAGE, 2005.

Gurr, Jens Martin. *Charting Literary Urban Studies: Texts as Models of and for the City*. Routledge, 2021.

Hein, Carola, and Dirk Schubert. "Resilience and Path Dependence: A Comparative Study of the Port Cities of London, Hamburg, and Philadelphia." *Journal of Urban History*, vol. 47, no. 2, 2021, pp. 389–419.

Heise, Thomas. *The Gentrification Plot: New York and the Postindustrial Crime Novel*. Columbia UP, 2021.

Hern, Matt. *What a City Is For: Remaking the Politics of Displacement*. MIT Press, 2016.

Herrmann, Victoria. "The Birth of Petroleum Path Dependence: Oil Narratives and Development in the North." *American Review of Canadian Studies*, vol. 49, no. 2, 2019, pp. 301–31.

Imarisha, Walidah. "How Oregon's Racist History Can Sharpen Our Sense of Justice Right Now." *Portland Monthly Magazine*, 25 Feb. 2020, https://www.pdxmonthly.com/news-and-city-life/2020/02/how-oregon-s-racist-history-can-sharpen-our-sense-of-justice-right-now.

James, Erin. *The Storyworld Accord: Econarratology and Postcolonial Narratives*. U of Nebraska P, 2015.

James, Erin, and Eric Morel, editors. *Environment and Narrative: New Directions in Econarratology*. The Ohio State UP, 2020.

Jaquiss, Nigel. "The Black Population of Inner North and Northeast Portland Continues to Shrink." *Willamette Week*, 25 Aug. 2021, https://www.wweek.com/news/city/2021/08/25/the-black-population-of-inner-north-and-northeast-portland-continues-to-shrink/.

Jonas, Andrew E. G. "Beyond the Urban 'Sustainability Fix': Looking for New Spaces and Discourses of Sustainability in the City." *The Politics of the Urban Sustainability Concept*, edited by David Wilson, Common Ground Publishing, 2015, pp. 117–35.

Kelleter, Frank, editor. *Media of Serial Narrative*. The Ohio State UP, 2017.

Koschorke, Albrecht. *Fact and Fiction: Elements of a General Theory of Narrative*. 2012. Translated by Joel Golb, De Gruyter, 2018.

National Low Income Housing Coalition. "Gentrification and Neighborhood Revitalization: What's the Difference?" 5 Apr. 2019, https://nlihc.org/resource/gentrification-and-neighborhood-revitalization-whats-difference.

Prosper Portland. "North/Northeast Community Development Initiative Action Plan: Fostering Economic Prosperity among African Americans and People of Color." 2017, https://prosperportland.us/wp-content/uploads/2016/08/NNECDI-Action-Plan-web.pdf.

Swart, Cornelius. "Priced Out: Portland's History of Segregation and Redlining—Full Documentary." 2017. *YouTube*, uploaded by Priced Out: Tales of Gentrification, 23 Oct. 2020, https://www.youtube.com/watch?v=vMZYiv_jf2U.

———. "[Remaster 2017] NorthEast Passage: The Inner City and the American Dream." 2002. *YouTube,* uploaded by Cornelius Swart, 28 Mar. 2017, https://www.youtube.com/watch?v=U83_LFs_q60&t=18s.

Throgmorton, James A. "Planning as Persuasive Storytelling in a Global-Scale Web of Relationships." *Planning Theory,* vol. 2, no. 2, 2003, pp. 125–51.

Wachsmuth, David, Daniel Aldana Cohen, and Hillary Angelo. "Expand the Frontiers of Urban Sustainability." *Nature,* vol. 536, no. 7617, 2016, pp. 391–93.

White, Hayden. *Metahistory: The Historical Imagination in Nineteenth-Century Europe.* Johns Hopkins UP, 1973.

Woloch, Alex. *The One vs. the Many: Minor Characters and the Space of the Protagonist in the Novel.* Princeton: Princeton UP, 2003.

Zapatka, Kasey, and Brenden Beck. "Does Demand Lead Supply? Gentrifiers and Developers in the Sequence of Gentrification, New York City 2009–2016." *Urban Studies,* vol. 58, no. 11, 2021, pp. 2348–68, https://doi.org/10.1177/0042098020940596.

PART 2

URBAN LITERATURE

CHAPTER 5

Scripting the Inclusive City, Narrating the Self

Contemporary Rust Belt Memoirs in Poetry and Prose

CHRIS KATZENBERG AND
KORNELIA FREITAG

Much has been written about America's "Rust Belt"—the term itself already sets a pessimistic tone. Anne Trubek's *Voices from the Rust Belt* (2018) revolts against this rush to regional judgment. Her anthology intervenes in a discursive context that is often dominated by misleading perspectives from the outside.

> We have created not only income inequality but also narrative inequality in this nation: some stories are told over and over while others are passed over, muted. So the writers in this book seek you and say: This is me and I am here. But more, they say: Please pay attention. Please listen. Let us tell you our story. We can tell it ourselves. (Trubek 5–6)

As its title already suggests, the anthology showcases voices from the margins of the American national (and literary) discourse. It aims to present previously unrecognized narrative self-descriptions of the region. Trubek insists that the anthology's writers are Rust Belt insiders who collectively construct a cumulative and shared regional self-narrative—and seek to present it to an external audience.

Anna Clark's *A Detroit Anthology* similarly collects "many voices" (9) that make up the Rust Belt. It focuses on the city that has come to be synonymous with the region's supposed complete failure—Detroit. The book was published in 2014, in the aftermath of the city's bankruptcy in 2013. As Clark points out in her introduction, much Detroit writing is, indeed, intended for readers from outside of the city and its surroundings. Yet, she knows that there is a second audience for her book: It presents "Detroit stories for Detroiters" (9–10).

> We may be lifelong residents, newcomers, or former Detroiters; we may be activists, workers, teachers, artists, healers, or students. But a common undercurrent alights the work that is collected here: These stories are for us. This is a city made of many voices, and so, too, is this book. (Clark 9)

Both anthologies start from the same premise: They collect recent writings by Rust Belt inhabitants who represent their life stories or histories, their experiences and thoughts in relation to their city and their region. And by making room for people's individual stories, they also create a space to voice larger, shared issues within the city region.

In this chapter, we will use memoir and cultural theory to study three texts from the two anthologies that are all set in Detroit. We will show how Jamaal May, Shaun Nethercott, and Marsha Music fashion self-descriptions of Detroit and Rust Belt city life between individual and collective concerns and pressures. We will inspect how each of their memoirs, as a specific form of "self-narration" (Eakin), constructs an account of regional urban self-formation. Moreover, we will start to demonstrate that the anthologies function in themselves as collectively authored (meta-)self-descriptions and self-narrations. They assemble numerous and often incoherent local perspectives on Detroit city life that ultimately exceed the narration of any single author.

In the next section of this chapter, we will briefly situate our project in the existing scholarship on memoir and autobiographical self-narration as well as on urban self-description. Subsequently, we will analyze how the three texts negotiate between self-narrations and self-descriptions, individual and collective views, internal and external points of reference, prescription, and agency. Finally, we will embed our findings into the wider field of research on the self-representations of big cities.

MEMOIRIST SELF-WRITING: FASHIONING SELVES IN LITERATURE

The terms *autobiography* and *memoir* are sometimes used interchangeably. Christiane Lahusen, however, has recently developed a useful narratological distinction between the two. Following influential twentieth-century narratologists like Bernd Neuman, Georg Misch, and Francis Russel Hart, she defines autobiography as typically more focused on the "psychic and personal development of the individual," while memoir rather places "an individual life story into a larger context of public or historic consequence," depicting "participation by an individual [. . .] in public life, in public events" (Lahusen 626). While memoirs do, of course, engage with a "subjective past," they focus mainly on "an event, an era, an institution, a class identity" (Hart 195 qtd. in Lahusen 626). As a fundamentally experience- and memory-based text type, they (re)present these events from an explicitly limited and unreliable perspective, with no claim to objectivity or completeness (Couser 19). Concerning these characteristics, the three texts to be analyzed here fall squarely into the category of memoir. Moreover, in all of them the roles of writer, narrator, and protagonist overlap. In Thomas Couser's terms, they are a form of "self-life writing" representing *"single-experience narratives"* (Couser 22) and match the broader trend in the memoir field "away from comprehensive scope toward narrower focus—either in time span or in 'thickness'" (23). The very fact that such texts from lesser represented, "literary second cities" (Finch, Ameel, and Salmela) like Detroit are increasingly being published, seems a consequence of the recent "memoir boom" in the US (Gilmore 2 qtd. in Lahusen 629; for a detailed account, see Rak). Local memories and experiences, penned by professional or amateur writers, have become bestsellers since the late twentieth century. Memoir has grown into an immensely popular "democratic genre, allowing for a diversity of voices, positions, styles, arguments, and subjects" (Danielewicz 6). It also empowers "previously silent group[s]" to narrate their lives publicly (Lahusen 630). The transformative potential of popular memoirs is high, as they call widespread attention to underrepresented issues, potentially swaying "public opinion" and even encouraging "collective action" (Danielewicz 6). As Clark's and especially Trubek's introductions indicate, their anthologies have exactly such aims. They want to shift the Rust Belt and its inhabitants from the margins to the center of public attention. They create the stage to intervene collectively in the ways the region has been and continues to be (mis)represented, poised to reduce the narrative inequality diagnosed by Trubek.

SELF-NARRATION IN MEMOIRS AND SELF-DESCRIPTION IN CITY WRITING

Danielewicz links memoirs' great attraction to its ability to "gratify readers' perpetual curiosity" about the lives of their fellow humans (6). Drawing on Paul John Eakin's work, she argues that memoirs' appeal is due to the genre's "referential (the author is a real person) and relational (the author's relationships to others are central)" qualities (6). Their referentiality situates memoirs, like any other autobiographical text, between claims of nonfictional grounding in "the real world" and the necessarily only mediated access to it through narrative (6). Their strong relationality anchors memoirists' referential self-constructions along the continuum between the individual and the social or collective life.

Eakin argues that by representing a process of self-fashioning in writing, memoirs may not so much perform a separate, highly specialized literary function than formalize a common human process, as one's self-narration is embedded in and foundational to aspects of a person's ongoing identity formation. This goes back to the cognitive psychologist Daniel Schacter's theory of "autobiographical memory" as a form of *"episodic memory"* that "allows us explicitly to recall the personal incidents that uniquely define our lives" (Schacter 17, qtd. in Eakin 107–8). If *"autobiographical memory"* is the "enduring chronologically sequenced memory for significant events from one's own life" (Nelson 162, qtd. in Eakin 108), Eakin proposes, language is needed to structure and order the events. He claims that an identity materializes in a "lifelong trajectory of self-narration" (113, see also 67–68, 99–141). Language is for Eakin the basis of an *"extended self"* (102, with reference to Ulric Neisser), the "self of memory and anticipation, the self in time" (102).

Eakin's understanding of self-narration as a process of referential and relational structuring of individual experiences via language is shared by Lahusen: She conceives of memoir-writing as "an act of ordering, through which the author directs herself towards a goal and presents her proposed identity. In this way, she positions herself in relation to the existing range of identities on offer, appropriates preexisting narratives, perpetuates them, or dispenses with them" (Lahusen 633). This is an ordering in time and place that happens within and toward a certain culture's social relations. Hence, city memoirists' self-narration may be understood as always both predefined by preexisting urban societal models and intervening in them. They are generated in a process of being inscribed, writing one's self, and redefining one's self via one's city at the "border between the individual and social groups" living in the city (Lahusen 634; see also Eakin 65–66).

This understanding of city memoirs suggests that they are an important part of the urban cultural texts that Barbara Buchenau and Jens Martin Gurr have defined as "city scripts": "proscriptive and descriptive systems of reading and writing" the North America city ("City" 396). And, given the interventionist aim of the two Detroit anthologies, it seems clear that their authors partake in but also consciously subvert "the normative ways of scripting the city, of rewriting and adapting cityscapes for new purposes and different users as well as audiences" ("City" 402).

Buchenau and Gurr explain how city scripts can lead to "re-scriptions of a city's past in the construction of (alternative) urban heritages, descriptions of its present in modes that look like 'the plotting of the everyday,' as well as prescriptions for its future" ("City" 405). They serve three "core functions" as a city's "self-description," "blueprint," and "procedural knowledge" (Buchenau and Gurr, "Development" 142). In city planning, policy, and marketing, city scripts are mostly geared toward an intended blueprint that, in turn, targets clearly defined procedural knowledge. The script of the smart, the green, the creative city is mostly not what the place in question is already; it is what the city hopes to become, or at least, what its town hall hopes to make it. These official self-descriptions of the future city are often everything but original: They are mostly invented somewhere else, and related blueprints and procedural knowledges are frequently imported. The imagined collective city disseminated on municipalities' websites, billboards, and media ads is streamlined to fit this kind of townhall script. In memoirs that focus on a city, the city's self-description instead gains center stage via the memoirist's self-narration. Urban planning blueprints are far away. The presented *city script* is based on personal experience that is transposed into a stand-in for the community in which the memoirist lives. Thereby it is much more provisional, more fragile, and less encompassing than a townhall script. "Self-narration" in memoir centrally understands and represents the self as changing over time, as Eakin makes clear (98). Hence, the city script in a memoir is circumscribed: It is what we call an *urban memoirist script,* a script that can be traced back to one individual and is based on that person's experience. Closely tied to the text type in which it emerges, it enacts very different generic conventions than the script formulated in the townhall's stable, (supposedly) all-encompassing plan, policy, or marketing image. We will demonstrate three ways of how self-narration in memoirs of city life addresses and turns into self-description in urban memoirist scripts in the next three subsections.

NARRATING URBAN SELVES, SCRIPTING RUST BELT CITIES: THREE CITY MEMOIRS

Jamaal May's short free-verse soliloquy "There Are Birds Here" captures the battle for representing Detroit life as a life worth living. It is no memoir in the usual sense, yet it undoubtedly places "an individual life story" of living in and defending one's hometown "into a larger context of public or historic consequence" and shows "an individual" actively engaging "in public life, in public events," as Lahusen defines memoir (626). The first-person speaker functions as the persona of the poet, who grew up in the city. The brief colloquial poem condenses May's positive experiences of contemporary Black life in Detroit into a quotidian city moment: A smiling boy observes a girl who feeds breadcrumbs to birds. The lively but peaceful scene is clearly meant to defy Detroit's stereotyped collective identity as a city of ruins and broken people. Yet the text literally traces the obstruction of peaceful everyday life within the city from the outside, by interrupting time and again the description of Detroit's birds and kids.

The poem's dedication, *"for Detroit,"* does not so much establish the setting but—as it turns out while reading—the arena of a battle about who gets to define the city. The speaker starts to declare "There are birds here" (l.1), underlining this with "so many birds here" (l.2), when, reacting to invisible antagonists, he has to interrupt himself for the first time in the poem to state "is what I was trying to say / when they said those birds were metaphors / for what is trapped / between buildings / and buildings" (ll. 3–7). With a strong "No," he returns to his original declaration and insists: "The birds are here / to root around for bread / the girl's hands tear / and toss like confetti" (ll. 7–11). Another "No" is followed by a jarring line break as he interrupts himself again to ward off the inappropriate interlocutor, then goes on to say: "I don't mean the bread is torn like cotton / [. . .] / not the confetti a tank can make of a building" (ll. 12–15). While the speaker stubbornly insists on the normality and livability of his hometown—with birds and happy kids—the interjections call up not just real-life urban restrictions ("trapped") and violence ("a tank" making "confetti [. . .] of a building"), but they highlight urban blight's continuation and aggravation by an overwhelming discourse that feeds on images of inner-city poverty, confinement, violence, and war.

The poem highlights the power of negative normative ways of scripting Detroit, in a Rust-Belt-specific version of the script of the Black inner city, a "racial script" in Natalia Molina's sense.[1] This city script, which May aims to counter with his life-embracing memoirist city script, is the flipside of one-dimensionally positive townhall scripts concocted by postindustrial cities' planning, policy, and marketing departments. May does not pretend bad things did not happen in Detroit or in Black history. In fact, he acknowledges them with words like "trapped," "cotton" (picking), and "tank" that allude to the well-known history of Black victimization. Thereby he gives his poem a precise racial setting. May shows that victimization occurs (also and again) due to debilitating city discourse, to a bleak racial [city] script that often seems inescapable for Black neighborhoods in its reductionism. He highlights

---

1. For "racial scripts," see Molina; for Black inner-city imaginaries in the US, see Anderson; for the specific racial script of Rust Belt Black-majority cities as doomed to decline, see Hackworth; Hamera.

how racialization exacerbates the "narrative inequality" that affects all of the Rust Belt.

After the speaker protests a last time the reversal of an utterance of life (the smile of the boy) into a simile of death ("like a skeleton") in lines 17 to 18, he finally gives up. In the last four lines of the poem, he acknowledges that "they won't stop saying / how lovely the ruins / how ruined the lovely / children must be in that birdless city" (ll. 28–31). The chiasm leads directly to the final sentence, literally sentencing the city to death. The racial city script of blighted Detroit is condensed into the figure of a "birdless city." It has finally drowned out the hopeful urban script of "birds here, / so many birds," an urban self-description the speaker knows to be true but is still unable to uphold against the onslaught of his imagined interlocutors. The vacuous last three lines are, in fact, a dead giveaway of the effects and the beneficiaries the "lovely [. . .] ruins" and the "ruined [. . .] lovely / children" in the "birdless city" of Detroit are meant to serve. The poem demonstrates the working of a powerful negative city script enacting symbolic violence: Line-by-line, a vivid scene of Black urban life in Detroit is condensed into metaphor, simile, and chiasm. It is inverted into dead people and deadly weapons. And it is newly assembled to make a "lovely" spectacle for consumption by unconcerned outsiders. The force of a negative, exclusionary city script is shown in (poetical) action.

The juxtaposition of external prejudice and insider experience is what the poem highlights: As its speaker attempts to hold on to his observation of happiness and hope, opposing negative scriptings of the city interject themselves. The poem structures this back-and-forth like an actual argument, artfully condensing many similar confrontations into one. Talking back is presented as an automatic habit for a (Black) citizen of Detroit. It is his interlocutors who put the speaker into the position of a representative of his city. He is forced to intervene, intercede, and speak for its collective self.

The speaker's interlocutors remain invisible and nameless, an anonymous collective of voices, the third-person plural pronoun "they." May's poem defies "their" eagerness to (mis)read Detroit and the Rust Belt as a symbol of a failed city rather than a real city with real people in it. This poem rejects both the external negative prescription and the crude reduction of Detroit: It seeks to set a local act of urban self-narration against the reductive constraints of external overdetermination. It tells a city story on the locals' own terms, to audiences both within and beyond the Rust Belt's borders.

Yet, the poem's bleak conclusion hints at the power of stereotyping city scripts that keep erasing Detroit's self-experience by misreading as symbolic what was meant to be literal and overwriting real-life events by rhetorical sleight of hand. This is not a hopeful ending, and it calls into question the effectiveness of both anthologies studied here. However, the poem's performative analysis of the mechanism of discursive expropriation is certainly eye-opening and empowering. It entertains no illusions regarding the ability of a single speaker—or text—to "flip the script" of downtrodden (Black) Detroit. Yet, it talks back defiantly, and effectively. Its "counter-scripting" exposes the clichés to raise the awareness of a tradition of exploitation and violence (Buchenau and Gurr, "Development" 125).[2] It shows how the denial of an ordinary life and of this life's presentation in simple stories victimizes Detroit's inhabitants. It performs the erasure of the memory that "there are birds here" by the mediated image of "that birdless city," replacing an (internal) memoir city script with a stereotypical, latently racialized (external) city script.

The prose text "The Detroit Virus" by the white Detroit playwright and activist Shaun Nethercott fits the category of "self-life writing" telling a *"single-experience narrativ[e]"* (Couser 22), although it is special in its division into two different sections with two distinct narrative voices. The first section is titled "Yes, But . . ." (214–16) and tells in the first-person singular about a slightly too long bike ride through Detroit that Nethercott is seemingly only able to finish because her husband Wes comes to her rescue. The second part, which shares the text's main title, "The Detroit Virus" (216–17), changes to the first-person plural and announces to a rhetorical "you," next to the couple's plan to cycle through America, the up- and the downsides of living in Detroit. This two-part structure seems to highlight Lahusen's definition of memoir by first showing "an individual life story," self-reflexively told by the individual itself, and then placing it "into a larger context of public or historic consequence," even addressing the public as "you." Nethercott clearly depicts "participation by an individual" (part 1) "in public life, in public events" (part 2, Lahusen 626). Yet, while this is undoubtedly her aim, a closer look at the structure and the function of her text raises some questions.

On the surface, "The Detroit Virus" works toward the same goal as May's text. It sets a positive vision against the negative image of the city. By way of her bike ride, the narrator aims to create a positive city script of an active and changing city "teeming with people":

> people of all ages, all colors, women in hijab and men in hard hats [. . .], youth with pants four sizes too big walking along hipsters with pants two sizes too small [. . .] grandmas [. . .] grandbabies, white-suited sailors, [. . .] even a few tourists having their pictures taken with [the] Underground Railroad monument. (214)

---

2. See Deckers and Moreno in chapter 1 of this volume on "scriptivity" and Black and LatinX practices of "counterscripting" through urban murals.

In this passage, the third paragraph of her text, she even manages to be much more encompassing than May—"all ages, all colors" and the "Underground Railroad monument." And later, the rhetorical vehicle of the bike ride also allows her to mention some less inviting parts of the city—a construction site and a stretch of shore she calls the "party zone," a "garbage zone" where trash piles up because the city can no longer afford to pick it up (215). Finally, exhausted, she summons her husband Wes and talks to him to catch her breath and regain her confidence, then bikes home safely. By way of the bike ride through nice and not so nice parts of the city, Nethercott strives to present the real, the full picture of the place.

Yet, instead of presenting herself in relation to her city and its people, she rather presents herself in a hermetically self-centered narrative. This is in part because she tells her ride as a quest narrative to meet a challenge: "I am going to take a long loaded bike ride [. . .] just to see if I can" (214). And while this challenge might have involved human interaction, it does not. It is herself against herself with Detroit as the stage for her self-experiment.

In the first two paragraphs, she tells how she sets out on a "blue spring day" (214)—with the pronoun "I" appearing eight times in nine and a half lines. The third paragraph describes the people and the city scenes quoted above— seen literally in passing, from her fast-moving bike. The next paragraphs turn back to the narrator, describing her feelings, her movements, her reactions— starting: "I am a bit of a spectacle," "I leave the waterfront," "I curve back," "I am still feeling good," and so forth (214–15). It seems that the narrator has no connection to "the teeming people" she observes. Each one and everything she sees somehow serves as a spectacle for her consumption—and, for the first part of her ride, serves to mirror her good mood. She describes the different people and notable city features in the manner of a female flâneuse—an aloof, white, middle-class, (st)rolling observer of street life. Unlike the stereotypical male flâneur, she is not invisible, yet still appears beyond immediate social censure (see D'Souza and McDonough; Nesci). Uninvolved, she enumerates all she encounters, people included, as an almost quaint, pastoral procession of sights. They may defy potential readerly expectations of Detroit as a dangerous ruinscape inimical to the white middle classes. Yet, the protagonist is in no way part of the picturesque city through which she rides.

As in every quest, she has to overcome obstacles. When she leaves the nice and acceptable part of the city, a "big mistake" (215), she rolls into a construction site that blocks the picturesque view of the Detroit River, and "workers stare at" her. She traverses the ugly stretch of shore full of party garbage and is exhausted, her "right leg is hurting." She "stop[s] in the shade"—and calls her husband for help. When she is on her way to meet him and waits at a red light, her only interaction with another Detroiter occurs: "A friendly fellow tells me,

'You don't need to wait for the light, there ain't no traffic.' I wait anyway, glad to be off my bike, even for a moment" (215–16). The advice is "friendly" but obviously redundant. The narrator is familiar with her body's needs, even if her weakened state is not obvious to the stranger observing from the outside.

On her way home, at the end of part 1, the narrator complacently answers the question she had posed to herself at the start: "'Can I do twenty miles in a shot?' The answer is 'yes, but . . .'" (216). This final statement recalls the title and is clearly meant to be read as implying a larger lesson on the limits of self-reliance and individual autonomy in the city of Detroit. Yet, the reading of the text has made it clear that, most likely contrary to her intention, Nethercott's representation of Detroit here is a place to consume, not to interact with. When, inadvertently, Detroit gets rough, what saves her are not just any Detroiters, but specifically her family—though she does identify herself with the city collectively, it appears that actual support networks function at a much smaller scale.

The surface message is that sticking with bold plans against all odds and better judgment is what it means to be a Detroiter. The self-centered, not at all relational or referential self-narration suggests a rather narrow idea of what that means for the city and its inhabitants. The first part translates into a full-fledged city script revolving around Nethercott, her husband, and people who are just like them.

In the second section of the text, the tone changes. While the memoiristic vignette of the bike ride is narrated in the first-person singular, the text then transforms into a narrative in the first-person plural, which lays claim to a larger Detroit identity. The new narrative "we" explains the titular "Detroit Virus," as a metaphor for the forces that drew the narrator and her husband to the city: "We moved here in 1989, one of the first to catch the Detroit virus. We fell in love with it, with its potential, with its stark and beautiful contradictions" (216). The figurative virus thus functions as both a self-description and an embodiment of procedural knowledge, condensing what it means to be a Detroiter. Yet this "we," far from encompassing all Detroit citizens, refers to the narrator-protagonist and her husband. It is also representative of "a number of people" that they "have transmitted the virus to" and who are said to do "really important work here that makes a real difference in people's lives and the shape of the city" (216). It is this group's vision of the city that Nethercott's text advertises, without openly admitting to its partial view. Thereby the activist newcomers are advertised as Detroit's future while the city and the people already living there are objectified, rendered as in need of shaping—or saving from the "ugliness" mentioned later in the text (217).

The rhetorical question "Is there a place that has more imminence, in which the future is more present? Or the past more painfully marked?" (216) is a perfect illustration of the workings of a hegemonic city script: In a single minimal narrative, the city's past is *rescripted* into "painfully marked" (alternative) urban heritages, its present is *described* as having "imminence," and its future is *prescribed* as "already present," demonstrating all three normative and temporal dimensions of city scripts.

Nethercott's request, "Want to break away from mindless consumerism, me-first-ism, and deadening conformism? Come on down," (217) displays an astonishing failure of self-awareness. Her self-centered city-consuming quest and the self-serving, streamlined city script in the two parts of "Yes, but" turn out to be just another race- and class-privileged white savior narrative—the claim that Detroit needs people like Nethercott to be saved. It is the flipside of the city script of the blighted inner city that May's poem dissected. Hence, it is no coincidence that Nethercott's text ends with a positive platitude that mirrors the negative false image of Detroit as the "lovely ruins [. . .] in that birdless city" that May portrayed: namely "the exasperating, endearing, delicious, delightful wreck of a city" (217). Nethercott voices the attitude of relatively new, mostly white and affluent professionals and members of the "creative class" (see chapter 10 by Rodewald and Grünzweig in this volume) who have been coming to Detroit over the last two decades or so, looking for cheap housing, an alternative lifestyle, or work in Detroit's redeveloped downtown. The bike ride illustrates unabashedly how gentrification and highly uneven development bypass most Black and most poor Detroiters and the wide swathes of the city they predominantly live in.

Direct critique of this attitude appears in several pieces in the anthologies, for instance in Aaron Foley's "Can Detroit Save White People?" (Trubek 115–18).[3] The problematic relationship between the Black and the white Detroit inhabitants is also addressed by Marsha Music, whose text is analyzed in the next part of this essay. It is devoted to Detroit's white flight as a historic counterpart to current trends of white gentrification.

Marsha Music's "The Kidnapped Children of Detroit" was anthologized in both collections, bespeaking the importance of its subject and Music's local fame as an African American writer, cultural historian, and former labor organizer. She is a Detroit native, assertively proclaiming herself a "primor-

---

3. The Detroit-based journalist Aaron Foley became Detroit's first official "chief storyteller" since 2017. The city government tasked him and his media team with developing and communicating new, alternative narratives for the city that break with its negative cliches (Bloomberg Cities).

dial Detroiter" on her website (Music "The Detroitist"). Her short, single-themed text is closest to a traditional memoir of the three texts studied here. It recounts the mid-twentieth-century "white flight" from the then racially mixed, "solidly middle-class" area of Highland Park, a "city within a city" in metropolitan Detroit (19), located in what is today the Black-majority area south of Eight Mile Road.

The text starts in medias res: "It happened suddenly. One day we'd be outside with our friends, black, brown, and white. [. . .] The next day, our white friends would be gone" (18). The beginning puts the phenomenon in a nutshell—from the perspective of "black and brown" kids who saw their white friends and playmates suddenly disappear, seemingly, as Music's title has it, "kidnapped" overnight. Starting from her own and her nonwhite playmates' childhood perspective, Music is able to highlight concrete consequences of white flight that are too often obliterated. White—together with the Black and Brown—children were victimized by the white parents' choice to leave the city. A community of children was destroyed. Far from claiming total recall, the narrator is quick to indicate the partiality, maybe even unreliability of her recollections in the second paragraph. The narrative "I" characterizes her reminiscences as fashioned from a "jumbled mishmash of childhood memories" (18).

After this unusual beginning, the text switches from the collective childhood "we" to an adult first-person singular perspective as the narrator-protagonist divulges her family background and upbringing (19). Thereby the dominant voice within the text is introduced. It will guide readers through the following memoirist account of Detroit's white flight, frequently commenting on and evaluating this part of city history she reconstructs. In the latter half of the text, the subject shifts to Detroit's present and its hoped-for future as it has developed in the wake of the narrated events. Comparable to May's poem, the narrative proceeds to highlight that today, there are still pockets of highly functioning neighborhoods and communities that have survived in Detroit proper. Proud Detroiters have stayed, "committed" to the city (26), and the protagonist-narrator's current neighborhood of Lafayette Park is presented as a "model of diverse urban living," bearing similarities to how the prewhite-flight Highland Park was described in the beginning (26).

Music intersperses personal and communal memories, seemingly supplementing them with insights from the scholarship on Detroit's postwar development. Thereby she guards herself against self-centeredness and creates a memoir that is at the same time, to use Danielewicz's phrase, "referential (the author is a real person) and relational (the author's relationships to others are central)" (6)—time and again bound back to the general historical context.

She explicitly seeks to set up a counternarrative against the dominant discourse on white flight from the city, which holds that it was triggered by the 1967 Detroit Rebellion. Instead, she traces the exodus to white anti-Black sentiments, manipulative real estate profiteering, and suburbanization trends in the postwar era. In so doing, she plausibly shifts the blame for Detroit's subsequent downturn from the Black population of Detroit, who stayed, to the white Detroiters, who abandoned the city (Music 21, 18–25).

In the course of her self-narrative, Music does not simply narrate the white flight as an unfortunate occurrence in her own life as a Black Detroiter. She intersperses her text with a speculative account of the events from the collective perspective of "the other," the "kidnapped" white children and their families. To do this, she relies in part on the personal testimonies of acquaintances from these groups and in part on her imagination. By writing about these "proximate other[s]," she makes sure to include "relational lives" in her memoir (Eakin 69, 176). This complicates the apparently clear-cut boundaries between "me/us" and "them" that were erected in both May's poetic condemnation of the stereotypical city script of the blighted inner city and Nethercott's white urban savior script, based upon an ultimately flawed flâneurial view of Detroit (which sharply contrasts with her collaborative artistic work with marginalized Detroit communities as a playwright, see LISC Detroit).

Music does not stick at all with the first, her childhood view that the whites fleeing the city simply lost their neighborhood-based collective identity as Detroiters and became "transfigured into new souls called suburbanites" overnight (26). She recounts that many of those ex-Detroiters still feel a sense of continued belonging and even ownership of their former city (27). While this sort of lingering sense of rootedness is not uncommon in personal memory, its introduction in the text muddles a unilateral view on the past and the present of Detroit—of who is responsible for it and to whom it belongs (see also Sattler in this volume).

Music relates that many Black Detroiters who stayed cannot "comprehend the sense of belonging or even entitlement that many whites feel toward Detroit even decades and states removed from living within the city boundaries" (27). The incompatibility of the views of the (white) ones who left and the (Black) ones who stayed is illustrated by "kidnapped children" who, upon occasional return to their erstwhile neighborhoods, find their parents' decision to leave justified by the deterioration (27). Music asks the rhetorical question of whether the returnees do not "sometimes [. . .] suspect that decision [*to leave the city*] itself [. . .] was at least part of the cause of all the mess here now" (27). Yet, far from just blaming "the other," she briefly envisions an alternate history of shared Black and white responsibility for Detroit life:

> I wonder what might have happened in Detroit if there had never been this flight—if whites had held on and resisted the racial manipulation; if blacks had been able to push back the plague of unemployment, drugs, and crime; if we had been able to live in Detroit, all at one time. (27)

If "we had been" responsible for the well-being of the whole community, Music suggests, the "mass evacuation" could have been prevented (27). The collective urban self not ruptured by white flight could have prevented the attendant urban erosion. As it is, the "unprecedented transfer of community" tore apart the collective urban self and created "Detroiters in exile" (27)—still feeling a part of, but apart from Detroit.

The self-critical memoir closes with reflections that anticipate a "redemptive" collective Detroit identity in the future (see chapter 8 by Ameel in this volume). Music discusses the influx of new generations of suburbanites to Detroit proper, who are often the descendants of those whites who fled the city decades earlier (27–28) and asks the familiar question: "*Will Detroit come back?*" (28). Yet, changing the interpretative context, she responds dryly that "Detroit never left—but three generations did" (28). This well-founded observation helps her to continue the argument that the right to the city lies with those who took and take responsibility for it. If "more and more of the children and grandchildren of the Kidnapped Children are finding their way home [...] they find the city already occupied, and these strangers in a strange yet familiar land must learn to share it with those who held on" (Music 27–28).

Based upon her critical historical re-vision of Detroit's history of segregation, she concludes her memoir envisioning a cautiously optimistic city script for the future (see Buchenau and Gurr, "Development" 142). It encompasses a hopeful self-description as an ethnically "shared" place (Music 28), an optimistic blueprint to become "the most exciting place in the world to live in diversity" (29), and it unfolds procedural knowledge that goes deeper and is more encompassing but also much more demanding than a quick image campaign or the newest silver bullet fix in urban planning:

> There is a need for atonement in Detroit and its suburbs. We need a restorative movement to heal what has happened here, as the working people in this town competed against themselves over the right to the good life. We have to share stories about the experiences of the past era. As we move forward in Detroit, there must be a mending of the human fabric that was rent into municipal pieces with the divisions of city and suburbs. Small, continual acts of reconciliation are called for here, as sections of the city rise again. (29–30)

This redemptive city script is Music's answer to the Detroit white savior discourse that she debunks. However, she does not simply condemn the return of white people to the city of Detroit it accompanies and prescripts. She rather artfully inverts it, while doing away with its underlying false assumptions about who took and takes responsibility for the city and who can and will save it. As her closing statement about young white people coming to Detroit suggests: "It is true that some say that they have come to save Detroit, but I say, they come to Detroit to be saved" (Music 30).

CONCLUSION

The three anthologized memoirs from and about Detroit and the Rust Belt analyzed here construct a complex, flexible relation between collective urban selves, in the sense of city- or neighborhood-level identities, and the individual selves and identities of city people, as they are fashioned in processes of self-narration. In so doing, the memoirs demonstrate the irreducible yet necessarily conflict-prone interplay between different levels of urban identities that are established in relation to each other, prescripted by various established urban self-descriptions, but also continuously rescripted and subverted.

All three texts seek to defend Detroit and its meaning for its citizens against more or less openly negative stereotypes from the outside. The anthologized memoirs show three different versions of what a narration of urban selves on Detroiters' own terms can look like. They "write back" from the Rust Belt as a metropolitan region too long either ignored or maligned in much US national discourse. They counterscript external narrative overdeterminations of individual or collective city selves caused by clichéd prescriptions. Thereby these urban self-writings reclaim agency over "self-narration" as a key aspect of human identity formation, in the postindustrial Rust Belt as elsewhere.

Yet, the analyses have also shown that none of the texts can simply bypass stereotypical ascriptions from the outside, although all aim to use individual self-narration to oppose such normative prescripting. While Jamaal May's colloquial poem ultimately illustrates the overwhelming power of the hegemonic Rust Belt script of the blighted inner city of Detroit, poetic condensation and allusion allow him to present a case study of the discourse of Black victimization, its history, and the tenacious Black opposition against it within sixteen lines. While Shaun Nethercott uses her careful self-narration of a bicycle ride through Detroit to call for joining in the progressive makeover of Detroit, her ahistorical and self-centered performative script for herself and the city turns out to be in many ways the well-meaning twin of the exclusive city script

May deconstructs in his poem. Marsha Music, on the other hand, intertwines individual and collective self-narration with local history in her account of *urban flight*. Through a revisionary rescripting of the local past, she fashions an inclusive city script of shared Black and white responsibility for Detroit's future. All in all, the analyses have shown how memoirist writing on a city may work in poetry and prose. We have demonstrated how different self-narrations, self-descriptions, and urban memoirist scripts may be produced in texts that all share the same aim—to write against the stereotyping of Detroit.

WORKS CITED

Anderson, Elijah. "The Iconic Ghetto." *Bringing Fieldwork Back In: Contemporary Urban Ethnographic Research*, edited by Elijah Anderson, Dana Ashbury, Duke W. Austin, Esther C. Kim, and Vani S. Kulkarni, *The Annals of the American Academy of Political and Social Science*, vol. 642, 2012, pp. 8–24.

Bloomberg Cities. "How Detroit's 'Chief Storyteller' Is Crafting a New Narrative for His City." *Bloomberg Cities*, 25 Apr. 2018, bloombergcities.medium.com/how-detroits-chief-storyteller-is-crafting-a-new-narrative-for-his-city-3c14d0fa559c.

Buchenau, Barbara, and Jens Martin Gurr. "City Scripts: Urban American Studies and the Conjunction of Textual Strategies and Spatial Processes." *Urban Transformations in the U.S.A.: Spaces, Communities, Representations*. Urban Studies, edited by Julia Sattler, transcript, 2016, pp. 395–420.

———. "'Scripts' in Urban Development: Procedural Knowledge, Self-Description, and Persuasive Blueprint for the Future." *Charting Literary Urban Studies: Texts as Models of and for the City*, by Jens Martin Gurr, Routledge, 2021, pp. 141–63.

Clark, Anna. "Introduction." *A Detroit Anthology*, edited by Anna Clark, Rust Belt Chic Press, 2014, pp. 9–10.

Couser, Thomas G. "What Memoir Is, and What It Is Not." *Memoir: An Introduction*, Oxford UP, 2012, pp. 15–32, https://doi.org/10.1093/acprof:osobl/9780199826902.003.0002.

Danielewicz, Jane. *Contemporary American Memoirs in Action: How to Do Things with Memoir*. Palgrave Macmillan, 2018.

D'Souza, Aruna, and Tom McDonough, editors. *The Invisible Flâneuse? Gender, Public Space, and Visual Culture in Nineteenth-Century Paris*. Critical Perspectives in Art History, Manchester UP, 2006.

Eakin, Paul John. *How Our Lives Become Stories: Making Selves*. Cornell UP, 1999.

Finch, Jason, Lieven Ameel, and Markku Salmela, editors. *Literary Second Cities*. Palgrave Macmillan, 2017.

Gilmore, Leigh. *The Limits of Autobiography: Trauma and Testimony*. Cornell UP, 2001.

Hackworth, Jason. *Manufacturing Decline: How Racism and the Conservative Movement Crush the American Rust Belt*. Columbia UP, 2019.

Hamera, Judith. *Unfinished Business: Michael Jackson, Detroit, and the Figural Economy of American Deindustrialization*. Oxford UP, 2017.

Hart, Francis Russell. "History Talking to Itself: Public Personality in Recent Memoir." *New Literary History*, vol. 11, no. 1, 1979, pp. 193–210.

Lahusen, Christiane. "Memoirs," translated by Roisin Cronin. *Handbook of Autobiography / Autofiction*, edited by Martina Wagner-Egelhaaf, De Gruyter, 2019, pp. 626–35.

LISC Detroit. "A Tale of Commitment and Community." *Local Initiatives Support Corps Detroit*, 6 Oct. 2019, https://www.lisc.org/detroit/regional-stories/tale-commitment-and-community/.

May, Jamaal. "There Are Birds Here." *A Detroit Anthology*, edited by Anna Clark, Rust Belt Chic Press, 2014, p. 76.

Molina, Natalia. *How Race Is Made in America: Immigration, Citizenship, and the Historical Power of Racial Scripts*. U of California P, 2014.

Music, Marsha. "The Kidnapped Children of Detroit." *Voices from the Rust Belt*, edited by Anne Trubek, Picador, 2018, pp. 18–31.

———. "Marsha Music—The Detroitist." *Marsha Music: The Detroitist*, https://marshamusic.wordpress.com/. Accessed 31 Mar. 2021.

Nelson, Katharine. *Language in Cognitive Development: Emergence of the Mediated Mind*. Cambridge UP, 1996.

Nesci, Catherine. "Memory, Desire, Lyric: The Flâneur." *The Cambridge Companion to the City in Literature*, edited by Kevin R. McNamara, Cambridge UP, 2014, pp. 69–84.

Nethercott, Shaun S. "The Detroit Virus." *A Detroit Anthology*, edited by Anna Clark, Rust Belt Chic Press, 2014, pp. 214–17.

Rak, Julie. *Boom! Manufacturing Memoir for the Popular Market*. Wilfrid Laurier UP, 2013.

Schacter, Daniel L. *Searching for Memory: The Brain, the Mind, and the Past*. Basic Books, 1996.

Trubek, Anne. "Introduction: Why the Rust Belt Matters (And What It Is)." *Voices from the Rust Belt*, edited by Anne Trubek, Picador, 2018, pp. 1–6.

CHAPTER 6

Whose Detroit?

Fictions of Land Ownership and Property in Postindustrial America

JULIA SATTLER

Due to large-scale deindustrialization and its long-term consequences, including the shrinkage of such cities as Gary, Indiana, or Detroit, Michigan, the US Rust Belt has been in a process of reconceptualizing its plans for the future since at least the turn of the millennium. Existing "in a liminal and contested state of ownership" (Safransky 1080), postindustrial lands and the built structures upon them have become the subject of public debates relating to ownership and responsibility as well as to possible redevelopment and the financial gains associated with this process. These sites are "simultaneously iconic reminders of the ongoing de-industrialisation, and locations to re-imagine, reinvent and recover landscapes as agents for cultural, social, economic and ecological change" (Langhorst, "Re-presenting" 69). In this context, and parallel to texts produced by city offices, city-owned agencies, foundations, the media, individual investors, or activists, fictional works have contributed to the discussion of a redemptive future. Postindustrial novels such as Philipp Meyer's *American Rust* (2009) or Christopher Barzak's *One for Sorrow* (2007) investigate the landscape that has been left behind by industrial companies and enter into heretofore closed industrial spaces, mediating on the remains of the past and the possible futures of the place. Other such novels, for example Alyssa Cole's *When No One Is Watching* (2020) or Lisa Braxton's *The Talking Drum* (2020), speak to the ongoing contentions about gentrification and ownership of the postindustrial city: What happens, for example, if a new population arrives that is unaware of the historical meanings of buildings and other grown structures and takes them over for economic profit, without considering their meaning to the locals? Entering into sites that have been left behind by the industry and by the population, they take a stand in relation to gentrification and the future use of formerly industrial spaces. They also ask questions relating to the American economy and the consequences of investor-led efforts at recovery on the ground level. They spell out what these processes of transformation in the Rust Belt mean for those who call these cities "home." Narratives of this kind are especially critical in terms of scripting Detroit's future(s) in both planning and literature.

This location is of particular interest to me due to the sheer force of its loss of capital and population and because of its complex positioning as "the central locus of the anxiety of decline" (Apel 6). While there are several studies of the Rust Belt's representation across the media, including essays on the gentrification novel and its specific literary form and the relationship of contemporary Rust Belt writing to working class literature (e.g., Strangleman; Linkon, *Half-Life*; Linkon, "Strukturwandel"; Strangleman, Rhodes, and Linkon; Peacock), there is as of yet no comprehensive analysis of how Detroit novels speak to urban transformation processes in the face of economic crisis and, specifically, the topic of gentrification. This is a conspicuous absence. Gentrification in Detroit plays out differently compared to places such as Brooklyn or the San Francisco Mission District because of the large-scale shrinkage of its population following deindustrialization and white flight (see Katzenberg and Freitag in chapter 5 in this volume). Further, the city and its declined spaces that lend themselves to urban regeneration efforts have become internationally visible due to coffee table books staging their ruination (for example Marchand, Meffre, Polidori, and Sugrue; Moore). John Patrick Leary even goes so far as to speak of the "Detroit Utopia" as a "major subgenre of the popular Detroit narrative" in the media and addresses how this particular kind of reporting gives the impression of a place "where bohemians from expensive coastal cities can have the one-hundred-dollar house and community garden of their dreams," which sounds suspiciously like gentrification (Leary n. pag.). Thus, in my discussion of two contemporary novels that were published after Detroit's 2013 bankruptcy and which speak to the contentions around ownership and gentrification in this particular city, I seek to begin filling this research void.

The first text I will discuss, Benjamin Markovits's *You Don't Have to Live Like This* (2015), is an account of a Detroit rebuilt via gentrification, while in the second one, Angela Flournoy's *The Turner House* (2015), the members of an African American family contemplate the fate of their home. From their unique standpoints, both novels speak to the city's present and potential future(s). Both recognize the role the past and its interpretation play for Detroit's future possibilities and explore how any intervention in the city comes with multiple implications. In that sense, they each allude to the idea of the "right to the city" as it is developed by alliances such as www.righttothecity.org and make evident the destructive potential of neoliberal urbanism and its associated policies.

REVISITING JAMESTOWN: COLONIZATION AND GENTRIFICATION IN *YOU DON'T HAVE TO LIVE LIKE THIS* (2015)

You Don't Have to Live Like This is set in a Detroit that has been heavily affected by deindustrialization, white flight, and neighborhood abandonment and imagines what were to happen if, indeed, a larger group of *creatives* or *gentrifiers* were to arrive and build a new community in the city that keeps mostly separate from the original inhabitants. Told from the perspective of a young white man named Greg Marnier, or Marney, who is part of this group of newcomers, the narrative plays with the idea of the city of Detroit as a contemporary *frontier*. The newly arriving group of gentrifiers follows the lead of entrepreneur Robert James into a quasi-wilderness, an urban environment in which some of the neighborhoods resemble "a war zone" (Markovits 17) and where "the city has given up on certain blocks" (17). This analogy to the frontier is not surprising in a novel about gentrification, since, as Neil Smith already proposed in 1996, "the social meaning of gentrification is increasingly constructed through the vocabulary of the frontier myth" (13), an idea with which the reader of this novel is certainly also familiar. However, *You Don't Have to Live Like This* takes the frontier myth to a new level.

Since the story is being told from a first-person perspective, and by a white man who has no history with Detroit but ends up there due to his misplaced sense of adventure—he comments that even in his childhood, he was fascinated by the idea of "gold-rushing or homesteading" (Markovits 3)—the reader participates in a situation in which outsiders try to understand Detroit, and even more so, try to take possession of it and its abandoned neighborhoods. At the same time, the narrator discredits his own authority over telling the story in the first lines: "When I was younger," he introduces himself, "I was never much good at telling stories [. . .]. I don't know that I've gotten any better at it" (1). This first impression creates a distance between the narrator and the reader and instills doubt about what they can learn from the protagonist, but it also warns them that there will be other perspectives to think about, which are not explicitly mentioned in the novel. Here, said reader has no choice but to engage with Marney's perspective that is at times strangely detached from what is happening on the ground, especially as Marney becomes more and more of an outsider in the community as the story progresses.

Other voices, such as those of the African American inhabitants of the neighborhood where Marney settles, only appear at the margins of the text—as so often, the story of Detroit's gentrification in this novel is the one told by the gentrifiers and not by the population that gets pushed out. This factor contributes to the novel's politics of storytelling and its strategy of critically commenting on the ongoing processes of urban transformation—while it tells a story of gentrification from the stance of the gentrifiers, *You Don't Have to Live Like This* overall looks at the process and its agents with skepticism and thus not only offers the reader an inside angle of sorts but also points out the problems of intervening in a city with which one is unfamiliar and taking economic approaches to recovery to their extreme end.

Several times in the novel, the protagonist is confronted with how the arrival of the group of gentrifiers is perceived by the long-term residents of the city. One Detroiter explains the locals' skepticism to the new arrivals in the following way: "Because you're trying to help and you haven't got a clue. In a place like Detroit that makes you one of the bad guys" (33). At least indirectly, this statement contains the advice to get to know the city first instead of blindly trying to help and thus potentially worsening the situation. This is a piece of advice the gentrifiers decidedly ignore in their attempt to get to know each other instead, to set up their community, and to make use of the opportunity Detroit represents to them, either in terms of growing a business, or in terms of living their lives as artists. Here, the novel directly picks up the idea that Detroit is "hip and cheap [. . .] the new Berlin" (27)—open for reinvention and with profit to be made.

As the main character, ironically an expert in colonial history and "a pretty average nerd" (2) interested in historical military strategy from the Civil War to the Africa campaign, explains to the reader, the newcomers refer to their settlement as "New Jamestown" in a nod to their founder Robert James, but also to the Jamestown colonial settlement, the first permanent European settlement on the American continent and the location that set the stage for American slavery. The parallel that is drawn between America's beginnings and Detroit is in tune with Jerry Herron's observation that Detroit is "probably the most important design project ever undertaken by Americans (after the Founding itself)" (n. pag.). Detroit is attractive to the newcomers in the novel because they perceive it as a canvas on which they are free to experiment: "There are still some beautiful, big houses standing empty. You could do whatever you want with them, set up any kind of society" (Markovits 17). In this context, Robert James is a kind of modern-day Great Gatsby, part of "a new breed of rich man who turn[s] not to philanthropy but to mediagenic projects designed to revitalize US society, while still making money" (Miller). He is not just involved with the locals but also with large international companies and foundations—the frontier that is Detroit is not simply a local space, but it is a space of national if not international importance and interest.

New Jamestown represents a kind of utopia to Robert James and the group at large. It is a city within a city, and the site of a steered gentrification effort referred to as "a Groupon model of gentrification" (Markovits 17). Like in the original Groupon voucher model where customers could sign up for an offer and if a certain number of clients was reached, the offer became available to everyone, Robert James suggests using social media to advertise homes in sections of Detroit that have been bought up by investors and making them available: "The consortium planned to rent out the houses, business units, and land very cheaply, not just to individuals but also to groups of people who would organize themselves over the Internet and put in bids" (57). In case the project takes off, the inhabitants also get "a share of the profit" (57). Basically, the model is one based on land speculation—if property values rise due to an increased interest in living in Detroit, the model will work and make Robert James a rich man, and Marney, who previously had unsuccessfully tried to start an academic career, a recognized historian (53).

The business model depends on raising interest among people from outside the city to live in Detroit in spite of its rather negative reputation—and to gain attraction, services have to be set up for them, and there need to be job opportunities, for example. This is the work done by the first "settlers" (126), who work on the houses, but also—in the case of Robert—find sponsors for the model (48). The website the group has set up in the context of the settlement is called "Starting-from-Scratch-in-America" (57), suggesting that there is indeed free and empty land where people can just begin their lives or start over again. In that sense, the project speaks to those Americans for whom living in their own house or starting a new business does not seem feasible in a place such as New York City, Chicago, or Los Angeles because of the money needed in the first place. The project gives them the opportunity to live in a semblance of small-town America and free from economic hardships. Here, the novel directly relates to the larger economic situation in the United States, which has made attaining a middle-class life standard much more difficult since the 1980s.

Gentrification in the novel is a business adventure—this is also how the group understands America's colonial foundations (53). The original taking of the land is linked to the ongoing project of rebuilding Detroit via a process of reinvention (17). Apparently, the context of the postindustrial city of Detroit or why it is in its current state does not matter here, but rather, what matters is the "small experiment in regeneration" (56) the consortium conducts. To expand and strengthen their apparent colony, the young-ish entrepreneurs consistently need to buy up more property. It is part of their strategy to directly address African Americans in transforming neighborhoods and persuade them to sell their homes, an idea that is certainly not welcomed by everyone alike (68). This is a process clearly reminiscent of land appropriation during the settlement era. Here, the undertaking is supported by businesses such as Goldman Sachs and several foundations as well as the city of Detroit and the national government, including the Obama administration, lending it much authority and ensuring media attention.

In a stance of bitter irony, the text even constructs a situation where President Obama comes to Detroit to applaud the "settlers'" efforts in the city (178) and claims that their efforts in Detroit make clear that "'the American experiment ain't over yet'" (179). The people coming to Detroit, he states, came there "'because there was a voice in [their] head saying, *You don't have to live like this. There's a better way to live*'" (179), with these lines ultimately lending the novel its title. Something this fictionalized Obama does not even allude to is the situation of Detroit's Black community—it is not just the newcomers being oblivious to them being left out of the experiment, but it is politics and all others involved as well. Apparently, here, what is good for the economy is good for the people, and not the other way around.

And apparently, there are certain people who are "better suited" for this effort than others: The newcomers to the project join from across the United States and Europe in a selective process (57) under the control of Robert James and a few others he trusts. While it is not entirely clear what the selection criteria are, those interested have to apply, and factually, are united by their whiteness and middle-class social status and *habitus*. The group members refer to themselves as "settlers" (126), and they evoke Crèvecœur's conception of the European transplant replanted in American soil in *Letters from an American Farmer* (1782). Here, it alludes to the idea of the postindustrial American nation being redefined and reinvented in Detroit—just like Detroit once used to be a prime site of "the American Dream" in the first half of the twentieth century.

Over time, the New Jamestowners give themselves a charter for their settlement to be more or less independent from the rest of the city and begin to set up security services and childcare, among other services. They conceive of their settlement and its potentially positive impact on its environs as a testing ground for fixing America's urban problems at large (Markovits 56). They consider themselves agents of progress and intend to export this model to other economically depressed cities. This is also why all advice by the locals is lost on them. By contrast, most of the so-called settlers have a rather arrogant attitude toward the African American inhabitants of the neighborhoods they perceive as "theirs": "There was a general feeling in the neighborhood, which I [the narrator] didn't totally share, that the old Detroit blacks should be grateful to us, for pushing up their property prices and giving some of them domestic employment" (151). The fact that Marney does not share the sentiment and realizes that "most of the old residents kept to themselves" (151) distances him from his fellow settlers and in the long run contributes to his skepticism toward Robert James and the project.

In following their visions, most settlers of New Jamestown only stick to the members of their own community and focus on the development and growth of the settlement in relative ease; only at times are they confronted with the perception that they are building their homes on "occupied territory" (139). By contrast, the idea is that the original population either leaves or adjusts to the new settlers. Marney, however, becomes more involved in Detroit because he starts teaching at a local school and, for a short time, becomes a replacement teacher in the Detroit school system. He begins to date one of the African American teachers in the school, Gloria, who had at one point also applied to become a member of the New Jamestown settlement but was rejected in the competitive process. The explanation Marney offers to her makes evident that Robert James's project is indeed not inclusive of those Detroiters who have been in the city for a long time but focuses on rebuilding the perceived frontier city only with the help of an entirely new population: "We were looking for people who wanted to change their lives. You have a life here already" (120). The settlers are aiming for a new inscription, not one based on Detroit's complicated history, which includes racial discrimination and racialized violence. The assumption is that there are only specific people from outside the city who are ready and able to *change their lives*. As becomes clear, even Marney keeps a certain unease in his interactions with the community in Detroit at large. He does not want to take sides, which is a point of contention between the couple: In Detroit, not taking sides is also taking sides (309, 322).

As the novel makes clear, at first, the settlers' business undertaking appears to go very well, as improvement work across the city is underway, and thus their plans seem to turn into reality (138). But as it turns out, while the gentrification effort is not financially successful in the long run, it does cover up spectacularly that the founder of the community, Robert James, is also involved in an aluminum deal where the material is stored in abandoned structures in

Detroit—the *colony* is "just the window dressing" (242), a fact that the gentrifiers, however, do not know. Still, this points to the actual intentions of the colony's leader: to make money out of misery and to use Detroit's "blight" for financial profiteering. The supposed philanthropist is thus revealed to be a dishonest businessman solely interested in his own gains.

In *You Don't Have to Live Like This,* there is no resolution between the "settlers" and those who have a history with the city of Detroit. Rather, and much to the opposite, the situation escalates due to a number of misunderstandings that go far beyond James's aluminum deal and point to the racism-infused fears of the white "settlers." Riots take place between the "old" and "new" populations of Detroit, and most of "New Jamestown" falls victim to this event. In a sense, Detroit's history repeats itself in this novel, and the twenty-first-century version of the colonial experiment goes just as terribly wrong as its predecessor during urban renewal. The novel ends on a decidedly ambivalent note: Some settlers leave, some stay. It appears that the predictions with which the newcomers were confronted in the first chapters were right: Learn about Detroit or leave (33).

Whether Marney, the specialist of US colonial history and the composer of New Jamestown's newsletter as well as its historian and archivist driven by the effort to script the postindustrial city as modern-day utopia, ever realizes that the *settlement* of Detroit is akin to a second process of urban renewal in Detroit complete with a riot is left open by the novel. He does feel discomfort when a local African American resident explains to him after he has already been there for some time that Detroit's urban renewal policy in the 1950s was equivalent to "N***** removal" (143) but does not appear to understand the connection of this explanation to his own actions, which is however evident to the reader. Overall, the reader, here as in the novel at large, is in a situation to judge his behavior along with the other settlers as one that is not culturally sensitive and shaped by a naïve trust in Robert James and belief in economic uplift.

Through the novel's play with frontier terminology and references to colonial history, it becomes undeniable to the reader that New Jamestown and its inhabitants are *colonizing* postindustrial Detroit. Original Detroiters—all those who are not "settlers"/"transplants"—in this equation are the "natives" who will have to make way for the newcomers, who do not feel safe in Detroit and do not rely on the existing structures. This does not serve the two communities' merging at all, but rather cements their separation. The "newcomers" do not live up to their vision of rebuilding Detroit and turning it into a better city and a model for others to follow—more to the contrary, they turn it into a site of economic contention and racial violence. The text points to the tensions associated with urban redevelopment projects in a city that has been harmed by urban renewal and in which the city's structure is strongly impacted by the vexed relationship between race, class, and property ownership at large. This tension is not sufficiently addressed by the self-proclaimed "transplants" to the city—and so, almost as if by force of nature, the *transplant* is rejected, with the text essentially issuing a warning to those trying to gentrify Detroit or perceiving of it as an empty canvas without a history.

As Neil Smith expressed for *Crocodile Dundee,* the frontier myth in *You Don't Have to Live Like This* is also "so clichéd" (13) that one cannot but recognize the irony of the storyline and wonder why none of the supposedly very educated and socially sensitive settlers wakes up at an earlier point in the story. The novel certainly makes fun of contemporary discourses about gentrification and economic processes of urban regeneration, but it does more than that: Through sidelining the local and African American characters within the text, it also points out exactly what is happening to these populations. Overall, it presents an inside view into processes of gentrification via the protagonist but leaves it to the reader to understand the destructions brought on by a neoliberal script for rebuilding Detroit.

THE HOUSES HOPE BUILT: ANGELA FLOURNOY'S *THE TURNER HOUSE* (2015)

Much in contrast to *You Don't Have to Live Like This,* which focuses extensively on a group of white newcomers trying to transform the Black city of Detroit in a situation of uncertainty, in Angela Flournoy's debut novel *The Turner House* the reader encounters an African American family with a significant history in the city. The story is told from a third-person perspective, turning the reader into an outside witness—not a family member, but someone who has intimate insights into the different members' lives due to the omniscient narrator. The reader knows more about the family members than they tell each other, leading to empathy for the different characters and their struggles that partly emerge from the situation in the city in 2008 and also partly stem from the past. In this novel, the reader understands that a situation may not be what it looks like from the outside—be it a family member's mental health or their economic position.

Having arrived in Detroit from rural Arkansas in the context of the Great Migration, the Turner family—the name most likely a reference to Frederick Jackson Turner, author of the frontier thesis—owns a home in one of Detroit's changing East Side neighborhoods, a neighborhood that is literally "turning," which certainly also has an impact on the residents. While the allusion to Turner and the frontier myth point to yet another novel constructing Detroit as urban frontier, the novel also speaks to the equally familiar depiction of Detroit as a ghost town. Still, the novel is not a traditional or conventional ghost story. Rather, it is a family novel that includes a haunting. As James Peacock has worked out in relation to Brooklyn gentrification novels, the idea of haunting is characteristic of novels addressing processes of gentrification, pointing to its "spectral realms" (131), "providing esoteric evidence of social transformations" (131). In *The Turner House,* the "haint" has followed the family to Detroit from the South and is a reminder of their origins. But it is also tied to the Detroit home as the location that shaped the family, or *turned it,* so to say, into what it is. Therefore, the state of the house and the unclarities relating to its future in 2008 necessitate a haunting.

The Turner family home on Yarrow Street is uninhabited at the time the novel is set but still owned by the family. It is associated with memories relating to the family's formation and growth. Upon their arrival in the city, the family moved from one location to the next, from a shabby tenement in the African American neighborhood Black Bottom to a house on Lemay and Mack Avenues on the East Side, "on the edge of a white neighborhood whites were quickly fleeing" (Flournoy 337), and finally to the Yarrow Street home, where they settled and gained more stability. The family's moving houses stands in relation to the improvement of their economic and social situation, while the present state of the house indicates decline. The family is very aware of their background in the South and of the progress they have made in the North (82)—the grandparents had been sharecroppers, and from there Francis, the family father, had worked his way up and to Detroit. Still, there is not a lot of open communication in the family, especially not about the past, which Cha-Cha, the oldest son, criticizes: "It was frustrating, the way his siblings worshipped their parents. What part of their worlds would crumble if they took a good look at their parents' flaws? If there was no trauma, why not talk about the everyday, human elements of their upbringing?" (83).

The novel shifts between the 1940s, the present the novel is set in—2008— and several other time periods in between. Here, the reader encounters a Detroit before bankruptcy, and a place that is brimming with history: Detroit "is the city with perhaps the most significant homeownership and ownership of property among people who have historically been denied property rights. Many Detroit homes are black going multiple generations" (Pedroni 213), a factor the novel pays close attention to. It contextualizes the situation in Detroit's East Side by including urban renewal as well as instances of racial unrest into its narrative. It describes how "by 1967 whites had already started their retreat to the suburbs" (Flournoy 91) and comments on the ongoing tensions between Black and white people since the first African Americans had arrived in the city (151). It mentions the burning of Detroit homes (172), the decline of the automobile industry (174), the discourses equating Detroit with "post-zombie-fucking-apocalypse" (183), and ongoing efforts at "reviving" the city (184), thus grounding the family story into a larger narrative of African American and local Detroit history. Without explicitly stating who is at fault for the present state of the city, the novel makes clear that the condition of the family home is not a result of the family's neglect. Rather, the text points to the complexity of factors shaping Detroit's property crisis, including social class and race. It becomes clear to the reader that in Detroit, "contentious land politics [. . .] follow socio-historical fault lines" (Safransky 1090).

By 2008, the problems of the neighborhood around the Turner family home are evident, despite the perception that "streets with this much new life could still have good in them":

> On both sides of the Turner house, vacant lots were stippled with new grass. Soon ragweed, wood sorrel and violets would surround the crumbling foundations, the houses long burned and rained away. The Turner house, originally three lots into the block, had become a corner house in recent years, its slight mint and brick frame the most reliable landmark on the street. (Flournoy 18)

The landscape described here sounds much like the postindustrial frontier landscape—nature is taking over the city and the structures change due to abandonment. Here, however, this development creates a feeling of threat among the characters; the text makes clear that there is no safety anymore in such an environment (Flournoy 252). This passage turns around the expectation that the supposed frontier landscape is inherently positive. At the same time, the personification of the house points out that it is persistent, that it has more endurance than many others, and that it is *reliable*—what is not, is its future.

When the reader enters the story, it is up to the thirteen Turner children to contemplate the fate of their house on Yarrow Street. This inheritance of property is not only a typical feature of gentrification stories but also points to the economic pressures under which the family lives. The year 2008 is a time of economic crisis, and for several members of the Turner family, it is also a time of personal crisis. The family matriarch, Viola, who had until recently lived there, has become too ill to take care of it herself and has moved in with her oldest child, Cha-Cha. Deciding what should happen next is not easy, as the siblings' understanding of the past and present—both of the house and the family—varies greatly, and they cannot agree on anything no matter how many times they address the issue. *The Turner House* speaks to the declining value of Detroit homes, which represents a problem for everyone wishing to sell their home, but especially for the Turner family, since they are already in debt (Flournoy 36).

For the members of the family, the house still holds value as it has been the site where all the children have grown up. It is the carrier of secrets, and the situation is further complicated because the house is haunted by the aforementioned ghost—or at least that is what some family members claim. While the deceased father, Francis, had always claimed that there "ain't no haints in Detroit" (Flournoy 3), pointing to the idea of a new start in the North following the Great Migration, some of the siblings are convinced that a ghost has followed the family from the South and remains a steady presence in Detroit. This is especially true for Cha-Cha, who claims that he got into a car accident because of the "haint," an incident leading him to consider his family's history and his role in it with the help of a therapist.

Overall, the ghostly presence points to the complex legacy of the past with which the African American Turner family members have to cope, and it will not rest until this legacy has been worked through by Cha-Cha and by the family at large. In his essay on haunting in Brooklyn gentrification fiction, James Peacock argues that hauntings provide "a means of exploring specific historical, political and geographical contexts" (138), but they are also important as they "mediate relations between the individual, the communities in which the individual participates, and wider history" (139). In the fictions he discusses, the spectral beings point to alternative paths, roads not taken and the fact that the past cannot be entirely cut out even in a situation of intense gentrification (Peacock 153). In contrast to this understanding of Brooklyn, the ghost in *The Turner House* relates to the importance of the African American history of Detroit that is about to be erased and to the long-term legacy of the Great Migration. The "haint" comes to haunt Cha-Cha because he, as the oldest son, is the carrier of family legacy. The ghostly presence calls for family secrets to finally be addressed; it forces open communication about what the house and the family mean to each of the members.

What the Turner children and the mother do not know or even suspect in their debate around the house and its sale or potential demise is that one of the siblings, Lelah, has been living in it since her eviction from her own home. Lelah is addicted to gambling, and Detroit's new casino—an effort at the city's recovery—is making this situation harder for her. She cannot share her addiction or eviction with her family, neither with her siblings nor with her daughter, because she wants to spare them from feeling obligated to help her or take her in (Flournoy 21). Thus, she has to make her childhood home her temporary accommodation without anyone noticing—her secret squatting adds to the other family members' perception that something is indeed *inhabiting* the home. Economic threat and the inability to speak openly about problems are literally coming to haunt the house and by implication, the Turner family.

In the novel, it is not only Lelah who is busy gambling. The family at large is very aware of the processes of speculation on land and gambling on property that are typical of the neoliberal city, and this impacts their ideas about what will happen to the family home in significant ways. At the same time, and in contrast to Markovits's novel, there are no *visible* gentrifiers exploring the neighborhood. Rather, gentrification is an invisible threat—another "haint"—to the house, the family, the neighborhood, and Detroit. When debating the future of the Turner house, the family members agree that "people are just walking away from their houses, and the city is making it too hard for other folks to buy them" (Flournoy 37). This is part of a process geared toward making land available for larger investments, for "land grabs" and the like. They assume that if they sell it for the amount it is supposedly still worth, four thousand dollars, "in ten years, Donald Trump or somebody will buy it, build a townhouse, and sell it to some white folks for two hundred grand" (Flournoy 37). This knowledge leads to the siblings ruling out selling the Turner house to anyone unrelated to the family. It would signify a betrayal of what they have inherited from their parents, no matter how insignificant its financial value. At the same time, the reference to Donald Trump shows that those in economic power might ultimately have the financial means to determine what happens to Detroit, without, of course, taking into account its complicated history, and its "haunting" (see Peacock 138–39).

Troy, one of the Turner sons, hopes that his partner can purchase the house—they are not married, and thus, she could appear as an interested stranger and make sure that the house remains with the family. Since a friend of his systematically purchases property in the city in the hope that this will make him rich, thus participating in the neoliberal tactics of land speculation, Troy knows about the dangers associated with such practices (Flournoy 183). Still, the family members vote against this procedure, deeming Troy's relationship with his partner too unstable for an investment of this kind under the given circumstances, but leading Troy to contemplate whether it may be worth betraying his siblings and just still selling the house (66 ff.). What makes the discussion about the house more difficult is that Viola, the mother, is still convinced that she will get better and be able to move back to Yarrow Street (40). The novel points to the decisive role of family loyalties and local histories, as well as what it means to live in Detroit at the turn of the twenty-first century—how decline shapes and sometimes enforces processes of decision-making, but also, what it means to stick together despite these difficulties and the threats of neoliberalism.

The novel has an open end, Viola accepts that she is dying from cancer, some of the children host a vigil for the Turner House "haint," and the family gives a party for everyone to take leave of the matriarch. In these scenes, the family members make peace with the past and with the present. It is only at this point that the reader learns why the house is so crucial for the family: A final flashback to the Great Migration and the family's arrival at Yarrow Street reveals that it was the place where the father for the first time since arriving from the South "allowed himself to hope" (338). This ending makes it seem impossible to simply leave the house behind or sell it. Pointing directly to the motto of the city of Detroit, "We hope for better things—it will arise from ashes" that is referenced throughout the novel, this ending alludes to the devastating Detroit fire of 1805, but more importantly to improvement and recovery because of those who are loyal to Detroit and consider it their home.[1] The novel suggests that any plan for the future will first have to deal with the past and with finding new hope for the city and its homes. Reconciliation is not the key to the future of Detroit, but attachment and atonement are.

LEARNING FROM FICTION

This paper explored how two recent novels set in Detroit enter into discussions about the future of the city and position themselves in relation to the developments at hand, such as the emergence of the "creative city script" inspired by Richard Florida (see chapter 10 by Rodewald and Grünzweig in this volume) that is often used by planning and marketing agencies to attract a new population to the Rust Belt, and to Detroit specifically, and that is also used in the efforts led by Robert James in *You Don't Have to Live Like This*. While it may be too early to speak of a new genre of Detroit-specific gentrification novels, these texts definitely speak to gentrification and associated processes from their own "Detroit" angle. What they are offering from quite

---

1. The novel thus speaks to the kind of postgrowth urban planning research that is found in *The City after Abandonment* (2013), an edited volume by Margaret Dewar and June Manning Thomas that focuses on "places where large levels of population and household loss have led to large amounts of property abandoned, manifested in a high percentage of vacant houses, buildings, lots, and/or blocks, which jeopardize the quality of life for remaining residents and businesses" (2–3).

distinctive vantage points is an understanding of this subgenre's need to speak to the reputation of Detroit as an "*un-city*" in conflict with both nonhuman and infrastructural matter (Herron n. pag.).

Both novels deconstruct the idea that the city of Detroit can recover via economic measures, and especially, via gentrification, which *You Don't Have to Live Like This* spells out to its extreme end. *The Turner House* explores how the emotional, affective value of property plays into processes of urban development and shows that an abandoned house may still be someone's "home." This runs contrary to the notion that "unused" parts of the city can simply be erased. In their investigation of the city and the neighborhood under conditions of neoliberal capitalism, these novels also speak to the concern that "finance has broken loose from its moorings in the so-called economy of manufacturing" (Knight 347) and issue a warning for what that might mean for individual people and individual places in the US.

Alluding to the period of urban renewal and the parallels to the present situation, both novels speak to the complexities of race, social class, and property ownership in Detroit and America at large, as well as to the danger of renewed erasure of an organically grown city and culture. Interestingly enough, and while both texts in their own ways comment on the 1950s and deal with the topic of colonization, neither speaks very explicitly to the original frontier that was Detroit during the colonial era and that led to the erasure of the Native population. Jamestown, after all, was a very different settlement as compared to Detroit with its French and English colonial settlers. What both novels do call up, though, is the 2012 plan for Detroit called "Detroit Future City," dedicated to "rightsiz[ing]" the city—to "fix the so-called spatial mismatch between surplus land and a reduced population" (Safransky 1080). Both novels discussed in this essay clarify that such city planning can never offer a redemptive practice, since it cuts some people off from infrastructures, urging them to move elsewhere. Both make clear that any script for the postindustrial city that is to be viable will have to engage with questions of property, ownership, and truly redemptive strategies of land use—beyond their economic dimension.

WORKS CITED

Apel, Dora. *Beautiful Terrible Ruins: Detroit and the Anxiety of Decline*. Rutgers UP, 2015.

Barzak, Christopher. *One for Sorrow*. Bantam Books, 2007.

Braxton, Lisa. *The Talking Drum*. Inanna Publications and Education, 2020.

Cole, Alyssa. *When No One Is Watching*. William Morrow Paperbacks, 2020.

Crèvecœur, J. Hector St. John de. *Letters from an American Farmer.* 1782. CreateSpace Independent Publishing Platform, 2012.

Dewar, Margaret, and June Manning Thomas. "Introduction: The City after Abandonment." *The City after Abandonment,* edited by Margaret Dewar and June Manning Thomas, U of Pennsylvania P, 2013, pp. 1–14.

Detroit Future City. *2012 Detroit Strategic Framework Plan.* Inland Press, 2013, https://detroitfuturecity.com/strategic-framework/.

Flournoy, Angela. *The Turner House.* Houghton Mifflin. 2015.

Herron, Jerry. "Motor City Breakdown: Detroit in Literature and Film." *Places Journal,* April 2013, https://doi.org/10.22269/130423.

Knight, Peter. "Economic Humanities: Literature, Culture, and Capitalism." *The Fictions of American Capitalism: Working Fictions and the Economic Novel,* edited by Jacques-Henri Coste and Vincent Dussol, Palgrave Macmillan, 2020, pp. 335–55.

Langhorst, Joern. "Re-presenting Transgressive Ecologies: Post-Industrial Sites as Contested Terrains." 2014. *Post-Industrial Urban Greenspace: An Environmental Justice Perspective,* edited by Jennifer Foster and L. Anders Sandberg, Routledge, 2016, pp. 68–92.

Leary, John Patrick. "Detroitism: What Does 'Ruin Porn' Tell Us about the Motor City?" *Guernica,* 15 Jan. 2011, https://www.guernicamag.com/leary_1_15_11/.

Linkon, Sherry Lee. *The Half-Life of Deindustrialization: Working-Class Writing about Economic Restructuring.* U of Michigan P, 2018.

———. "Strukturwandel erzählen—Arbeiterliteratur nach der Deindustrialisierung." *Arbeit—Bewegung—Geschichte: Zeitschrift für historische Studien,* vol. 19, no. 2, 2020, pp. 12–30.

Marchand, Yves, Romain Meffre, Robert Polidori, and Thomas J. Sugrue. *The Ruins of Detroit.* Steidl, 2010.

Markovits, Benjamin. *You Don't Have to Live Like This.* Harper, 2015.

Meyer, Philipp. *American Rust.* 2009. Simon & Schuster, 2013.

Miller, Laura. "You Don't Have to Live Like This by Benjamin Markovits Review—Utopianism Meets Racial Distrust in Detroit." *The Guardian,* 5 Aug. 2015, https://www.theguardian.com/books/2015/aug/05/you-dont-have-to-live-like-this-benjamin-markovits-review.

Moore, Andrew. *Detroit Disassembled.* Damiani, 2010.

Peacock, James. "Those Dead Left Behind: Gentrification and Haunting in Contemporary Brooklyn Fictions." *Studies in American Fiction,* vol. 46, no. 1, 2019, pp. 131–56.

Pedroni, Thomas C. "Urban Shrinkage as a Performance of Whiteness: Neoliberal Urban Restructuring, Education, and Racial Containment in the Post-industrial, Global Niche City." *Discourse: Studies in the Cultural Politics of Education,* vol. 32, no. 2, 2011, pp. 203–15, https://doi.org/10.1080/01596306.2011.562666.

Safransky, Sara. "Rethinking Land Struggle in the Postindustrial City." *Antipode,* vol. 49, no. 4, 2017, pp. 1079–100.

Smith, Neil. *The New Urban Frontier: Gentrification and the Revanchist City.* Routledge, 1996.

Strangleman, Tim. "'Smokestack Nostalgia,' 'Ruin Porn' or Working-Class Obituary: The Role and Meaning of Deindustrial Representation." *International Labor and Working-Class History,* vol. 84, no. 1, 2013, pp. 23–37, https://doi.org/10.1017/S0147547913000239.

Strangleman, Tim, James Rhodes, and Sherry Linkon. "Introduction to Crumbling Cultures: Deindustrialization, Class, and Memory." *International Labor and Working-Class History,* vol. 84, no. 1, 2013, pp. 7–22, https://doi.org/10.1017/S0147547913000227.

CHAPTER 7

To the Bodega or the Café?

Microscripts of Gentrification in Contemporary Fiction

MARIA SULIMMA

According to a by now notorious expression, it has become easier to imagine the end of the world than the end of capitalism. The catchy phrase is likely a paraphrased version of Frederic Jameson's quip: "It seems to be easier for us today to imagine the thoroughgoing deterioration of the earth and of nature than the breakdown of late capitalism; perhaps that is due to some weakness in our imaginations" (xii). Gentrification is intimately related to capitalism—it is arguably the most visible way in which (late neoliberal) capitalism plays out in urban environments.[1] Yet, unlike for capitalism generally, we *can* imagine an end to gentrification. Several contributions of this collection investigate alternatives to gentrification as they are conjured up by scripts to mitigate or counter its devastating socioeconomic effects for low-income groups. An abundance of stories crafting alternatives to gentrification should not distract from the issue that motivates this article: a lack of understanding of what it is

---

1. Ever since sociologist Ruth Glass coined the term in her 1964 study of a middle- and upper-class "gentry" displacing London working classes (see xviii), academia and activism have been struggling to pin it down. For some, it has become a "dirty word" (Smith 30, in reference to a *New York Times* advertisement of 1985) that should be replaced with euphemisms such as urban renewal, revitalization, or renaissance, though others argue that these terms cannot capture the ways gentrification destroys a city's affordable housing stock (see Smith 30–47). Even though gentrification is felt around the globe, it depends on national and local circumstances; for example, (not only) in US-American cities, racial exclusion is nearly always an aspect of gentrification that disproportionately affects communities of color.

that we mean by gentrification and how, consequently, contemporary fiction engages with the multifaceted phenomenon.

For decades, social studies have tended to follow either a macro or a micro approach to explain the causes, breadth, or consequences of gentrification (see Brown-Saracino). Depending on their approach, scholars (and activists) target either sociostructural capitalist frames—such as privatization, corporatization, real estate investment and speculation, capital mobility, and globalization—or certain "gentrifier" population segments and their behaviors, including issues of consumption, taste, responsibility, and "authenticity." In her review of quantitative and qualitative scholarship, Japonica Brown-Saracino finds that "driving these differences is an anxiety that fuels (and goes beyond) the gentrification debates: namely, an anxiety about broad economic and spatial shifts that are underway" in most global cities (517). Many scholars express the need to overcome the standoff between macro and micro approaches. As the authors of the autoethnographic study *Gentrifier* (2017) ask, "how can we respect this structure while creating space for our agency within it? When asking the question 'where do we go from here?' there are few satisfying answers in the present dialogue" (Schlichtman, Patch, and Hill 173). The division between macro and micro approaches is much more than a mere difference in methodology, scale, or research interest in the social sciences. Rather it points to issues of the imagination—and the necessity to interrogate the stories that circulate about gentrification and what these stories reveal about the phenomenon itself.[2]

Further, the limits of imagination especially affect the practice of storytelling, of that which can or should be told. In narratology, such concerns are closely related to what Robyn Warhol—drawing on Gerald Prince's notion of disnarration—conceptualizes as the unnarratable. Warhol differentiates between Prince's "disnarration," "telling what did not happen," and "unnarration," her term to describe "what did happen [that] cannot be retold in words, or explicitly indicating that what happened will not be narrated because narrating it would be impossible" (222). She further classifies different types of unnarration: the "subnarratable," the "supranarratable," the "antinarratable," and the "paranarratable" (Warhol 222).

Of particular relevance for my purpose is the subnarratable, "that needn't be told because it's 'normal'" (Warhol 222) and thus absent from the text, and the supranarratable, "what can't be told because it's 'ineffable' [. . . and defies] narrative, foregrounding the inadequacy of language or of visual image to

---

2. Within literary studies, there are sustained explorations into the ways contemporary fiction develops certain themes, characters, and narrative scenarios to depict gentrification (see Peacock, *Brooklyn Fictions*; Henryson; Heise; Gurr).

achieve full representation, even of fictitious events" (223). We can understand the lack of imagining an end to capitalism in theory and activism as resulting in the latter, in such a kind of unnarration. In other words, the struggle of scholars, activists, or storytellers to represent gentrification is so hard because their attempts scrape supranarratability.

Building upon Warhol's conceptions, this contribution turns to contemporary fiction and identifies a narrative phenomenon related to storytelling about and imaginings of gentrification: the evocation of seemingly trivial activities or places tied to the consumption of characters as embodiments of gentrification. Understanding such literary depictions as trivial further recalls the criticisms leveled against the US-American literary tradition of realism in the late nineteenth century. Naturalist writer Frank Norris expresses his concerns toward realist fiction in terms of not a coffee but teacup: "It is the drama of a broken teacup, the tragedy of a walk down the block, the excitement of an afternoon call, the adventure of an invitation to dinner" (215). A few years after Norris, George Santayana coined the term "the genteel tradition" and expressed similar skepticism toward the everydayness of such literary scenes. Contemporary fiction's coffee-drinking gentrifier and realism's "genteel" tea-drinker both serve as literary explorations of status, class, and societal conflict—in ways that are distinctly urban. These representations appear small-scale and invested in individual characters' banal consumerism; hence, they border on the subnarratable—because they appear to be inconsequential or even boring statements of consumption.

Again, what Warhol calls "subnarratable" is so, because it is too unremarkable, banal, "normal," or uninteresting to be worthy of inclusion in a narrative, and hence, is absent from the text (222). Paradoxically, in stories about gentrification, such seemingly subnarratable moments become a means to represent gentrification; that is, they are included solely on the basis of being a shortcut to overcome the supranarratability of gentrification. Hence, instead of supranarratable, the *nature of gentrification* becomes understandable and knowable in these passages. I will describe specific narrative passages as microscripts because they offer depictions or lists of leisurely activities that are immensely recognizable (possibly even boring) but also imply a deep sociopolitical impact that is related to the imagination of gentrification.

Whereas city scripts seek to inspire grand visions of/for a city's past, present, or future, microscripts are short and condensed moments in a larger story that in an off-hand and incidental manner transport an observation or insight about life in a city. They are invested with contested sociopolitical and economical meanings for the reader to identify. What Ruth Mayer argues about short literary formats applies to stand-alone passages inspiring microscripts as well. For Mayer, smallness is not a feature of length or scope of a text but should be conceived of in terms of style, gesture, and self-awareness: "Their smallness is characterized by these texts' ability to reconfigure established literary spaces or to open up new spaces for literary exploration" (Mayer 205) because their forwardness and fragmentariness alert readers to the reduction of complexity undertaken for the sake of brevity.[3] These marginal passages exceed micro and macro frameworks of gentrification, serve characterization or plot construction, and complicate narrative practices related to *tellability* in Robyn Warhol's sense.

Specifically, this contribution turns to depictions of urban cafés and bodegas, as sites of buying and drinking coffee. Contemporary fiction often relies on the ominous "death by latte/cappuccino"-narrative popularized in journalistic discourse that targets how specialty cafés "have sprouted like mushrooms across cities in areas that are usually in the process of gentrification or in existing gentrified areas" (Felton 10). Passages surrounding the buying of coffee in contemporary fiction offer striking condensations, or microscripts, of how fiction refers to discourses surrounding gentrification, individual responsibility, and structural change. I demonstrate how four contemporary novels, written and published before the COVID-19 pandemic and set either in New York City or Oakland, evoke microscripts of drinking coffee. The first section focuses on moments in which a narrating character's feelings of inclusion or exclusion from specific urban spaces, bodegas or cafés, serve as implicit characterization and demonstrate belonging to or expulsion from the gentrified city. In the second part, I am interested in how such snapshot-like passages relate to the plot of a novel, that is, what kind of plots such microscripts may inspire. The article purposefully pairs novels with gentrifier characters (see Henryson and Sulimma) with works written from the perspective of characters who are displaced by gentrification.

CHARACTERS: HAVING COFFEE WITH/AS GENTRIFIERS

In general, fiction may present gentrification from the perspective of those displaced by it, working-class populations struggling to remain in a changing neighborhood, or from the perspective of gentrifier characters, that is, characters who find their needs accommodated for in a gentrified neighborhood. To

---

3. "Die Kleinheit weist sich dadurch aus, dass die Texte einen literarisch erschlossenen Kulturraum neu inszenieren oder unvertraute Raume erschließen" (Mayer 205).

think about fictional characters and gentrification recalls many interests of literary sociology, such as class, habitus, social-economic mobility, and interpersonal relationships. I contrast two recent novels, both of which were critical and commercial bestsellers, Tommy Orange's *There There* (2018) and Ottessa Moshfegh's *My Year of Rest and Relaxation* (2018), as examples of these different concerns.

My Year of Rest and Relaxation is Ottessa Moshfegh's third novel and continues her interest in exploring "unlikeable," misanthropic protagonists and their abject bodily realities. The novel's unnamed narrator-protagonist is a normatively beautiful, rich white woman in her mid-twenties whose trust fund enables a comfortable life on Manhattan's Upper East Side in the early 2000s—an urban setting already thoroughly gentrified and culturally homogenous. The protagonist's sardonic and nihilistic narrative voice betrays her to be an insightful observer of her surroundings who, however, is either bored by or hateful toward everyone in her life. This alienated "female Anti-*American Psycho*" (Drügh 130) is only passionate about one thing, unconscious, dreamless sleep—a state not typically depicted in fiction. She seeks a pharmaceutical drug–induced hibernation as a way to rebuild herself. This kind of recovery is in turns fleshed out as grotesque wellness treatment, self-induced coma, abstract art project, or extreme body modification: "My hibernation was self-preservational. I thought that it was going to save my life" (7). Set from June 2000 to September 2001, *My Year of Rest and Relaxation* recalls the promotional hook of self-help books, guides, or memoirs that take a year as a stylistic device to accomplish a feat, undertaking, or adventure. However, its title should be approached with distanced irony (Greenberg 191), and, ultimately, the novel dismisses any self-realization or self-optimization related to such a "year"-structure as "hollow and commercial" (Greenberg 193; see also Drügh).

Cheyenne and Arapaho author Tommy Orange generated considerable journalistic and scholarly buzz with his bestselling first novel *There There* that also rejects any form of nostalgia or sentimentality.[4] Taking its title from Gertrude Stein's remark about Oakland, "There is no there there," Orange's novel reframes the fact that "for Native people in this country, all over the Americas, it has been developed over, buried ancestral land, glass and concrete and wire and steel, unreturnable covered memory. There is no there there" (39). Claiming the city as a site of Native urbanity, Orange's novel counters the erasure of Indigenous people in US-American settler cities and highlights how gentrification continues in the legacy of colonialism.

---

4. James Cox draws attention to the lineage of Native American fiction and especially urban Native fiction that Tommy Orange stands in—and often intertextually pays tribute to—in his debut. For instance, its polyvocal structure recalls the multiple narrative voices of Louise Erdrich's novels *Love Medicine* (1984), *Tracks* (1988), and *Four Souls* (2004) (Cox 255).

The novel introduces readers to a group of twelve Indigenous Oakland natives of different genders, ages, professions, and class backgrounds and their more or less connected lives. *There There* has forty-two chapters narrated from the perspective of these characters in either third person (thirty-four chapters) or first person (seven chapters). Only one chapter is narrated in the second person, and therefore warrants particular attention: "You walk outside your studio apartment to a hot Oakland summer day" (213). As with any second-person narration, this style includes the reader but also focalizes the perspective of middle-aged drummer Thomas Frank. Unlike most of the other characters whose (estranged) family relationships come into focus as the book progresses, Thomas is the most socially isolated character. He also struggles with addiction: To cope with a painful skin condition (eczema), Thomas drinks excessively—and as a consequence loses his job as custodian at the Indian Center.

The readers of both novels will realize mid-book that the plots are racing toward a significant diegetic event that will disrupt everything for the protagonists and will end the story in a moment of shock and surprise. In *My Year*, the unnamed protagonist awakens in time to witness the impact of the terrorist attacks of 9/11 and sees a female figure whom she assumes to be her friend Reva jump to her death from one of the burning twin towers. In *There There*, a powwow held at the Oakland Coliseum turns into a mass shooting when some characters rob it with 3D-printed guns—and Thomas is among those killed.

As a further connection, both novels undertake a study of urban characters struggling with addiction and, at the same time, a study of a gentrified city. To do this, these novels feature relevant passages in which characters realize how their gender identity, race, class status, and professions impact how they are able to belong to certain spaces and excluded from others—when they seek to purchase and drink caffeinated beverages.

> I could have gone to any number of places for coffee, but I liked the bodega. It was close, and the coffee was consistently bad, and I didn't have to confront anyone ordering a brioche bun or no-foam latte. [. . .] The bodega coffee was working-class coffee—coffee for doormen and deliverymen and handymen and busboys and housekeepers. The air in there was heavy with the perfume of cheap cleaning detergents and mildew. [. . .] Nothing ever changed. (Moshfegh 5–6)

> You pass a coffee shop you hate because it's always hot and flies constantly swarm the front of the show, where a big patch of sun seethes with some invisible shit the flies love and where there's always just that one seat left in the heat with the flies, which is why you hate it, on top of the fact that

> it doesn't open until ten in the morning and closes at six in the evening to cater to all the hipsters and artists who hover and buzz around Oakland like flies, America's white suburban vanilla youth, searching for some invisible thing Oakland might give them, street cred or inner-city inspiration. (Orange 214–15)

Thomas and the narrator of *My Year* are two drastically different characters with divergent experiences of the city. Their likes even implicitly feature in each other's passages. Thomas is the kind of working-class "handyman" assumed by the narrator to frequent the bodega. Meanwhile, to Thomas, the narrator of *My Year* easily would appear as a young white "hipster" new to the city, a privileged gentrifier through and through. Both passages unfold microscripts through an affective reaction to urban space in a particularly gendered fashion: Thomas explains why he "hates" the specialty café when immediately confronted with it; the narrator describes why she "likes" the bodega as a consequence of her personal consumer choices. These reasons are surprisingly compatible and complementary. Both react to issues of accessibility and the patrons associated with a place, and both project anxieties surrounding a class-based kind of *coffee tourism*.

Here, access refers to an urban space being either closed in a moment of need (such as the café with its working hours that are only convenient for customers with a flexible schedule) or reliably open (such as the bodega). In his discussion of the novel, Jonathan Greenberg reads *My Year*'s bodega as "seemingly immune from time" because it is "open twenty-four seven, it is a small miracle of capitalism, unaffected by the diurnal cycles of waking and sleep" (189). The bodega may appear as an expression of a capitalistic imperative of constant consumption and availability, yet it also curiously seems to exist outside of capitalistic processes of gentrification, because of its resistance to change. The bodega is a space that the narrator can shuffle into in any physical state and at any time of day or night to buy large coffees—before countering the caffeine with sedatives and antidepressants to return to sleep. And yet, again, access also depends on intersectional factors relating to race, class, and in this case, age. *My Year*'s narrator has a choice ("I could have gone to any number of places"), whereas Thomas's anger stems from not being the intended clientele of the café and even possibly being fetishized as "authentic" in the eyes of hipster newcomers to the neighborhood. Indeed, in her valorization of working-class professions as fellow patrons of the bodega, the narrator exhibits a similar fascination with "authenticity" that she in her self-chosen unemployment can easily opt out of.

Both passages respectively highlight the perspective of their narrator protagonists and disregard that of the relatively invisible minor characters, such as the staff and patrons of the bodega and café. These minor characters are present not as individuals but as an unnamed crowd characterized by their profession as deliverymen, busboys, housekeepers, or hipsters and artists. Yet, as Alex Woloch demonstrates in his readings of the asymmetrical relationship between protagonists and minor characters in the nineteenth-century realist novel, "real life is full of uneven matches, but fictional representation can uniquely amplify such disparities within the narrative form itself" (8). Despite the reductive exclusion of minor characters, these passages draw attention to their relevance for the narrative and the influence that they have on the protagonists.

Because the narrator emphasizes her frustration with, disinterest in, or hatred toward almost everyone and everything in her life, the confession of "liking the bodega" is especially surprising. Heinz Drügh finds that the character's preference of the bodega and "working-class" coffee (similar to her love for Whoopi Goldberg's acting) should be understood as an aesthetic appreciation bordering on parody, akin to Susan Sonntag's notion of *camp* as a "coarsest, commonest pleasure" (qtd. in Drügh 130–31). In addition to her disassociation from her neighborhood, and the complete disregard of her position as a wealthy newcomer to Manhattan, the narrator's preference for "working-class coffee" (Moshfegh 6) over the coffee served at a more upscale café has little to do with morals or political behaviors (for example, to support the bodega over the café, to avoid being labeled a gentrifier or hipster), or the coffee on offer. Instead, whether described as aesthetic or conceptual, her preference amounts to a preference for the microscript of bodega coffee over that of upscale hipster coffee. It is this understanding of convenient bodega coffee as something that can be chosen for the story it inspires that demonstrates the privilege of *My Year*'s protagonist, especially when considering how Thomas would never perceive bodega coffee along such lines. Further, even the smells of mildew and cleaning products in the bodega become an ingredient of this script and serve to evoke authenticity.

By contrast, Thomas evokes an abject physical experience when he describes the heat and the flies buzzing around the only available seat in the café. Whereas in *My Year*'s bodega the mildew is present and perceivable, Thomas cannot see or smell the "invisible shit the flies love" (Orange 214). Symbolically, the bodega projects honesty, whereas the café's repulsive aspects are hidden and "invisible." Further, Thomas links the flies and the hipster patrons of the café, to be read as gentrifiers, who are similarly "buzz[ing]"

(Orange 215) around Downtown Oakland, drawn to some invisible appeal that to him is similarly repulsive, "invisible shit." This "street cred or inner-city inspiration" (215), it is implied here, is something these newcomers may associate with his Indigenous urban masculinity and seek to culturally appropriate. The term Thomas uses to describe the café-goers, "white suburban vanilla youth," is further relevant since it identifies this antagonistic presence as unrightfully there, a newcomer from the suburbs, as well as of a common, bland, and uninteresting flavor, "vanilla." A stand-in for whiteness, the reference to vanilla matches the setting of the café. To sweeten his coffee with vanilla syrup could to Thomas seem unnecessary, indulgent, or even feminine. And, the sticky-sweet vanilla syrup used in coffee preparation would be attractive to the café's flies, another kind of "invisible shit" to which they are drawn.

Stylistically, the second-person narration of Thomas's passage invites readers to assume his perspective, to put themselves in his shoes, and to understand the exclusion and repulsion caused by the café. Whereas, the first-person narration of *My Year* reveals the omissions and partiality of its narrator and the lack of thought that goes into her fetishization of "working-class coffee" (Moshfegh 6), the bodega, its staff, and its customers. Even though similar preferences are articulated by both characters narrating these passages, they differ significantly when it comes to questions of access, inclusion, and exclusion. As microscripts of gentrification, these passages trigger their reader's understanding of gentrification and consumerism, as well as the positions of gentrifiers and victims of gentrification. Extending from such subnarratable notions of gentrification for characterization purposes, the next section expands on questions of plot as related to gentrification.

LOCALIZED PLOTS:
A BEFORE AND AFTER OF GENTRIFICATION?

Frequently, there is an implicit assumption that gentrification follows certain inevitable stages or phases that are the same in different locations. Building on geographer Sharon Zukin's work on urban "authenticity," literary scholar James Peacock highlights how flawed and inaccurate chronologies of gentrification are: "Gentrification is not a simplistic matter of befores and afters, of an authentic past supplanted by an inauthentic present. Rather, it is about the interpenetration of competing discourses, a continual dialogue between visions of authenticity rooted in economics and culture" ("Those the Dead Left" 135). Similarly, sociologists Schlichtman, Patch, and Hill argue against uniform temporalities: "Gentrification is not an event with a singular start and finish. Gentrification is produced, reproduced, expanded, and sometimes stalled" (85). How can the stand-alone, fragmentary nature of microscripts of gentrification be related to the temporal and spatial concerns of fictional plots?

The question of how narratives translate the theme of gentrification into a plot structure is an interest of urban literary studies and has tended to focus on specific genres. The contemporary crime novel is at the forefront of such analyses (see Heise; Peacock, *Brooklyn Fictions* 93–122), which explore how crime fiction turns gentrification into a particular kind of whodunit. Thomas Heise finds that this "gentrification plot" is typical of contemporary crime fiction, which "tells stories of urban displacement, racial conflict, class grievance, community erosion, and cultural erasure, stories that are traceable in one form or another to the socioeconomic transformations of the city" (8). Aside from crime fiction, it is interesting that gentrification is often turned into a plot in genre fiction, like science fiction or dystopian futuristic fiction. Such popular genres expand the singular, fragmentary observations of gentrification microscripts into larger plot structures and do not shy away from playful and often simplistic explorations of gentrification. This section will look at a crime novel, *Maggie Terry* (2018), next to an urban science fiction novel, *The City We Became* (2018), both of which also feature passages that develop microscripts of gentrification through coffee from the bodega or the café. My interest here is less in aspects of characterization or narration but in how such passages can be related to the plot developments of the rest of the novel, that is, what kinds of plots may be inspired by microscripts of urban coffee drinking.

Maggie Terry (2018) is the eleventh novel by activist and writer Sarah Schulman. Even though they differ significantly in narrative style, genre, and themes, taken together Schulman's novels serve as a chronicle of queer communities in New York City's East Village from the 1940s until today. In the four days of July 2017 when *Maggie Terry* is set, its eponymous protagonist, a white, cis female, and lesbian former NYPD detective, returns to New York after a stint in rehab for her decades-long alcohol and narcotics addiction.[5] Back in Manhattan, she takes a job as a private investigator and is tasked with the case of a murdered actress. Further, Maggie is preoccupied with a second

---

5. With the unnamed protagonist of *My Year,* self-proclaimed "WASP Queen" (14) Maggie shares several biographical features: Both are normatively beautiful, white cis women with a liberal arts education, and an upper-class background who are alienated from not only their families, coworkers, friends, and former romantic partners but also their entire urban surroundings.

murder years earlier: that of an innocent Black man shot by a police colleague of hers, a murder she is complicit in covering up.[6]

Further, as a central theme running through all of her work, Schulman draws attention to the lack of remembrance of HIV and AIDS as well as the decades of activism it fired up.[7] In what is probably her most frequently quoted work, the intellectual memoir *The Gentrification of the Mind* (2013), Schulman describes how the AIDS-related deaths of thousands of gay men contributed to gentrification when their deaths horrifyingly freed up physical space in the form of subsidized apartments that went to market rate or were converted into luxury condos. As a "spiritual gentrification" (*Gentrification* 14), the replacement of diverse populations with more homogenous groups for Schulman leads to a homogenization of urban culture, including queer and artistic subcultures: "With this comes the destruction of culture and relationship, and this destruction has profound consequences for the future lives of cities" (*Gentrification* 14). When Maggie walks through the city, she notices the absence of signs to commemorate the people who have either died from drug use or AIDS: "The oral history passed down by drug addicts told of days before Maggie's time. [. . .] No plaques saying 'A person in this building died of AIDS.' No sign. It never happened at all" (187–88). As a queer woman, and someone struggling with addiction, Maggie has not forgotten this queer history, but it also does not impact her life significantly. By including the lack of commemoration of the HIV/AIDS crisis and its forgotten relevance for New York City, Schulman's novel hints at the possibility of an alternative commemoration. About the narrativity of commemorative street names, signs, and plaques, narratologists Ryan, Foote, and Azaryahu argue that "it is a function of their belonging to master narratives of history and, not less important, to their capacity to evoke the stories of historical events or persons" (141). Presented from Maggie's perspective, the above passage allows readers to reflect on how the city's built environment makes the lives of some inhabitants visible and erases the fate of others.

Throughout her travels around gentrified Manhattan, Maggie serves the reader as a kind of neighborhood guide. Her narrative voice depicts the subnarratable and documents urban change in a snapshot-manner with individual moments combining to create a panorama of gentrification. Returnee Maggie had been physically absent from the city during her rehab and men-

---

6. Through the perspective of a white officer, Schulman thus incorporates into the novel an example of the racially motivated, corrupt police violence that catalyzed the Black Lives Matter movement.

7. A long-time activist, Schulman has been involved with the New Yorker collective ACT UP since the 1980s, coordinates the ACT UP Oral History Project, and published *Let the Record Show: A Political History of Act Up New York, 1987–1993* (2021).

tally absent for much longer. During her self-involved struggles with addiction, she was too intoxicated to notice the demographic shifts, the rebuilding and upscaling of the city around her. Similar to *My Year*, Maggie's personal crisis occurred before the book's plot, and it seeks to capture the diegetic process of rebuilding a self. In *Maggie Terry*, the replacement of the city population and closing of urban landmarks has already taken place, whereas in the chronologically earlier *My Year* these developments are occurring, and our narrator seeks to remove herself from these structural changes just as much as from her personal trauma.

Maggie also frequents her local bodega as a lifeline or sole connection to her neighborhood. Unlike *My Year*'s narrator, she does not perceive her relationship with the bodega's owner, Nick, and his customers in purely aesthetic terms. The minor story of Nick's Deli frames the developments of Maggie's case and her journey of sobriety. She starts each day with a visit to the bodega. These visits begin each chapter and complement Maggie's daily attendance of Alcoholics Anonymous or Narcotics Anonymous meetings to stabilize her sobriety. Rather than the healthier morning tea that she decides should replace her coffee, Maggie craves the ritualized daily encounter with Nick, the only person in her life who knew her before rehab. However, the novel does not depict their casual acquaintance in sentimental terms. Maggie cannot delude herself about the transactional nature of their relationship. "Instead of an old friend, she found a kind of looming clown. He was, after all, a bored person playing a role, trapped in service to people like her. The neighborhood guy" (7). This awareness of her responsibility in "trapping" Nick counters the romanticization that often accompanies the bodega, specifically in popular culture or stories connected to New York City.[8]

The *New York Times*' Willy Staley calls New Yorkers' attachment to their local convenience stores "bodega fetishism" and ties their appeal to the now unique purpose they embody in gentrified environments:

> As the rest of the city's character has been sanded away, bodegas have proved surprisingly resilient and have become, in many ways, a portal to a New York that no longer exists: unvarnished, idiosyncratic, sometimes illicit. [. . .] You might get to know the proprietor a little bit, make small talk, maybe even stash an extra house key there. A lot of businesses used to foster this sort of low-stakes relationship, but now it's just the bodegas, which must bear the burden of a whole generation's yearning for the very stuff their presence in New York has eliminated.

---

8. In Germany, similar discourses exist surrounding the Trinkhalle in the Metropolitan Ruhr Region or the Spätkauf/Späti in Berlin.

Staley's argument is exemplary of the ways that bodegas are perceived as pre-gentrified spaces or spaces immune to gentrification in popular urban discourse. As just one recent iteration, the highly anticipated film adaptation (2021) of Lin-Manuel Miranda's Broadway musical *In the Heights* centers on protagonist Usnavi de la Vega's family business, a bodega in the gentrifying Washington Heights neighborhood of Upper Manhattan. As such, bodegas are diametrically opposite to specialty cafés as embodiments or motors of gentrification. Both Maggie and *My Year*'s narrator would be examples of the kind of gentrifiers who Staley finds to have eliminated the kind of local neighborly interaction that bodegas continue to stand for. Nick's presence connects Maggie to her past life in a neighborhood that she has lived in for a long time and that is now changing. Maggie shows some awareness of this change and her privileged position of being able to remain living in the neighborhood. However, in this crime novel, despite her interest in understanding the whodunit of New York's gentrification, when it demands a victim close to her—Nick's bodega—Maggie cannot muster enough interest to respond.

At the end of the novel, she finds the bodega closed from one day to another because Nick could not afford the rising rents. This violates one of the appealing aspects of the bodega as constantly available and open, providing a tragic turn as Maggie stands in front of the shut-down storefront. Instead of a moment of neighborhood solidarity or activist coalition building, this loss registers with her solely as a personal defeat:

> Maggie let go of the last person who had known her before. The last caring, intimate, friendly face. She crossed the street to the cold-pressed juice place, and bought a cheddar scone, a soy latte, and a kale juice. [. . .] Maggie's old world was completely dissolved. (222)

Undertaking a subnarratable-turned-profound act of literary consumption, Maggie quickly becomes a patron of the upscale café that Nick had complained to her about at the beginning of the novel and even purchases the exact items that left Nick puzzled:

> You know what they got? Something called cold-pressed juice. Ten dollars. They have scones, made with cheese. Four dollars. Iced soy lattes. A pastry, coffee, and juice and you have to hand over a twenty. If you need soy, why do you buy cheese? (6)

The speed with which Maggie moves on from Nick's to this café is jarring to the reader—and remains unquestioned by her narration—amounting to a cynical, climactic punchline that ends Maggie's relationship with Nick and the narrative's serialized opening passages in the bodega. The absurdity of consuming a nondairy coffee with a cheddar scone echoes *My Year*'s narrator's disdain for a "no-foam latte." Again, the bodega is presented as a more honest, cheaper, and consistent alternative to overthought and unnecessary indulgences offered by specialty cafés. While the whole novel presented Maggie's quest for understanding the changed city and remembering those displaced by gentrification (such as the missing plaques for the victims of AIDS), in this last scene, Maggie's complicity as gentrifier allows her to move on unscathed. Her status as gentrifier grants her the luxury of forgetting what she had been so critical of before.

N. K. Jemisin's urban science fiction novel *The City We Became* (2020) relies less on sarcasm and more on straightforward humor and exaggeration to depict urban change.[9] The novel's New Yorker protagonists are aware of gentrification, as well as the scholarship on it and activism against it, and do not shy away from launching the term to describe threats to their hometown. It is the somewhat demanding premise of the novel that cities can be "born" into sentience through a complex symbiosis with one of their inhabitants as their human embodiment. Their connection awards the city sentience and the human magical superpowers. An antagonistic force seeks to prevent the symbiosis of New York City by manifesting as a multitude of threats: tentacles, horrific monsters, racist police officers, gentrified storefronts, and, most prominently, white femininity. I have analyzed elsewhere how *The City* employs intertextuality to present "gentrification as a Lovecraftian evil that makes the ways that global neoliberal capitalism is gendered and racialized more understandable by connecting it to fictional horrors and the science fiction genre's racist past as a literary institution" (Sulimma 13). The novel's diverse superhero characters face off against Woman in White, a supernatural conglomeration of intersectional threats related to racism, sexism, or homophobia. The image of gentrification in this novel by Jemisin is simplified, but it very effectively communicates a shared evil that characters have to face not only in superhero fight scenes but everyday experiences of discrimination, some of which take place in a café.

The City begins with a prologue that is stylistically different from the rest of the novel: In first-person narration, it presents the perspective of a homeless queer teenager of color who is treated to breakfast by an acquaintance

---

9. N. K. (Nora Keita) Jemisin is one of the most proficient contemporary science fiction writers. Aside from the first installment in a planned trilogy, the novel is an extension of a short story ("The City Born Great") that Jemisin first published in 2016 and republished in her short story collection *How Long 'til Black Future Month?* (2018).

in an upscale café. Very similar to the above-cited passage from Orange's *There There*, he describes how the other visitors of the café are "eyeballing me because I'm definitively black, and because the holes in my clothes aren't the fashionable kind. I don't stink, but these people can smell anybody without a trust fund from a mile away" (2). Tellingly, in this café, neither Maggie nor *My Year*'s narrator would catch a second glance (as white women with trust funds), whereas both the unnamed teenager and *There There*'s Thomas are acutely aware of being watched and judged. Unlike Thomas, the teenager enjoys his visit to the café.

> I sit there for as long as I can, making the sandwich last, sipping his leftover coffee, savoring the fantasy of being normal. I people-watch, judge other patrons' appearances; on the fly I make up a poem about being a rich white girl who notices a poor black boy in her coffee shop and has an existential crisis (3).

Even though he expresses a desire for "being normal," it is through artistic creation, "making up a poem," that the teenager seeks to establish his belonging in this exclusive space and sarcastically targets the socioeconomic and racial bias implicit in it. Similar to Thomas's attack of "vanilla" youth frequenting the café in Oakland, he imagines a "rich white girl" as the invented face of the excluding atmosphere he feels in this space. Again, the actual visitors and staff of the café remain an unmentioned crowd ("these people") whose microaggressive attention creates pressure for the protagonist ("eyeballing me"). Despite their lack of actual interaction, through the overlap of the teenager's and the minor patrons' respective "character spaces" (Woloch 14) in the charged setting of the café, much is revealed about the unequal access to resources and class-related separation of consumer spaces in gentrified neighborhoods. Tellingly, it is art that here is invoked as a potential to reflect on such inequality: The "existential crisis" of the teenager's fictional poetic "rich white girl" character is caused by the confrontation with her (white) privilege and complicity as a gentrifier.[10]

Later in the novel, a group of characters drives by bodegas in Harlem, and the third-person narrator describes them as "sentinels of The City That Never Sleeps And Occasionally Needs Milk At Two A.M." (381). The next sentence immediately contrasts the bodegas with upscale cafés:

---

10. Later in the novel, an exhibition of photographs taken of the teenager's street art provides the chance for a less paralyzing realization and connectivity for those displaced by gentrification, not unlike the street art counterscripts described by Deckers and Moreno in chapter 1 of this volume.

Gentrification here has taken the form of endless coffee shops. For the last few blocks these have been indie places, proudly touting their locally roasted pour-overs, all with different decor and sign fonts. Then comes the proof that it's all over for the neighborhood's original character: they pass a Starbucks on the corner. (381)

Again, bodegas as neighborhood lookouts and signposts of pregentrification are immediately contrasted with specialty cafés as embodiments of gentrification and culminate in global franchises as the ultimate indicator of the kind of cultural homogeneity that Sarah Schulman refers to as "gentrification of the mind." In an over-the-top spin, in *The City,* these coffee franchises become sentient, too. They grow legs, scales, feathers, or wings and turn into animalistic predators chasing the protagonists' car through the city. Hence, the novel's manifestation of gentrification as concrete evils to be battled offers comic relief. However, it does not absolve white femininity as the most dominant personification of gentrification, since it is this shape that the antagonist adopts to weaponize white privilege (see Sulimma 4).

Altogether, whether gentrification is unfolded within the genre conventions of a whodunit for a detective character to investigate or as a superhero quest in which a powerful evil must be battled by intrinsically good antigentrifiers, plots build upon marginal passages that I refer to as microscripts of gentrification. Some novels expand such seemingly trivial moments beyond characterization purposes and link them as narrative events that through their serial repetition connect larger plot structures.

CONCLUSION

Because the urban changes subsumed under the label gentrification are not solely economic, social, or even spatial, but also narrative processes, this contribution has explored one of the strategies with which contemporary fiction takes up the imaginative issues surrounding gentrification.

By turning subnarratable—quotidian, trivial—developments into microscripts, contemporary fiction surpasses the supranarrative dilemma of gentrification (the notion that gentrification defies narrative), which exceeds micro and macro frameworks of cause and effect (see Warhol for terminology). Microscripts occur in marginalized descriptions of sites of consumption. These sites' narrativity evokes readers' understandings of sociopolitical changes connected to gentrification. In their brief fragmentary nature, such microscripts serve important purposes. I have explored how microscripts of buying and drinking coffee trigger questions of responsibility, complicity, access, exclusion, and fetishization. The cultural imagining of the bodega and the café as diametrically opposed urban spaces here stands in for the scriptive materiality of urban spaces that function similarly: In the bodega and in the café, the reader learns metonymically how urban infrastructure limits access on economic and performative grounds, how it actively excludes or includes specifically marked urban dwellers. It is through this opposition imagined by focalizing characters that readers are confronted with the everyday banal practices of gentrification.

In three of the novels, characters battle with alcohol or narcotics addictions, further complicating their consumer practices and capacity for self-reflection. In three of the discussed novels, white women are positioned as dominant embodiments of gentrification. Meanwhile, in the two novels presented from the perspective of characters excluded from the benefits of urban change or displaced through gentrification, the polyvocal narrative structure creates a representation of urban multiplicity under threat. Finally, marginal microscripts of gentrification offer literary studies a means to understand literature's contribution to the intense gentrification debates wielded in so many areas of public life, as well as how to study small-scale representations with large aspirations for readerly interpretation.

WORKS CITED

Brown-Saracino, Japonica. "Explicating Divided Approaches to Gentrification and Growing Income Inequality." *Annual Review of Sociology*, vol. 43, no. 1, 2017, pp. 515–39.

Cox, James H. "Tommy Orange Has Company." *PMLA*, vol. 135, no. 3, 2020, pp. 565–71.

Drügh, Heinz. "Ästhetik der *pulchritudo adhaerens*: Zur Form der Warenwelt." *Formästhetiken und Formen der Literatur: Materialität—Ornament—Codierung*, edited by Torsten Hahn and Nicolas Pethes, transcript, 2020, pp. 115–38.

Felton, Emma. *Filtered: Coffee, The Café, and the 21st-Century City*. Routledge, 2019.

Glass, Ruth. "Aspects of Change." *London: Aspects of Change*, edited by the Centre for Urban Studies, 1964, xiii–xlii.

Greenberg, Jonathan. "Losing Track of Time." *Daedalus*, vol. 150, no. 1, 2021, pp. 188–203.

Gurr, Jens Martin. *Charting Literary Urban Studies: Texts as Models of and for the City*. Routledge, 2021.

Heise, Thomas. *The Gentrification Plot: New York and the Postindustrial Crime Novel*. Columbia UP, 2021.

Henryson, Hanna. *Gentrifiktionen: Zur Gentrifizierung in deutschsprachigen Berlin-Romanen nach 2000*. Peter Lang, 2021.

Henryson, Hanna, and Maria Sulimma. "'Nothing Was Solved, Only Accelerated': Gentrification as Apocalypse in Contemporary Dystopian Berlin Novels" (in preparation).

Jameson, Fredric. *The Seeds of Time*. Columbia UP, 1994.

Jemisin, N. K. *The City We Became*. Orbit Books, 2020.

Mayer, Ruth. "Kleine Literaturen als globale Literatur." *Handbuch Transnationalität & Literatur*, edited by Doerte Bischoff and Susanne Komfort-Hein, De Gruyter, 2019, pp. 203-14.

Moshfegh, Ottessa. *My Year of Rest and Relaxation*. Penguin Press, 2018.

Norris, Frank. *The Responsibilities of the Novelist, and Other Literary Essays*. Doubleday, 1903.

Orange, Tommy. *There, There*. Knopf, 2018.

Peacock, James. *Brooklyn Fictions: The Contemporary Urban Community in a Global Age*. Bloomsbury, 2016.

———. "Those the Dead Left Behind: Gentrification and Haunting in Contemporary Brooklyn Fictions." *Studies in American Fiction*, vol. 46, no. 1, 2019, pp. 131-56.

Prince, Gerald. "The Disnarrated." *Style*, vol. 22, no. 1, 1988, pp. 1-8.

Ryan, Marie-Laure, Kenneth Foote, and Maoz Azaryahu. *Narrating Space / Spatializing Narrative: Where Narrative Theory and Geography Meet*. The Ohio State UP, 2016.

Santayana, George. "The Genteel Tradition in American Philosophy." *The Genteel Tradition: Nine Essays by George Santayana*, edited by Douglas L. Wilson, Harvard UP, 1967, pp. 72-76.

Schlichtman, John Joe, Jason Patch, and Marc Lamont Hill. *Gentrifier*. U of Toronto P, 2017.

Schulman, Sarah. *The Gentrification of the Mind: Witness to a Lost Imagination*. U of California P, 2013.

———. *Maggie Terry*. Feminist Press, 2018.

Smith, Neil. *The New Urban Frontier: Gentrification and the Revanchist City*. Routledge, 1996.

Staley, Willy. "'High Maintenance' and the New TV Fantasy of New York." *New York Times*, 30 Jan. 2020, https://www.nytimes.com/2020/01/30/magazine/new-york-tv.html.

Sulimma, Maria. "Scripting Urbanity through Intertextuality and Consumerism in N. K. Jemisin's *The City We Became*: 'I'm Really Going to Have to Watch Some Better Movies about New York.'" *Critique: Studies in Contemporary Fiction*, vol. 63, no. 5, 2022, pp. 571-86, https://doi.org/10.1080/00111619.2020.1865866.

Warhol, Robyn R. "Neonarrative; or, How to Render the Unnarratable in Realist Fiction and Contemporary Film." *A Companion to Narrative Theory*, edited by James Phelan and Peter J. Rabinowitz, Blackwell, 2005, pp. 220-31.

Woloch, Alex. *The One vs. the Many: Minor Characters and the Space of the Protagonist in the Novel*. Princeton UP, 2003.

CHAPTER 8

Redemptive Scripts in the City Novel

LIEVEN AMEEL

The promise of redemption, of past faults redeemed and virtue in the world restored, is one of the most prominent themes in the history of American literature.[1] In the literature of New York City, the promise of redemption is developed in close dialogue with the forces of urbanity and modernity. Such forces may elevate individuals or communities as well as corrupt them, all within a spatial setting in which individual fate can be seen as symbolic of the fate of ethnic or social communities of America or indeed all of Western modernity. The redemptive narratives examined here—from Edith Wharton's short story "Autres Temps . . ." (1911) to F. Scott Fitzgerald's *The Great Gatsby* (1925) and Colson Whitehead's *The Intuitionist* (1999)—are treated as providing persuasive *scripts,* formulaic narrative sequences that may be called upon in particular circumstances. Scripts can be seen as serving three functions: "They activate procedural knowledge, they serve as self-description, and they provide blueprints for the future" (Buchenau and Gurr 142). The examples discussed are specifically *urban* scripts, gesturing toward possibilities of redemptive urban community or possible urban lives. In most of these texts, the suggested possibility of redemption remains ultimately out of reach. A measure of redemption, however, can be found in the very act of narrating

---

1. For an example of the dimension of individual and collective atonement, see chapter 1 by Deckers and Moreno; for the postindustrial and urban dimension of this promise, see chapter 6 by Sattler.

and finding a voice. Redemptive scripts are also at work outside of literary fiction, and the final part of this article briefly examines redemptive scripts in urban planning, contemporary music, and popular culture set in New York.

REDEMPTIVE NARRATIVES

While this article is most interested in redemptive narratives as they appear in the context of American—and specifically New York—literature, a redemptive impulse is ingrained in all narrative structures. Narrative tends to be set in motion by the introduction of an imbalance into a storyworld, and readerly interest is bound up with the desire to see such imbalance corrected. The view of imbalance as central to narrative progression is well-established and runs from formalist views of narrative structure to more recent rhetorical approaches to narrative functions (see Todorov; Kafalenos). James Phelan, for example, has pointed to the introduction of "unstable relationships" as generating the progression of the narrative and sees textual narrativity as bound up with the "dynamics of instability-complication-resolution" (Phelan 16, 225). At the background of such readings of narrative, of course, is Aristotle's view of classical tragedy's development as moving through complication toward resolution. All narrative can be seen as involving a progression (in innumerable sequential and chronological varieties) from an imbalance (or revelation of an imbalance) through complication toward the possibility of a restoration of that imbalance. Readerly interest is bound up at least in part with an understanding of the importance of the imbalance within the storyworld: Readers may be invested in seeing restoration brought about—or not. Closure, ideally, brings resolution, although there have always been works that deliberately deny the reader an image of balance restored.

The idea of resolution can be aligned with the notion of redemption, to the extent that some critics have argued that, whereas "the introduction of plot conflict corresponds to the problem of evil, the movement toward resolution corresponds to redemption" (Middleton and Walsh 64). But how can redemption (as an essential part of plot development) be defined in more precise terms, and how does it complicate the notion of resolution? The *Oxford English Dictionary* gives a range of meanings for the term "redemption." Among these, three meanings stand out: first, the notion of payment of some sort of debt (specifically to free a prisoner, captive or slave; *OED* 1.a), second, the theological notion of "deliverance from sin and damnation, esp. by the atonement of Christ; salvation" (*OED* 2.a), and third, "expiation or atonement for a crime, sin, or offence; release from punishment" (*OED* 3.a). The understanding of the redemptive plot as it is developed here is based not exclusively on the second, theological meaning but on all three meanings.

Drawing on this three-fold definition of redemption, the main features of a redemptive plot can be outlined: The plot is set in motion by an imbalance or the realization of an imbalance. This may also entail an experience of a breach and/or loss, including the loss of freedom, loss of coherence, or loss of stability in the storyworld. A debt is incurred, a sin committed, or an offense perpetrated, or all three can occur. The action of the plot is driven in part by a desire for the restoration of balance (and/or the desire to understand the roots and repercussions of the imbalance), which may take the more specific form of the redeeming of a debt, the deliverance from sin, atonement for past mistakes, or all three. In the course of these activities, the protagonist, narrator, or central characters are led to understand some of the symbolical meanings (communal/national/universal) of the foundational imbalance that set the plot in motion. In the resolution, balance is restored, continued, or further complicated. If balance is restored, this not only atones for an evildoer's wrongs but restores the protagonists and their community to a just and good world. It should be noted that in the texts discussed here, redemption is present as a possibility but rarely realized. But even if the resolution of the plot does not offer a restoration of balance or a sense of deliverance or atonement, an experience of redemption may be located on the level of the narrative voice: A character or narrator who was lacking narrative agency at the outset may gradually achieve the voice with which to recount the events experienced, providing in narrative form the coherence, balance, and atonement that the storyworld continues to lack. The narrative can be seen in this case not as a description of events that aim at redemption, but rather as a description of the gradual acquiring of voice. This is arguably the most powerful dimension of the redemptive scripts discussed here: the possibility for a narrative to find ways to give meaning, through the very act of narrating, to traumatic or destabilizing experiences.

Redemption may also be located in the perspective of the actual reader (see Bersani for a discussion of this notion) or in the perspective of the actual author (for example in writing therapy). Both of these two last perspectives entail a much more figurative understanding of the notion of redemption than the one used here, and they largely fall outside of the scope of this article.

The notion of a loss of balance, a fall from grace, and the tentative possibility of redemption has particular resonances within the literature of modernity. In the limited space of this chapter, only some general points may be noted here. The processes of modernity can be described as a series of accelerating imbalances and experiences of loss: of authenticity, of enchantment, or

TABLE 8.1. Features of a redemptive plot (compiled by the author)

PLOT	Imbalance, breach, or loss	Development, driven in part by urge for the restoration of the balance and specifically by redemption of debt, deliverance, atonement, or all three	Resolution, with balance restored, continued, or complicated
	Imbalance may involve debt or loss of freedom, a sin committed, or a crime or offence		Redemption of debt, deliverance, or atonement—or lack thereof
NARRATIVE VOICE	Lack or loss of voice	Development of voice	Achievement of voice—or failure to fully achieve voice
READERLY PERSPECTIVE	Reading/reception as redemptive experience		
WRITERLY PERSPECTIVE	Writing as redemptive experience (e.g., as part of writing therapy)		

of perceived natural bonds with one's environment. Developments in literature over the past two centuries can be seen as powerful engagements with such experiences of loss, from romanticism's investigation of increasingly fraught relationships to the natural environment or the historical avantgarde's expression of a loss of cohesion to contemporary climate change literature that searches for new literary forms to come to terms with the possibility of life's extinction. Following Lukács, the novel form, as it developed in the nineteenth and twentieth centuries in the shadows of modernity, can be seen as an expression of "transcendental homelessness" (41). This modern experience is not without a measure of guilt, a sense of being complicit in the processes that have brought about the fateful rupture in the world. In consequence, the literature of the modern city has been seen as dominated by the combined fascination for, and sense of collective guilt about, modernity's Promethean achievements (see Pike). By addressing expressions of loss and guilt, it could be argued, redemptive scripts draw on the ability of scripts to "assume the role of *scriptures* in the old sense of the term: as declared foundational texts of a shared faith," which "might become canonical, authoritative, communally binding, and prescriptive" (Buchenau and Gurr 146–47).

As recent studies by Fessenden and Ferraro have convincingly shown, redemptive plots carry special meanings in the cultural narratives of the United States. This may in part be related to the continued role of Christian frames of meaning in public life in the US, as well as to the puritan roots of the American republic and American founding myths. Early modern Puritan views could see America as the place where earlier evils (left behind in the Old World) could be atoned for; but America is also the place where new evils were carried out, from the expulsions of Indigenous peoples to the historical crime of slavery. In the American context, redemptive narratives can be seen as central narrative resources outside of literary and cultural representations: In everyday storytelling, redemptive scripts have been identified as the dominant kind of scripts used by Americans in the telling of their own lives (see McAdams).

REDEMPTION AND *THE GREAT GATSBY*

All of the key elements of the redemptive plot, as outlined above, can be found in F. Scott Fitzgerald's *The Great Gatsby* (1925), a novel that has repeatedly been read as redemptive (although often in terms of Gatsby's love relationship and Fitzgerald's Catholicism; see Gindin 81 ff.; Fessenden 181 ff.; Ferraro 143 ff.). The instability that the plot of the novel aims to resolve can be located on a number of different levels. With the figure of Gatsby, shifting class identities, as well as a threat to the institution of marriage are introduced in Long Island, but he is also a figure who announces the disruptive experiences of America's participation in the Great War. The car trips back and forth to New York City and the outings in the "Valley of Ashes" link the instability at the heart of the novel to the disruptive effects of modernity and industrialization. On the personal level of Gatsby, the desire for a new beginning, and for past mistakes redeemed, centers on the figure of Daisy and his endeavors to regain her favor against all odds. In the assertion of Gatsby: "'I'm going to fix everything just the way it was before,' he said, nodding determinedly. 'She'll see'" (Fitzgerald 117).

This compulsive urge to dream of a new beginning in Gatsby's personal life is connected in the final paragraphs of the novel to America's self-image of the continent and nation that will allow mankind (or at least its Western sphere) a new beginning, a symbolical return to a lost Eden. In these final moments of the novel, the landscape of Gatsby's mansion appears to the narrator Nick Carraway as a vision of "the old island here that flowered once for Dutch sailors' eyes—a fresh, green breast of the new world" (187). But this vision remains elusive: By this time, Gatsby is dead, his house deserted, his dream proven to be a dangerous and destructive illusion.

One could say that in the end, nothing in *The Great Gatsby* is redeemed: No debts are paid (literally, since Gatsby's debts to organized crime, it is suggested, remain unpaid), no past mistakes set right. The destructive forces of industrialization and modernity are unremittingly at work; the marriage of the Buchanans is saved but proven to be hollow in the process; the returning veteran is not reintegrated into society. If anything, the drive toward redemption, which the novel connects powerfully to America's foundational narrative, is revealed as both illusory and destructive.

But the instability and its resolution can also be located on the level of the narrative voice, with the narrative as a gradual development of a voice to describe what has happened. Nick Carraway, the narrator of *The Great Gatsby*, gradually appears to the reader not only as an observer but as someone who is actively trying to write down the events he has witnessed. By the end of the novel, he has not only produced a coherent account of the events and of the riddle that is Gatsby but has succeeded in transcending the aspirations of Gatsby by casting Gatsby as the embodiment of the "American dream" itself. In his final utterance, Gatsby's dream, finally, is connected by Carraway to what is posited as the universal urge to beat on against the currents, including the reader (through the sudden use of the personal pronoun *we*) in the process: "So we beat on, boats against the current, borne back ceaselessly into the past" (188).

In *The Great Gatsby*, redemption remains out of reach for Gatsby. For America, Fitzgerald's novel suggests, the promise of redemption, and the dream of starting again from the beginning in a landscape untainted by past mistakes, constitutes a dangerous illusion, complicit in bringing about new violence. But in the novel, the perspective of Nick Carraway adds an important dimension to the redemptive script: finding one's own voice as a redemptive experience that lends meaning to otherwise traumatic or enigmatic events.

FINDING A VOICE IN REDEMPTIVE SCRIPTS

In several New York novels of the twentieth century, redemption is not achieved by coming to terms with past trauma or past mistakes or becoming integrated into community, but rather in finding one's voice, a language with which to share and thereby transcend one's experiences. A key novel in this respect is Henry Roth's *Call It Sleep* (1934), a novel that describes the early twentieth-century Jewish immigrant experience in the coming-of-age of young David in New York's Brownsville. The climactic scene in the novel, in which David tempts electrocution by touching an electrified train rail and experiences something akin to a mystical epiphany, has frequently been read as indicative of the redemptive plot in the novel (for a critical overview of this tradition, see Materassi). But the novel's progression is also, and crucially, about finding one's language. Biblical David, as Hana Wirth-Nesher points out, is also the writer of the psalms, and in the course of the novel, Roth's protagonist is described as negotiating between different languages to reach a mature voice of his own (98).

In the context of the American city novel, redemptive plots that include a finding of voice and a maturing of language have particular importance. This goes especially for what has been called the "ecological novel" by Blanche Gelfant—a quintessentially New York subcategory of the city novel, which focuses on unpacking a specific urban neighborhood, and in which redemptive plots tend to oscillate around escaping the bounds of one's social and ethnic neighborhood. Betty Smith's classic *A Tree Grows in Brooklyn* (1943), which focuses on the coming-of-age of young Francie Nolan in an impoverished Williamsburg neighborhood, is a case in point. In the resolution of the novel, hard work, perseverance, and education will eventually redeem the painful generational transition from Old Continent to New Continent as well as the imbalances at work both in the family and the social neighborhood. As Llyod Michaels notes, the book—as well as the movie adaptation by Elia Kazan—is a "synthesis of bildungsroman and kunstlerroman" (406), with Francie finding her voice as a writer outside of the tenements. In the final pages of Smith's novel, the tree that has again bloomed into life after being stumped and burned is also the symbol of Francie's—and the working-class block's—ultimate redemption: "But this tree in the yard—this tree that men chopped down [. . .] this tree that they built a bonfire around, trying to burn up its stump—this tree lived! It lived! And nothing could destroy it" (442–43).

LIMITS TO REDEMPTIVE SCRIPTS

If redemption in New York novels is about coming to terms with reintegrating into, or escaping from, the constraints of social and/or ethnic communities, New York novels also repeatedly offer tragic stories in which redemption remains impossible or illusionary—*The Great Gatsby* a classical example. The oeuvre of Edith Wharton can be seen as one set of literary works that often pivot around New York communities, and in which the possibility of redemption is held out only to be denied. I have elsewhere (with Markku Salmela) examined Wharton's short story "Autres Temps . . ." (1911) from the perspective of the themes of self-transformation and rebirth (323). But the short story could just as pertinently be described as one about redemption. Its opening sees the elderly Mrs. Lidcote return by steamer to New York City from Italy, where she has been in self-imposed exile, pondering the possibility of reinclusion into New York society years after the events that have seen her ostracized. Is it possible that times have changed—as the title suggests—and that the moral landscape has changed as well? In part, the question is the same as in *The Great Gatsby*: Is it possible to make a new start, to make up for the mistakes of one's youth, this time in a way that leads to integration and a process of healing? To these questions are added the inflections from the novel of manners: Can Mrs. Lidcote be returned to New York's fashionable society, and will it turn out that that society has mended its ostracizing ways (especially toward women)? For Mrs. Lidcote as well as for the reader, the interest of the short story revolves around this question, which is resolved in the negative in two separate instances on the final pages. First, when Mrs. Lidcote expresses her inability to escape—even when leaving the country—the constraints of society. She recounts to the sympathetic Franklin Ide how "I thought I'd got out of it once; but what really happened was that the other people went out, and left me in the same little room. The only difference was that I was there alone" (Wharton 272). And the second, and more final awareness of the continuing imbalance comes when Mrs. Lidcote realizes that Mr. Ide also continues to be afraid of being tainted by his acquaintance with her, a realization described as "the veil of painted gauze [. . .] torn in tatters" after which "she was moving again among the grim edges of reality" (276). In Wharton's short story, the redemptive script attunes the reader to possible future forms of urban community. If there is a possibility of redemption at the end of this short story, it will be claimed by the generation following Mrs. Lidcote.

AFRICAN AMERICAN ELEVATION AND REDEMPTION IN *THE INTUITIONIST*

In African American literature, redemptive plots have a particular, if fraught, resonance, in part because of redemption's significance in African American historical slave narratives but also because of the way in which African American texts question and complement cultural narratives of American redemption. Can American redemptive scripts, as they have developed in nineteenth-century and twentieth-century US literature and culture, be squared with African American scripts of redemption (see Moses; Giggie)? And conversely—to what extent can African American stories of redemption become part of American scripts, grounded as these are in experiences of European settlers and puritan republicanism? Such questions continue to be relevant in the twenty-first century. One important starting point is the meaning of redemption not only as a remittance (personal, communal, societal) of the sins of society but more specifically as the making of a payment to free a slave from bondage (see *OED* 1.a). Numerous African American authors have drawn on religious tropes to create personal and communal stories of redemption (see Brooks and Mabry 81). But powerful American scripts of redemption have also historically functioned as ways to exclude certain groups—African Americans among them—from American forms of storytelling (see Fessenden).

Several of the most iconic African American novels of New York City, perhaps most notably Ralph Ellison's *Invisible Man* (1952) and James Baldwin's *Go Tell It on the Mountain* (1953), are structured around the possibility, and the limits, of redemptive scripts. I want to focus here, however, on a more recent American novel that examines the possibility of redemption: Colson Whitehead's *The Intuitionist* (1999). The novel is set in an alternative New York City in the second half of the twentieth century, in a world in which elevators have taken on special importance. The protagonist, Lila Mae, becomes embroiled in the infights between two elevator technician guilds with their own distinct philosophical approaches to elevator maintenance, the Intuitionists and the Empiricists, and much of the plot revolves around her investigations into the writings of legendary elevator inventor James Fulton. The redemptive plot is set in motion in the opening pages, with the mention of something that is ominously broken: elevator nr. 11 in the Fanny Briggs Memorial Building (Whitehead 35). Elevators, in turn, are presented as the technological innovations that have been designed to mend a broken world, or more precisely, the fraught modern city. The dreamed-of-perfect elevator, according to Fulton, "will deliver us from the cities we suffer now, these stunted shacks" (61). The urban environment and the elevators in Whitehead's novel are deeply symbolical of the broken promises of modernity, but also, as the location of the original—and literal—breach in a building called "Fanny Briggs" (named after "a slave who taught herself how to read"; 12) indicates, of fraught American race relations.

The elevator is what will lift up, literally and symbolically, what will enable modernity to run its triumphant course and mend its flaws. But it is profoundly uncertain in the novel whether this message of redemption is understood to be universal, or how racialized minorities are to see their own role in such universalist visions of redemption. A subtle passage in this respect is the long quote, in the novel, from the US vice president's speech at the 1853 Exhibition of the Industry of All Nations:

> We are living in a period of most wonderful transition, which tends rapidly to accomplish that great end to which all history points—the realization of the unity of mankind. The distances which separated the different nations are rapidly vanishing with the achievements of modern invention. (80–81)

The quote is an actual quote by Prince Albert, husband of Queen Victoria, and pronounced at the opening of the Great Exhibition in London in 1851—the first of the World Exhibitions. The speech announced universalist ideas such as that of a universal "brotherhood of man," but was also a showcase of—among others—imperialism, the triumphant advance of Western civilization, and Christian ideals; and already in contemporary satire, Western advancements at the exhibition were criticized for being built, as Tanya Agathocleous points out, on "the debasement of black bodies" (48). In this light, the gradual uncovering by Lila Mae of Fulton's prophecy of a coming "second elevation"—a better future that will be brought about by a new kind of elevator, a mysterious "black box" (61), with promises of a "new beginning," a "renegotiation of our relationship to objects" (62)—is fraught with uncertainties. A turning point in the novel, and for Mae's understanding of the nature of a possible "second elevation," is when she learns that James Fulton was "colored" and passing as white (134). Redemption, in Lila Mae's thoughts reflecting on Fulton's fate, turns out to be impossible, because racial boundaries remain unsurpassable: The idea of universal redemption is no more than a dangerous lie.

> There was no way he believed in transcendence. His [Fulton's] race kept him earthbound, like the stranded citizens before Otis invented his safety elevator. There was no hope for him as colored man because the white world will not let a colored man rise, and there was no hope for him as a white man because it was a lie. [. . .] He knows the other world he describes does not exist. There will be no redemption because the men who run this place do not want redemption. (240)

In its final pages, the novel does not offer a clear resolution, no unequivocal key to how the elevator allegory would have to be read.[2] Lila Mae has become the guardian of Fulton's secret and is working on the advancement of his ideas, the completion of the new elevator that will change and redeem the world at last: "She returns to the work. She will make the necessary adjustments. It will come. She is never wrong. It's her intuition" (255).

It remains profoundly unclear whether Lila Mae's hope is illusory, or how the promised "second elevation" would be able to resolve the tensions at the beginning of the novel—ingrained as they are in the "first elevation" of modernization and urbanization as well as structural racialized inequality. In the storyworld, redemption—on the level of community—remains out of reach, but, crucially, a measure of redemption is reached in how Lila Mae finds her

---

2. For more on allegorical readings of the novel, see, for example, Huehls 115.

voice and her agency in the course of the novel. I have argued above—in the case of *The Great Gatsby* and *Call It Sleep*—that to find one's voice to narrate a pathway informed by the promise of redemption can be seen as one important aspect of redemptive scripts. In *The Intuitionist,* Lila Mae's self-realization as heir to Fulton's work is described not as learning how to write, but as a way of finding literacy, an ability that is explicitly—through the figure of Fanny Briggs—related to transformative slave narratives:

> In her room at the Friendly League Residence, she reads *Theoretical Elevators,* Volume Two. Reads, *The race sleeps in this hectic and disordered century. Grim lids that will not open. Anxious retinas flit to and fro beneath them. They are stirred by dreaming. In this dream of uplift, they understand that they are dreaming the contract of the hallowed verticality, and hope to remember the terms on waking. The race never does, and that is our curse.* The human race, she thought formerly. Fulton has a fetish for the royal "we" throughout *Theoretical Elevators.* But now—who's "we"?
>
> She is teaching herself how to read. (186)

Lila Mae teaches herself to read, and as the novel progresses, the reader, too, is learning to read and learning to question universalist narratives of redemption. For both, this reading process is guided by a redemptive script that gestures toward personal "uplifting" but also toward possible urban futures in which past and present societal wounds can be redeemed.

NEW YORK CITY PLANNING AS REDEMPTION

As these examples from a range of texts from twentieth-century literature of New York show, the possibility of redemption provides a powerful script with which to model a literary protagonist's experiences of the city, their hopes and aspirations, achievements, and disillusions, in ways that anticipate the urban future of the location in which the texts are set. More often than not in these texts, redemption proves elusive or problematic, and redemptive plots are actively critiqued and disrupted, for example, in the way characters experience their own progress within a world that remains broken. The predominance of texts that draw on the possibility of redemption while problematizing it can be seen as in tune with the more general predominance of tragic and satiric plots (in the terms of Frye) in the literature of modernity. Since the advent of the realist novel (and with Honoré de Balzac's *Illusions perdues* [1837–43] as one example), literature tends to consistently cast doubts on the transformative benefits of modernization and urbanization. Such fiction expresses a profound uneasiness about what technological, industrial, and social "elevation" has wrought in terms of moral, spiritual, or societal forms of a fall from grace.

In this context, it is all the more striking that in urban planning and policy visions, redemptive scripts have retained a peculiarly solid ground. Or rather, that redemptive scripts have returned to urban planning and policy visions toward the end of the twentieth century, after having been out of favor in the postwar years, when a systems approach and "rational planning" were arguably preferred above far-reaching visions that aimed at an idealized end-state (see Taylor 63). As many of the chapters in this book indicate, redemptive patterns tend to be especially pronounced in the case of American postindustrial urban revitalization plans. In the case of New York City planning, the promise of new beginnings and redemption of past mistakes can be seen at work in the consecutive New York comprehensive waterfront plans. The promise of new beginnings is most explicit in the first comprehensive waterfront plan from 1992, which introduces the changes it proposes as a new beginning in the preface: "Taken together, the land use changes, zoning text amendments, public investment strategies and regulatory revisions recommended in this plan signal a new beginning for the city's waterfront" (xi). The very title of the plan, *Reclaiming the Edge*, emplots the planned changes in terms of a past loss that will be made good. The vision of a possible new beginning, enacted within a landscape that has become a byword for the past mistakes of urbanization and industrialization (and of the short-sighted endeavors to maximize profit), returns time and again throughout the planning document. And the restoration of a balance "between commerce and recreation" that has been lost is explicitly named as the aim of the plan, with the ultimate goal "to balance these competing interests" (i; see Ameel, "Sixth Borough" 253–54).

In the second comprehensive waterfront plan, *Vision 2020*, a similar vision of renewal and restitution appears. The plan emphasizes, for example, that these new and beneficial developments come after "decades of turning our back on the shoreline—allowing it to devolve into a no-man's land of rotting piers" (*Vision 2020*, 6). In the media representations of specific parts of the waterfront development—notably the development of Willets Point—the trope of a new beginning was explicitly cast as a redemption of past mistakes and connected to metaphoric images from *The Great Gatsby* (see WNYC). The reference to *The Great Gatsby* is no coincidence: In a century of planning visions for New York, metaphors ("the Green Breast"; "the valley of ashes") from Fitzgerald's novel have been used time and again to suggest the possibility of new beginnings at the waterfront (see Ameel, "'Valley of Ashes'").

To a degree, *Vision 2020* goes some way toward an acknowledgment of the continuing challenges that have to be contended with, even if all the plans it proposes will be completed: "Building resilience to coastal storms and flooding anticipated in the future does not lend itself to quick or simple solutions. [...] Because certain risks are unavoidable, a resilience strategy should not seek to eliminate all risks" (106). The wording of *Vision 2020*—acknowledging the lack of "quick or simple solutions," pointing to the continuing presence of risks, regardless of planned measures—explicitly evades closure and signposts to the reader that a clean, new beginning at the waterfront is not achievable. The text is an interesting showcase of a planning text that activates a redemptive script while remaining open-ended, eluding the desire for closure.[3]

REDEMPTIVE SCRIPTS: SALVAGING MEANING FROM THE WRECKAGE OF THE WORLD

In the first decades of the twenty-first century, experiences of loss have accumulated in and around New York City, from 9/11 to Hurricane Sandy to the events of the COVID-19 pandemic at the time of writing. Literature, representational art, and audiovisual media have continued to draw on the possibility of redemptive scripts to come to terms with such real-world events. Redemptive scripts may be drawn upon to come to terms with specific traumatic events and may be used to transform such experiences and to provide them with meanings. This may involve a reactionary ethos that wants to provide the relief of closure rather than to explore, in narrative form, the ongoing causes and effects of traumatic experiences. Guy Westwell points out how, in the wake of 9/11, revenge films "formed part of a broader raft of cultural production that extended patriotic and nationalist discourses of rescue and redemption" (56). But American cinema has always included the possibilities of exploring themes of redemption in more subtle terms, from the 1954 film *On the Waterfront* (often read as an explicit Catholic redemption story, see Fisher x) to Scorsese's oeuvre, from *Taxi Driver* to *Gangs of New York* (see Miliora 142 ff.).

Redemptive scripts in cultural representations of New York have come in various guises, one notable example from contemporary music being the album *Landfall* by Laurie Anderson and Kronos Quartet (2018). The album, which documents the landfall and aftermath of Hurricane Sandy (2012), is structured as an effort to retrieve what is of worth in this catastrophe and to find a measure of redemption in the flotsam and jetsam left by the experience. One reviewer described the album as creative salvaging, "the sound of a quintessential New Yorker processing a New York tragedy, salvaging something

---

3. For planning without closure, see Ameel, *Narrative Turn* 118.

from the sad wreckage, internalizing the debris of a creative life, showing how human memory can be stronger than catastrophe" (Pelly). In *Landfall,* too, the redemptive progression is in part about gaining voice, with the album culminating in an almost ten-minute-long monologue by Anderson.

Redemptive plots, then, continue to be important narrative frames of meaning in American lives and American cultural representations. Such plots are hinged upon the desire to see balance restored, sins atoned for, freedom gained. Redemptive plots are also about finding a voice to salvage something meaningful from the broken world order. Some authors will hope that this redeeming aspect will be replicated in their readers or audiences. Other texts will engage with redemptive plots in ways that draw the readers' attention to the dangers of believing that order can be restored painlessly—*The Great Gatsby* and, more recently, the planning document *Vision 2020* gesture toward the possibility of redemption while warning the reader not to be blinded by the promise of new beginnings or easy solutions. In the American context, redemptive scripts are also the arena for processes of exclusion and differentiation, and in a work such as Colson Whitehead's *The Intuitionist,* the promise of redemption is considered in light of its universalist pretenses and complicated by connecting it to America's history of racialized inequality. Moving into the present century, new challenges—such as catastrophic man-made climate change—will undoubtedly further complicate how redemptive scripts are drawn upon to deal with past traumas and future threats.

WORKS CITED

Agathocleous, Tanya. *Urban Realism and the Cosmopolitan Imagination in the Nineteenth Century: Visible City, Invisible World.* Cambridge UP, 2011.

Ameel, Lieven. *The Narrative Turn in Urban Planning: Plotting the Helsinki Waterfront.* Routledge, 2020.

———. "The Sixth Borough: Metaphorizations of the Water in New York City's Comprehensive Waterfront Plan *Vision 2020* and Foer's 'The Sixth Borough.'" *Critique: Studies in Contemporary Fiction,* vol. 60, no. 3, 2019, pp. 251–62.

———. "The 'Valley of Ashes' and the 'Fresh Green Breast': Metaphors from *The Great Gatsby* in Planning New York." *Planning Perspectives,* vol. 34, no. 5, 2019, pp. 903–10.

Bersani, Leo. *The Culture of Redemption.* Harvard UP, 1990.

Brooks, Joanna, and Tyler Mabry. "Religion in Early African American Literature." *A Companion to African American Literature,* edited by Gene Andrew Jarrett, Wiley Blackwell, 2013, p. 75–89.

Buchenau, Barbara, and Jens Martin Gurr. "'Scripts' in Urban Development: Procedural Knowledge, Self-Description and Persuasive Blueprint for the Future." *Charting Literary Urban Studies: Texts as Models of and for the City,* by Jens Martin Gurr, Routledge, 2021, pp. 141–63.

Ferraro, Thomas J. *Transgression and Redemption in American Fiction.* Oxford UP, 2020.

Fessenden, Tracy. *Culture and Redemption: Religion, the Secular, and American Literature.* Princeton UP, 2007.

Fisher, James T. *On the Irish Waterfront: The Crusader, the Movie, and the Soul of the Port of New York.* Cornell UP, 2009.

Fitzgerald, Scott F. *The Great Gatsby.* 1926. Penguin, 1950.

Gelfant, Blanche Housman. *The American City Novel.* U of Oklahoma P, 1954.

Giggie, John M. *After Redemption: Jim Crow and the Transformation of African American Religion in the Delta, 1875–1915.* Oxford UP, 2007.

Gindin, James. "Gods and Fathers in F. Scott Fitzgerald's Novels." *Sin and Redemption,* edited by Harold Bloom, Bloom's Literary Criticism, 2010, pp. 81–104.

Huehls, Mitchum. *After Critique: Twenty-First-Century Fiction in a Neoliberal Age.* Oxford UP, 2016.

Kafalenos, Emma. *Narrative Causalities.* The Ohio State UP, 2006.

Lukács, Georg. *The Theory of the Novel: A Historico-Philosophical Essay on the Forms of Great Epic Literature,* translated by Anna Bostock. MIT Press, 1971.

Materassi, Mario. "Shifting Urbanscape: Roth's 'Private' New York." *New Essays on Call It Sleep,* edited by Hana Wirth-Nesher, Cambridge UP, 1996, pp. 29–60.

McAdams, Dan P. *The Redemptive Self: Stories Americans Live By.* Revised and expanded ed. Oxford UP, 2013.

Michaels, Lloyd. "A Tree Grows in Brooklyn." *QRFV,* vol. 27, no. 5, 2010, pp. 406–7.

Middleton, J. Richard, and Brian J. Walsh. *Truth Is Stranger Than It Used to Be: Biblical Faith in a Postmodern Age.* InterVarsity Press, 1995.

Miliora, Maria T. *The Scorsese Psyche on Screen: Roots of Themes and Characters in the Films.* McFarland, 2004.

Moses, Wilson Jeremiah. *Black Messiahs and Uncle Toms: Social and Literary Manipulations of a Religious Myth.* Pennsylvania State UP, 1994.

New York City. *Reclaiming the City's Edge: New York City Comprehensive Waterfront Plan.* Department of City Planning, 1992.

———. *Vision 2020.* Department of City Planning, 2011.

Pelly, Jenn. "Laurie Anderson—Kronos Quartet—Landfall." *Pitchfork,* 27 Feb. 2018, https://pitchfork.com/reviews/albums/laurie-anderson-kronos-quartet-landfall/.

Pike, Burton. *The Image of the City in Modern Literature.* Princeton UP, 1981.

Phelan, James. *Experiencing Fiction: Judgments, Progressions, and the Rhetorical Theory of Narrative.* The Ohio State UP, 2007.

"redemption." *Oxford English Dictionary Online,* Oxford UP, December 2021, https://www.oed.com/view/Entry/160259?redirectedFrom=redemption#eid. Accessed 13 Jan. 2022.

Roth, Henry. *Call It Sleep.* 1934. Penguin, 1977.

Salmela, Markku, and Lieven Ameel. "New York Fiction." *The Palgrave Handbook of Literature and the City,* edited by Jeremy Tambling, Palgrave, 2016, pp. 317–32.

Smith, Betty. *A Tree Grows in Brooklyn.* 1943. Popular Library, 1962.

Taylor, Nigel. *Urban Planning Theory since 1945.* Sage, 1998.

Todorov, Tzvetan. *Grammaire du Décaméron.* Mouton, 1969.

Westwell, Guy. *Parallel Lines: Post-9/11 American Cinema.* Wallflower Press, 2014.

Wharton, Edith. "Autres Temps . . ." 1916. *Roman Fever and Other Stories,* Collier Books, 1993, pp. 235–72.

Whitehead, Colson. *The Intuitionist.* Anchor Books, 1999.

Wirth-Nesher, Hana. *Call It English: The Languages of Jewish American Literature.* Princeton UP, 2006.

WNYC. "Mayor: Valley of Ashes in 'Great Gatsby' Was Inspired by Willets Point." *WNYC News,* 15 June 2012, https://www.wnyc.org/story/216534-blog-mayor-valley-ashes-great-gatsby-was-inspired-willets-point/.

PART 3

URBAN HISTORIES OF IDEAS

CHAPTER 9

Patterned Pasts and Scripted Futures

*Cleveland's Waterfronts and Hopes
of Changing the Narrative*

JOHANNES MARIA KRICKL AND
MICHAEL WALA

In 2019 the Cleveland-based organization Share the River proclaimed that "a new narrative for Cleveland was blazed as 250 paddlers on kayaks, paddleboards, and canoes took part in a historic celebration on the Cuyahoga River, 50 years to the day since the 1969 fire ignited the environmental movement" ("2019 Blazing Paddles"). With its annual Blazing Paddles Paddlefest, Share the River has been trying to shape a more positive image of Cleveland as a waterfront city with an abundance of recreational and leisure activities on offer for visitors and locals alike. Hinting at what this new narrative is or could be, Share the River stylizes elements of Cleveland's past to propose a perceptible shift in what sociologist Martina Löw has described as the "intrinsic logic" of a city (40). In the past, the notoriety of the 1969 Cuyahoga River fire not only served as the punchline for corny jokes about Cleveland's postindustrial struggle, but also fed public perceptions about the Cuyahoga fire's supposed role in kickstarting US environmentalism in the 1970s. If there is a new narrative of Cleveland seeking to script a different, a better future as a waterfront city, then this case of a symbolic recourse to the burning river clearly contributes to it. Narrative—or with every oar stroke the embodiment of narrative—not only represents the possibilities of change but seems to be the very catalyst of change.

In addition to Share the River's promotion of the Cuyahoga River as a source of urban recreation, urban scholars Aritree Samanta and Wendy

Kellogg observe that the "intentional transformation of the narrative of loss to an asset-based narrative was key" in transforming the river and the city (206). Widening the scope of their study beyond the lower, industrial Cuyahoga Valley to the whole watershed, Samanta and Kellogg state that "based on the origin story and legacy of the river, the city, and the region, this narrative provided a novel and sustainable organizing policy and governance framework for restoration and revitalization efforts" (206). They argue that the strategic placement of new narratives, in a profound entanglement with the river's urban, environmental, and regional history can prompt the policy-making necessary for the river's ecological comeback and shape the image of a more livable city.

Narrative here emerges as a practical, hands-on *method* to identify, and at the same time solve, postindustrial challenges. In the case of Cleveland, complexities of urban depletion and environmental pollution that became apparent in the wake of deindustrialization are schematized into a reductionist logic of two oppositional narratives. Plainly put, a narrative of decline is followed by a narrative of renaissance, without which prospects for urban revival remain unarticulated and virtually inconceivable. These narrative strategies appear to be grounded in a desire to tame the consequences of deindustrialization, cushion the rages of neoliberal market radicalism, and make contingencies manageable by breaking them down into coherent narrative strands. Storytelling provides order, sequence, and final closure; narratives promise to fill an otherwise overwhelming or incomprehensible void with meaning. Yet, narrative strategies do have their blind spots and weaknesses. By conjuring a causality between narrative change and urban revival, the deliberate prescription of new narratives not seldomly overrides the ambiguities and intricacies that stem from an industrial past, which are undoubtedly representative of a city caught in the tribulations of postindustrial transformation.

More than dwelling on narratives' function as a strategic coping strategy, this chapter proposes an understanding of narrative as open to complexities and ambiguities. As official planning documents and feasibility studies often insist on a clean slate unencumbered by the city's industrial past, these are challenged by other proposals for Cleveland's revival using that very past as part of their legitimization. Any change of narrative ultimately rests on decisions and selections of what is being narrated and promoted as a city's new identity. We argue that urban revival narratives are inevitably historicizations, that these narrative identity constructions can hardly be radically cut loose from the weight of an industrial past. Using Jörn Rüsen's typology of historical narratives and his concept of "historical thinking," we claim that hands-on, local narratives employed by urban actors such as Share the River have a universal cognitive as well as a cultural function, which transcends modes of mere representation (*Evidence* 25–26). Setting Rüsen's philosophy of history in relation to Juri Lotman's theory of cultural semiotics allows us to show that historicizations always activate a moment of cultural semiosis, i.e., meaning-generating processes through and beyond the account of a narrative. In synthesis, we will delineate a conceptualization of patterned pasts and scripted futures, understanding the pattern-script-interrelation as a basic operation in how historical narratives shape cultural meaning. By way of bringing together theory and exemplary application, this chapter looks at two phases of Cleveland waterfront reconfigurations: the promotional phase leading to the construction of downtown's North Coast Harbor (1980–89) and Share the River's Blazing Paddles Paddlefest as a combination of citizen grassroots and entrepreneurial activism. We will analyze their respective historical recourses in order to illustrate our theoretical approach to the role of historical narrative in the discourse of urban planning.

USES OF THE PAST—CULTURAL ORIENTATION IN URBAN DEVELOPMENT

Although urban planning has a strong tradition in Cleveland, the city has lacked the tenacity required for implementing a grand vision for repurposing its lakefront and riverfront. Ambitions, of which there have been many, were always hampered by a sheer jumble of dissatisfactory "piecemeal development" (Keating, Krumholz, and Wieland 145). Steven Litt, longtime art and architecture critic of Cleveland's only surviving daily newspaper, the *Plain Dealer,* echoes this assessment. In a 2022 online article, he recaps Cleveland's history of waterfront planning as temporally situated in "decades when big visions languished or went bust." Other cities such as Baltimore, New York, or Pittsburgh had long before capitalized on their waterfronts as planning targets, especially when the waning impact of heavy industries on the cities left vast stretches of property vacant or dilapidating along their shorelines and riverbanks. Lake Erie and the Cuyahoga River, however, presented very little leverage in implementing the city's urban revival. For decades, they had been barred off by traffic infrastructure, polluted by heavy industry, occupied by warehousing, and thwarted by administrative inaction. Picking up on the public mood of the time, when calls for an integrated river- and lakefront swelled again, the *Plain Dealer* lamented in an article in March 1980: "There is not one bench on the lakefront from E. 9th Street to Gordon Park where a Clevelander can sit and watch the lake" (Miller 30-A). This stretch of sixty-three blocks on Cleveland's eastside offered virtually no public access to the lake. Clearly, Cleveland missed out on this planning trend for a while, a major setback to an asset-based urban revival of the postindustrial city.

Nonetheless, the 1980s proved a pivotal decade in Cleveland city planning, when missed chances and persistent neglect of the city's waterfront could no longer be tolerated. Firm in his belief that restoring Lake Erie's shoreline was indispensable for Cleveland's reputational turnaround, Mayor George V. Voinovich vowed in late 1985 that his waterfront plan would be "not another pie-in-the-sky effort that will fade in a few years" ("News Release, Lakefront" 1). Voinovich was inaugurated in January 1980 and immediately had his administration join forces with the New Cleveland Campaign, a marketing association launched by the *Plain Dealer* publisher and editor Thomas Vail two years earlier to counter the city's lingering bad reputation, upon which national media had unrelentingly fixated following the event of the 1969 Cuyahoga River fire (Souther, *Believing* 198). During Voinovich's ten years in office, the New Cleveland Campaign and city hall meticulously avoided any reference to the 1969 Cuyahoga fire and the city's legacy of water pollution. Rather, they framed the restoration of the shoreline and downtown's North Coast Harbor in light of a different history.

Voinovich regarded waterfront reconstruction as a steppingstone into Cleveland's future. Severing the nostalgic ties to the glories of Cleveland's industrial heyday, the mayor conceded that "we can't be the same city we were in the 50s and 60s. We can't plan backwards, attempting to duplicate the past" ("Participation '84" 20). Instead, the development of downtown's North Coast Harbor was supposed to guide Cleveland into the 1990s and 2000s, with Voinovich proposing a grand city planning vision he regarded as sorely missing since World War II. Voinovich never promoted the new lakefront as an antidote to Cleveland's ongoing deindustrialization and urban depletion but rather sought out different ways to embed redevelopments into a historical grand scheme of the city.

With the groundbreaking of downtown's North Coast Harbor in 1986, Voinovich cast a historical arc to Cleveland's Great Lakes Exposition from 1936 and 1937.[1] "At that time," Voinovich said in a presentation to the Waterfront Steering Committee, "the lakefront was a popular and exciting 'people place'"

---

1. Echoing the Chicago World's Fair three years earlier, the Great Lakes Exposition commemorated Cleveland's centennial as an incorporated city in the summers of 1936/37. The Expo sought to offer fair-style entertainment for Clevelanders and visitors and promote the city's and northeast Ohio's industrial portfolio in the midst of the Great Depression. Held on a landfill shoreline stretching from East Ninth Street to East Twenty-Fourth Street, it was also conceptualized to spur new lakefront and downtown rebuilding efforts.

("News Release, Remarks" 1). This he wished to see restored. Alluding to the symbolic power of jubilees (see also chapter 2 by Borosch and Buchenau in this volume), Voinovich continued that "1986 would mark the beginning of our waterfront development so that the city's gift to itself in 1996, on its 200th birthday, would be the completion of our waterfront development" ("News Release, Remarks" 3). Cleveland's new lakefront, at least according to the mayor, fell in sync with the city's origin, when Cleveland became the hub of the Connecticut Western Reserve. On another occasion, at a lobby luncheon of the Cleveland Mid-Day Club, Voinovich made this clear with a solemn reminder: "Let us never forget that our roots are set here at the water's edge, and that our city's founder, Moses Cleaveland, landed here because we had a strong river flowing into a large lake. Without those elements, Moses would have went somewhere else" ("News Release, Lakefront" 3). In the late eighteenth century, the surveying, indexing, and selling of land in the Northwest Territory was a measure to refurbish the United States treasury after a costly Revolutionary War. Cleveland's founding and settling was part of this US expansionist strategy when Moses Cleaveland, a large shareholder of the Connecticut Land Company, landed with his band of surveyors at the mouth of the Cuyahoga River on July 22, 1796. The decision to line up Cleveland's future with its preindustrial history suggests that in the 1980s the city's recent industrial past offered little identificatory currency on which to build an urban revival. The wounds inflicted by deindustrialization were still too fresh, the damage done by plant closures and industrial flight too dismal to draw any hope from this era. Cleveland's renaissance—embodied in a new waterfront and a downtown building boom—could not be built on an industrial legacy conflicted by processes of deindustrialization but trusted instead, partially and symbolically, on the city's founding myth.

In the context of city planning, the decision of whether the past is considered "an important resource for the future" or "a burden to be shed as much as possible" is often a political one (Berger and Wicke 16). If valued, the past carries meaning; if shunned, it remains unarticulated and meaningless. Mayor Voinovich's decision to circumvent Cleveland's recent past of industrialization and deindustrialization presents a case that confirms that "cities and regions enjoy a certain freedom to choose their historical legacies" (Berger and Wicke 10). In this sense, the New Cleveland Campaign painted a surprisingly self-confident picture of Cleveland, contrary to the predominantly negative press the city had been receiving, for years epitomized in the grave imagery of heavy water pollution, a dying Lake Erie, and a burning Cuyahoga River (Souther, "Best Things" 1105–10). Consequently, the narrative coupled with Cleveland's new lakefront was not one of ecological recovery and redemption—or only implicitly so—and did not dwell on the struggles of overcoming postindustrial urban decline but rather pointed to the dormant potential of Lake Erie's shoreline for development, which up to that point apparently no one managed to fully activate or even recognize. Like virgin land—recast in the hue of a bucolic frontier land in the Connecticut Western Reserve—the lakefront was to be discovered, appropriated, and cultivated yet again.

Voinovich's historical recourse to Cleveland's founding myth is a search for the city's old and new identity and an attempt to use it as a means of orientation. Historian Jörn Rüsen describes this search for orientation as a universally cognitive process of "historical thinking," where historical narrative is the means of accessing and producing cultural meaningfulness (*Evidence* 168–89). Much more than ensuring a referential claim of historical truth, "historical thinking" unfolds its cultural value only insofar as history becomes a valuable resource for orientation in the present and for the future. This can be a highly selective practice, as was the obvious case in Voinovich choosing Cleveland's preindustrial past over its industrial past in connection with the city's lakefront. Matters of historical truth—fact or fiction—are not irrelevant. But they do not necessarily inform, or define, the cultural value and the means of orientation we find in historical narrative.

To equip our analysis with some terminological accuracy, we draw on Jörn Rüsen's typology, which identifies four historical narratives. Although this typology works with ideal types, which limits its applicability, it nevertheless offers an analytical toolkit helpful for scaling the different purposes of historical narratives. Rüsen's typology differentiates whether the past reigns over the present and the future, or whether the present elaborates on a particular past to inform future development. The distinction thereby evoked is that of teleological versus constructivist dimensions and the respective historical narratives they spawn. "In a teleological view," Rüsen wrote, "the present is aligned with an established and set principle of time based on long-term and future-directed developments" (*Evidence* 72). Therefore, past, present, and future combined form a symmetry that becomes legible as temporal continuity.

The decision to choose Cleveland's founding myth as the inception for the lakefront's repurposing, thus, creates this sense of temporal and meaningful continuity. As a teleological narrative, it embeds present circumstances in a temporal scheme with an origin that predefines a later course of action. In this regard, Cleveland's identity construction as a waterfront city attains stability and legitimization, which it draws from the depths of the past. "The further we reach back into the past," says Rüsen with regard to teleological constructions of meaning, "the more certain the foundations of our temporal orientations in the here and now appear" (*Evidence* 74). This may explain the mayor's recourse to the city's very beginnings: With the onset of deindustrialization, Cleveland had experienced disruption rather than continuity; hence, the restoration of the lakefront could be promoted as nothing less than the continuation of Cleveland's oldest legacy, as an encompassing pursuit endorsing the city's entire history. According to Rüsen's typology, this particular case of teleological construction of meaning presents an *exemplary* type of historical narrative. It "opens up the horizon of experience in historical thinking and turns all its accumulated experience and evidence into a pillar of orientation in the present" (*Evidence* 159). "Experience" here is not to be understood in the strict sense of subjective, empirical firsthand relatability. In the case of Mayor Voinovich's anecdotal recourse to Cleveland's founding—which serves as the exemplary template of the past—this would be absurd. Rather, experience needs to be seen as the communicative, dialogic context where

> our view of history becomes open to everything that happened in the human past. Historical thinking approaches these events as a plethora of events or situations that, despite their spatial and temporal diversity, present concrete cases that demonstrate the *general rules of action with timeless validity*. (Rüsen, *Evidence* 159)

Voinovich's colloquial comment, that "Moses would have went somewhere else" if the Cuyahoga River and Lake Erie had not made settlement attractive, utilizes a rhetorical register that endows this exemplary historical narrative with immediacy and intimacy despite the obvious temporal gap of almost two hundred years. Casual and romanticized as Voinovich's anecdote may sound, it imparted Cleveland's North Coast Harbor plans with the impression of a historical obligation to continue a legacy of progress connected with the city's origin. The *traditional* historical narrative is one other type of teleological construction of meaning according to Rüsen. It differs from the exemplary narrative in that historical experientiality is exempt from processes of constructing meaning. Its primary purpose is to convey a sense of "continuity through the ages" by trusting in a "continuously reproduced agreement about the validity of universal origins" and "prompting us to accept the predefined world orders" (Rüsen, *Evidence* 159). Almost axiomatic, the traditional type of historical narrative offers universal validity instead of a full-fledged plot. It becomes a narrative only as the perceived connection of the past with the present establishes the sequence of events (Koschorke 43–45). The strength of the traditional narrative type lies in its inviolability and its invariability. Yet, this also marks its greatest weakness, namely that it only presents a rigid and overblown scheme of historical sense-making.

Cleveland's North Coast Harbor plans were undergirded by such teleological narratives, which surfaced in promotional texts and the public relations material rallying for citizen support. This is also the case with, for example, a promotional brochure from the Cleveland Waterfront Coalition, a nonprofit citizen organization for the advancement of a comprehensive lake- and riverfront plan and part of Mayor Voinovich's North Coast Development Corporation. Seeing the momentum of lakefront development grow in the mid-1980s, the Coalition boasted that "Cleveland's beginning to enjoy something that's been out there all along" (1). Reaching even further back in time, the Waterfront Coalition satisfied the need for orientation not in the preindustrial era of eighteenth-century westward expansionism of the early republic, or nineteenth-century industrialism, but in the depths of prehistory. "The lake, of course, has been here all along," the brochure reveals on the opening page. "What is new, though, is Cleveland's Inner Harbor" (Cleveland 2). Cleveland's North Coast Harbor here seems to converge with the long-cast trajectory of Lake Erie's ancient natural history.

The teleological reasoning behind this traditional narrative is neither very compelling nor is it quite refutable as non-sense since it is borne on a tautological truth. However, lining up postindustrial lakefront redevelopment with the precultural history of Lake Erie also obscures the conflicted and controversial histories of the Great Lakes cultural area as well as the tribulations of postindustrial life. Rüsen notices that "these histories are relatively lacking in evidence since they refer to information that is relevant for the human community and disregard all other possible ways of forming the human way of life" (*Evidence* 159). Remarkably, Native American history finds little to no voicing in the mnemonic discourse of legacy cities in the Great Lakes region, even when these discourses explicitly reference the preindustrial past. Historical tributes to Native American culture and the recognition of displacement practices of US expansionist imperialism are omitted as sources for identification. In the same fashion, the scenario drawn up by the Waterfront Coalition's historical narrative belies the reasons why Cleveland's lakefront was hitherto unenjoyable and neglects a recent past that continued to trouble Clevelanders and their reality of an inaccessible lake. In this regard, a remark found in a 1980 *Plain Dealer* article is dead-on with its assessment that "the public has been denied downtown access to Lake Erie for so long that the people have forgotten that they have a right to be there" (Miller 30-A). We can see that public perception paints a diametrically different picture from what the Waterfront Coalition's brochure construes as the natural course of history and its apparent culmination in the development of a new downtown with an integrated lakefront: Access to Lake Erie was restricted and contested, something that strenuously had to be regained and, in a way, learned again.

Obviously, the history of Cleveland, the Cuyahoga River, and Lake Erie is much more complex than city hall and the planning corporations tried to contrive it in their rather boosterish texts to advocate a downtown revival. In the face of deindustrialization, the symbolism attached to Lake Erie and the Cuyahoga River was incompatible with the city's ambitious renaissance endeavors. The symbolic dimensions not only indexed Cleveland's unsettling history of environmental pollution, but the burning Cuyahoga River conflated a host of ills into one apocalyptic image. The burning river became a shorthand for everything that troubled a city hit hard by deindustrialization: racial unrest in the late 1960s, few desegregated schools, poverty, inner-city decay and population drain, suburbanization, vacancy, vast demolition for the purpose of urban renewal, property-tax deficits, and finally Cleveland's municipal default in 1978 (Souther, "Best Things" 1092). Therefore, the Voinovich administration rolled out its comeback bid by countering and avoiding this symbolism and by casting Cleveland's waterfront redevelopment in a light emphasizing the ancient pristine beauty of the city's surrounding natural environment. While showing some signs of success, this attempt at a symbolic inversion of Lake Erie and Cleveland's waterfronts had no long-lasting effect. "Over the years, Cleveland's economic deterioration continued, and the story of a burning river somehow seemed explanatory. It echoed for decades, with no competition from a similarly flammable river running through a similarly deindustrialized landscape" (Stradling and Stradling 531). The broadly spread optimism that grew with Voinovich's mayoralty—the "Comeback City" pride and the confidence boosts of three All-America City Awards—dwindled and turned into disenchantment.[2] Urban historian J. Mark Souther notes that Cleveland's "1980s comeback ran out of steam in the 1990s," and the image of the burning Cuyahoga—despite efforts to muffle this reputational harm—resurged after the Voinovich years with a new quality ("Best Things" 1092).

THE SEMIOSIS OF PATTERN-SCRIPT-INTERRELATIONS

The 1969 Cuyahoga River fire, David and Richard Stradling write, "has attracted considerable referencing but little research" (519). In their work,

---

    2. In the late 1970s and throughout the 1980s, national media garnished Cleveland with the moniker "Comeback City," an epithet usually associated with Pittsburgh or Baltimore (Souther, *Believing* 1–5, 197–204). The success of private-public partnerships in revitalizing downtown and distressed neighborhoods as well as a catalogue of political and financial reforms were reasons for Mayor Voinovich to enter Cleveland in the competition for the National Civic League's All-America City Award, which it won it in 1982, '84, and '86 (Souther, "Best Things" 1109).

they trace the evolution of the interpretation that this historical event has experienced over the decades. When Cleveland was bustling and brimming with industrial brawn, a burning river was primarily a threat to production and traffic infrastructure with high financial liabilities. The reality of deindustrialization, however, shifted the ecological damage done to the river to the forefront and was, henceforth, regarded as most concerning. "In 1969 Clevelanders were not ready to think of a burning river as an apocalyptic symbol of a rapidly developing ecological crisis," comment David and Richard Stradling, who continue, "this symbolism would be learned over time" (521). With deindustrialization as a foil and hopes for an urban renaissance setting a new pace, historical interpretations of the burning Cuyahoga River took on ever new meanings: Over time the '69 fire evolved from a threat to heavy industries to an environmental catastrophe, then to the epitome of postindustrial failure, and later to a glaring emblem of the need for ecological recovery, as well as the strategic key asset of a sustainable waterfront city. In these different shapes, the multitude of the Cuyahoga's symbolic applications were always anchored in the river's ecological nadir, explicitly or implicitly—*ex negativo*—evoking the image of the burning river but meaning much more than this signifier alone.

When the Cuyahoga River burned for approximately twenty minutes on June 22, 1969, it could actually be interpreted as "a rather unexciting event," as David and Richard Stradling relate (518). There had been bigger and more destructive fires on the Cuyahoga before, but the message formulated in the aftermath of the '69 fire was clear and has been repeated often: "In the press, and in popular conception, it wasn't much more complicated than that; the Cuyahoga fire ignited a national movement to improve the nation's waterways" (Stradling and Stradling 519). Cast in this light, the Cuyahoga became an issue of national interest and at the same time an indicator of how bad off Cleveland presumably must have been. The question of whether Cleveland was on a path to recovery or still caught in a downward spiral of urban decline, or saw itself somewhere in between, was negotiated on many occasions in a variety of narrative recourses to the burning Cuyahoga. While city officials steered clear of what they perceived as detrimental imagery—as did the Voinovich administration—public and popular references were not contained by such strategic obligations.

The multitude of historicizing stories told about the last Cuyahoga fire do not comply with one normative interpretation. Historical narratives springing from Cleveland's burning river are conceived under a constructivist mode of historical thinking. Jörn Rüsen's typology provides further narrative types that explicate this mode of historical sense-making. Integrated in *genetic* narratives, claims Rüsen, "events of the past in their temporal movement no longer appear within the confines of fixed practical principles of human ways of life. Rather they establish a dynamic process of transformation that takes the edge off change in the human world and shakes off the eternal value of accepted norms" (*Evidence* 160). During the second half of the twentieth century, cities such as Cleveland were confronted with incisive shifts; long-held reassurances found in industrial growth and prosperity faltered with a feeling of uncertainty nourished by the onset of economic and urban crises. The questioning of old truths and dynamics of change became the modus operandi of identity constructions in the era of deindustrialization. Therefore, we see the constellation of historical experience and expectations about the future diverge in an asymmetrical fashion. In this sense, Rüsen's antinormative type of historical narrative is particularly interesting for a historiographic analysis of Cleveland's deindustrialization as it displays the greatest narrative freedoms in the formulation of cultural meaning. The *critical* narrative "destroys and deconstructs culturally predetermined [. . .] interpretive patterns. It focuses on events that challenge established historical orientations" (*Evidence* 162). The event of Cleveland's burning river engendered the critical narratives that drove the paradigmatic shift in cultural orientation. "A critical narrative of history," Rüsen writes, "is about deviating points of view, differentiation, rebuttals and the transformative power of 'no'" (*Evidence* 162). The disruptions and uncertainties of a liminal state define Cleveland's postindustrial identity gap at a time when many critical narratives of the burning Cuyahoga River proliferate. Over time these narratives sediment in the form of a cultural memory from where they are occasionally revived.

"Memory and history are not the same thing. But we cannot think of history without memory," postulates Rüsen (*Evidence* 175). Memory is a medium through which historical experience inevitably becomes a means of cultural orientation through narration. Memory, Rüsen continues, "charges historical consciousness with the vitality of a past made present" (*Evidence* 176). Hence, the historical inventory (*res gestae*) of the river fire of 1969 is liberated from its chronological isolation. As an epistemological incentive, it produces an enhanced state of historical consciousness, which is made present in an array of narrative manifestations (*narratio rerum gestarum*). As such, the material and formal dimensions of historical thinking merge and thus elicit the cultural meaning of the '69 fire, as it is set in relation to the present through the narrative formulations and the interpretations they allow. Jörn Rüsen defines this as the *functional* dimension of historical thinking, where the cultural significance of history becomes apparent through the transcendence of the mere mimetic principles of narrative; these are the constraints of referential content and formal expression (*Geschichte denken* 103–4; 115). In its functional dimension, historical narrative is endowed with what narratologist Stephan Jaeger described as a "poietic ability," exacting the creative impulses life asks of us when forming meaningful accounts of the past (30). Narrative constructions in this sense widen the horizon beyond mimetic representations and allow for creativity and new, that is, higher orders of experience. Jaeger indicates that "one of the tasks of historiographic narrative is to construct or simulate historical experience" (36). In doing so, historical experience is detached from its time-bound origins, letting first-order experiences diffuse into the plethora of cultural story-constructs with which the "recipient is led to experience history as if it happened presently, while being aware that this is a secondary experience of a construct" (Jaeger 31). Memory, in this respect, is the cognitive exchange market of historical narratives and their trade-ins in the form of meaningful modifications, add-ons, or reductions.

Concordant with the idea of an exchange market, cultural theorist Aleida Assmann perceives memory as a medium where "mental images become icons, and narratives become myths, whose most important property is their persuasive power and affective impact. Such myths largely detach historical experience from the concrete conditions of its origin and recast them as time-removed stories" (2, our translation).[3] The significance of the lessening impact of industrial wastewater on the Cuyahoga River and Lake Erie's ecological wellbeing congealed in the affective imagery of waterborne flames winding through the Flats. David and Richard Stradling speak, with good reason, of the 1969 Cuyahoga River fire as a myth, as public perception bends the historical account to align with expectations people foster in hopes for improved water quality and a more sustainable life in the city of Cleveland. The more impressive and graphic the imagery, it seems, the more effective, recognizable, and reassuring becomes the power of its symbolism.

In outlining the possibilities of a postindustrial, sustainable, and recreational life in Cleveland, the organization Share the River amply draws on the potent symbolism of the burning Cuyahoga. Since 2018, stand-up paddlers, kayakers, canoeists, and rowers gather annually on the river on June 22 (later moved to Cleveland's founding date, July 22). They race away in the name of environmental protection, sustainability, and improved public access to the city's recreational bodies of water. As Share the River's founder Jim Ridge indicates, the name of the event, Blazing Paddles Paddlefest, leans on Mel Brooks's

---

3. The German source reads: "Im kollektiven Gedächtnis werden mentale Bilder zu Ikonen und Erzählungen zu Mythen, deren wichtigste Eigenschaft ihre Überzeugungskraft und affektive Wirkmacht ist. Solche Mythen lösen die historische Erfahrung von den konkreten Bedingungen ihres Entstehens weitgehend ab und formen sie zu zeitenthobenen Geschichten um" (2).

FIGURE 9.1. Blazing Paddles Paddlefest logo, as sported on T-shirts, social media, and the event's website. Used with kind permission of Jim Ridge.

1974 comedic Western, *Blazing Saddles* (Ridge). This pop cultural reference echoes the ironic attitude many Clevelanders have adopted in embracing their hometown's ambiguous history of industrial decline. In proclaiming the last fire on the Cuyahoga as the moment spurring US environmentalism, the event sports a logo (see fig. 9.1) that depicts silhouettes of stand-up paddlers and kayakers racing in front of a Cleveland skyline engulfed in licking flames.

While the design's rendering of flames reverberates with an interpretative pattern of Cleveland's pollutive past, the pleasure rowers in the foreground suggest the recreational possibilities, which become intelligible in narrative spin-offs. Mimetic and referential accounts of the past are enriched by an instance of cultural semiosis. Symbols are of great importance in mnemonic constellations like these. To use the terminology of cultural theorist Juri Lotman, "the symbol serves as a condensed programme for the creative process. The subsequent development of a plot is merely the unfolding of a symbol's hidden possibilities. A symbol is a profound coding mechanism, a special kind of 'textual gene'" (101). Just as the Blazing Paddles logo references specific narratives of ecological catastrophe or industrial decline connected with the city of Cleveland, the symbolic implementation of the burning river also offers semiotic revolutions in the form of alternative imaginaries. Summarizing

Lotman's idea of a symbol as a "textual gene," Batiashvili, Wertsch, and Inauri explicate that

> the symbol embodies the potential for a new semiosis and in this way perform[s] as a hidden script for the unfolding of meaning. The idea of a plot-gene concerns the ability of a symbol to organize consciousness and thus to impose order or fit the textual content in which it is used in some kind of a structured schema. At the same time, it suggests that a symbolic expression has the potential not just to hint at, or allude to[,] the voluminous content hidden behind its expression, but to generate plot lines that are expressive of the prefixed meanings, while at the same time having variability in the ways in which they reconfigure these prefixed meanings. (386–87)

Lotman's "textual gene" builds the focal point of semiosis, where patterned perceptions of the past render the creative agency of scripting alternatives, resumptions, amplifications, or denials. It is an anthropological desire to come to terms with the world by way of trusting in reproducible experiences and structures of the familiar.[4] Yet, in the sense of Rüsen's idea of historical thinking and the functional dimension of historical meaning constructions, there can hardly be a pattern without a script.[5] As cultural beings, we need "the temporal relationship that systematically connects the interpretation of the past to an understanding of the present and the expectations of the future" (*Evidence* 50). True to Rüsen's philosophy of history (*Historik*) and to Lotman's theory of cultural semiotics, we understand that patterned pasts transition into scripted futures, with the present defining the creative agency necessary to do so; only then does this interplay of patterns and scripts provide the cultural orientation we seek in the formulation of historical narratives.

Defining a methodological nexus of cultural and literary studies with postindustrial urban studies, Barbara Buchenau and Jens Martin Gurr propose that scripts "activate procedural knowledge, they serve as self-description, and they provide blueprints for the future:" Past events evoke patterned renditions

---

4. Literary scholar Daniel Fulda argues that "what is perceived is perceived because the cognitive apparatus checks it against 'internally stored' schemata" (n. pag.). Analogously, Jörn Rüsen points out Friedrich Schiller's idea of *Universalgeschichte* and hints at an aphorism by Gustav Droysen, which is helpful here: "Geschichte über den Geschichten," translated as "History over the (hi-)stories" (*Geschichte denken* 46). Our understanding, however, is that Fulda's notion of schema falls short of including the creative agency and semiotic impulse transported with—and inherent in—our conceptualization of the interrelation of patterns and scripts.

5. From the standpoint of cognitive narratology, Daniel Fulda notes that "it becomes possible to describe history narratologically as both a pattern for reception and a product of reception" (n. pag.).

and perceptions of their meaningfulness ("narrative, medial [and] figural acts of framing"); thus, they provide a practical sense of cultural orientation and present a means of identification ("self-description") and align historical experience with expectations that design a serviceable future path ("blueprints for the future") (Buchenau and Gurr 142).

Put to the test, the 2019 Blazing Paddles event description offers a germane example to demonstrate how cognitive pattern-script-interrelations render a historical event, in its functional dimension, to serve as a means of cultural orientation for the present and the future:

> Blazing Paddles is a celebration of how the Cuyahoga River has risen like a phoenix since the 1969 fire ignited the environmental movement. [. . .] At one time in American history, hundreds of rivers were used as sewers for the byproducts of industrial processes. Yet the Cuyahoga River stands alone as the symbol for the ravages of a bygone era. More rigorous environmental regulations and engaged citizen stewardship have helped fuel the recovery of tributaries that now support not only a widening array of fish and wildlife species, but they also serve as a sustainable economic driver for their regions: tourism and recreation. When you participate in Blazing Paddles and recreate on the Cuyahoga River, you'll be making a national statement about the value of protecting our nation's natural resources. ("Blazing Paddles")

The historical exposition of industrial America as a "bygone era," when concerns about environmental protection took a back seat to economic growth and industrial mass production, provides the groundwork for the metaphor of the rising phoenix to take effect. In itself, the metaphor already stimulates a plot, driven by the tension of utter destruction and subsequent, if not transcendent restoration. Installed as a "symbol" then, the Cuyahoga transports a mix of patterns that not only describe a past state of affairs but also signal a relief of tension, as the river now stands in for environmental consciousness and as a token of further responsibilities to be lived up to. Virtually redeemed of collective, past irresponsibilities, today's pleasure seekers—be it paddlers, anglers, tourists—are the living manifestation of a river that has come a long way. As they paddle and "recreate," they perform and create a script that not only strengthens a national memento but also serves as "a sustainable economic driver" and a brand for a city that styles itself as a postindustrial waterfront city. After all, it seems that paddlers and kayakers are not just paddling for paddling's sake, but for the environment, for biodiversity, for boosting the local economy, for public access to bodies of water, for a more just, more creative, more inclusive, more sustainable, and more livable city of Cleveland.

CONCLUSION

Has Blazing Paddles really blazed a new narrative for Cleveland? And could Mayor Voinovich's retelling of the city's founding myth change perceptions, so that people actually believe that Cleveland was finally making reasonable use of its two waterfronts? The numbers, as the *Plain Dealer* recaps, speak a sobering language in that regard: In 2022 "78% of the Lake Erie shoreline within [Cuyahoga County], or 23.4 miles, are rendered inaccessible by private property, rail lines, highways, and Burke Lakefront Airport" (Litt). But then again, what story do bare numbers really tell? In search of orientation and grounded legitimization for their visions of urban futures, we see planners, entrepreneurs, and citizen stakeholders appropriate history and narrative as political and strategic instruments. However, Cleveland's urban revitalization efforts teach us that attempts to domesticate history for the purpose of technocratic and measurable planning implementations can be somewhat shortsighted undertakings. Changes to the narrative cannot be executed with surgical precision and processed with definite predictability of its effects. When history attains meaning through a narrative, the two are subject to the centripetal forces of cultural semiosis. Targeted interventions will more likely be interferences; new means of identification cannot be "planned" reliably. Nevertheless, historical narratives unfold cultural meanings in messy settings: They are stimulated by competing narratives, ambiguities, and contradictions, as much as by long-lasting reinforcing narrative traces in the cultural whole. When history is tapped as a source of orientation, its meaning is always negotiated in a moment of semiosis, where patterns of the past overlap with scripts for the future. The joint application of history and narrative as a collaborative strategic instrument in the discourse of urban planning and development deserves a solid grounding in both, the philosophy of history and the theory of cultural semiotics.

WORKS CITED

"The 2019 Blazing Paddles Paddlefest Blazes a New Cuyahoga River Narrative." *Share the River*, 3 July 2019, https://sharetheriver.com/blog/2019/6/27/the-2nd-annual-blazing-paddles-paddlefest-burns-a-new-cuyahoga-river-narrative.

Assmann, Aleida. "Soziales und kollektives Gedächtnis." *British and American Studies Universität Konstanz,* https://cms.uni-konstanz.de/fileadmin/archive/litwiss-personen/fileadmin/litwiss/ang-ame/AA%20Download%20Aufsatz%20SozKultGed%C3%A4chtnis.pdf. Accessed 16 Apr. 2021.

Batiashvili, Nutsa, James V. Wertsch, and Tinatin Inauri. "Lotman and Memory Studies." *The Companion to Juri Lotman: A Semiotic Theory of Culture,* edited by Marek Tamm and Peeter Torop, Bloomsbury Academic, 2022, pp. 379–89.

Berger, Stefan, and Christian Wicke. "Deindustrialization, Heritage, and Representations of Identity." *The Public Historian,* vol. 39, no. 4, 2017, pp. 10–20.

"Blazing Paddles Paddleboard, Kayak, & Canoe Paddlefest." *Share the River,* http://sharetheriver.com/blazing-paddles. Accessed 6 June 2019.

Buchenau, Barbara, and Jens Martin Gurr. "'Scripts' in Urban Development: Procedural Knowledge, Self-Description, and Persuasive Blueprint for the Future." *Charting Literary Urban Studies: Texts as Models of and for the City,* by Jens Martin Gurr, Routledge, 2021, pp. 141–63.

Cleveland Waterfront Coalition. "Cleveland's Beginning to Enjoy Something That's Been Out There All Along, Brochure." 1985/1986, Container 126, Folder 1, MS 5048 Records of the Mayor of the City of Cleveland, George V. Voinovich. Western Reserve Historical Society, Cleveland, OH, transcript, pp. 1–4.

Fulda, Daniel. "Historiographic Narration." *The Living Handbook of Narratology,* 25 Mar. 2014, https://www-archiv.fdm.uni-hamburg.de/lhn/node/123.html.

Jaeger, Stephan. "Poietic Worlds and Experientiality in Historiographic Narrative." *SPIEL,* vol. 30, no. 1, 2011, pp. 29–50.

Keating, Dennis, Norman Krumholz, and Ann Marie Wieland. "Cleveland's Lakefront: Its Development and Planning." *Journal of Planning History,* vol. 4, no. 2, 2005, pp. 129–54.

Koschorke, Albrecht. *Fact and Fiction: Elements of a General Theory of Narrative.* 2012. Translated by Joel Golb, De Gruyter, 2018.

Litt, Steven. "5 New Lakefront Projects Led by Cuyahoga County, Cleveland Metroparks Gain Support, Accelerating Drive to Open Up Shoreline." *Cleveland.com,* 28 Feb. 2022, https://www.cleveland.com/news/2022/02/5-new-lakefront-projects-led-by-cuyahoga-county-cleveland-metroparks-gain-support-accelerating-drive-to-open-up-shoreline.html.

Lotman, Yuri M. *Universe of the Mind: A Semiotic Theory of Culture.* Translated by Ann Shukman, Indiana UP, 1990.

Löw, Martina. "Eigenlogische Strukturen—Differenzen zwischen Städten als konzeptuelle Herausforderung." *Die Eigenlogik der Städte: Neue Wege für die Stadtforschung,* edited by Helmuth Berking and Martina Löw, Campus, 2008, pp. 33–54.

Miller, William F. "Development for Public Slow Here, Planner Says." *Plain Dealer,* 2 Mar. 1980, p. 30-A.

Ridge, Jim. "Blazing Paddles and Share the River." Transatlantic Rust Belts—Scripting Urban Futures, 10 Sep. 2021, online symposium, Detroit, MI. Presentation.

Rüsen, Jörn. *Evidence and Meaning: A Theory of Historical Studies.* Translated by Diane Kerns and Katie Digan, Berghahn, 2017.

———. *Geschichte denken: Erläuterungen zur Historik.* Springer, 2020.

Samanta, Aritree, and Wendy Kellogg. "Back to the Beginning: The Resurgence of the Cuyahoga River and Cleveland." *Legacy Cities: Continuity and Change Amid Decline and Revival,* edited by J. Rosie Tighe and Stephanie Ryberg-Webster, U of Pittsburgh P, 2019, pp. 205–20.

Souther, J. Mark. *Believing in Cleveland: Managing Decline in "The Best Location in the Nation."* Temple UP, 2017.

———. "'The Best Things in Life Are Here' in 'The Mistake on the Lake': Narratives of Decline and Renewal in Cleveland." *Journal of Urban History,* vol. 41, no. 6, 2015, pp. 1091–17.

Stradling, David, and Richard Stradling. "Perceptions of the Burning River: Deindustrialization and Cleveland's Cuyahoga River." *Environmental History,* vol. 13, no. 3, 2008, pp. 515–35.

Voinovich, George V. "News Release, Lakefront Development Funds, Remarks to the Mid-Day Club." 21 Oct. 1985. Container 126, Folder 1, MS 5048 Records of the Mayor of the City of

Cleveland, George V. Voinovich. Western Reserve Historical Society, Cleveland, OH, transcript, pp. 1–3.

———. "News Release, Remarks at the Waterfront Steering Committee." 12 Mar. 1985. Container 126, Folder 1, MS 5048 Records of the Mayor of the City of Cleveland, George V. Voinovich. Western Reserve Historical Society, Cleveland, OH, transcript, pp. 1–5.

———. "Participation '84." 16 Nov. 1984. Container 4, Folder 11, MS 5048 Records of the Mayor of the City of Cleveland, George V. Voinovich. Western Reserve Historical Society, Cleveland, OH, transcript, pp. 1–21.

CHAPTER 10

The Creative Democracy

A Critique of Concepts of Creativity in Contemporary Urban Discourse

HANNA RODEWALD AND
WALTER GRÜNZWEIG

> As long as art is the beauty parlor of civilization, neither art nor civilization is secure.
>
> —John Dewey, *Art as Experience*

THE ENIGMA OF THE CREATIVE CITY

In November 2019, Dortmund-based artist Janna Banning presented a large-scale multimedia art project titled *Wir arbeiten für Gentrifizierung ehrenamtlich* (We are volunteering for gentrification). At ten different locations along the Rheinische Strasse, a part of the historically important European trade route of the medieval Hellweg that runs westbound of Dortmund's city center, the artist installed various stations that addressed emerging processes of creative development and gentrification in a rapidly changing neighborhood. For one month, Banning's installations raised questions about the role of art in urban development and of artists as supposed initiators of gentrification.

With her oftentimes sharply observant and pointedly sarcastic installations such as a fake pop-up burger shop, a banner on a fence reminiscent of a realtor advertisement, and commentaries on vacant shop windows, Banning aims to disrupt the perception of interested visitors as well as the neighborhood's residents. Keen to showcase and criticize processes of gentrification, she wants to irritate her spectators and initiate conversations because she understands art primarily as a form of conversation. In dialogue with the recipients, she wants to find answers to pressing issues of urban transformation. On the project's website, she asks: "Is the pattern of enhancing a neighborhood with the help of creatives and the accompanying displacement of its original residents a mandatory process? Or are there alternative approaches by intervening early and interrupting or disrupting this process or cycle?" (Banning, "Art"; our translation).[1]

What Banning describes as a distinctive "pattern" of creative urban enhancement, which seems almost mandatory in its realization, and which apparently imposes itself onto the neighborhood like a vicious "cycle" that seems inescapable, represents the global phenomenon of an urban creative imperative also known under the less favorable term of gentrification. Whereas mechanisms of gentrification have been proven to generate processes of social exclusion and displacement due to rising rents and property speculation, creative urban development seems to positively mystify the same underlying processes. Wherever urban planners use the word "creative" in their strategies to reinvigorate the postindustrial city, the term remains curiously opaque. They usually do not define it, as if its meaning must be obvious to everybody to whom it is presented. Oftentimes readers of such planning documents need to "unearth" (Throgmorton 129) the larger story behind this *creative city script,* as Jamie Peck (2007) and Dzudzek and Lindner (2013) have labeled it, from other sources. If at all, city officials address it indirectly, usually instrumentally, explaining what creativity should accomplish.

Today's creativity mantra, as it is widely applied in cities around the world, stems mostly from a self-proclaimed guru of this creative urbanism, the American economist Richard Florida. From the mid-1990s onward the idea of the creative city evolved into a replicable blueprint for cities needing to adapt to a changing economic structure.[2] In particular, Richard Florida's books *The Rise of the Creative Class: And How It's Transforming Work, Leisure, Community, and Everyday Life* (2002), *Cities and the Creative Class* (2005), and *The Rise of the Creative Class, Revisited* (2012) have had a decisive impact not only on the discourse of a "creative" makeover of the city but also on actual city development itself. It is hard to estimate the many billions of various currencies that have been expended to turn Florida's notions into a gentrified reality.

The underlying story that is told around such development follows a rather simplistic narrative. It is based on the claim that the new economy of the twenty-first century is no longer centered around mass production or the

---

1. "Muss das Muster, mit der Aufwertung eines Viertels durch Kreative und die oft damit einhergehende Verdrängung der ursprünglichen Bewohner, immer gleich sein? Oder kann man es individuell gestalten, indem man frühzeitig eingreift und den Prozess oder Zyklus unterbricht oder stört?"

2. Focusing mainly on the United Kingdom and Europe at large, it was actually Charles Landry who was the first to promote creative city development with his publications on *The Creative City* (cowritten with Franco Bianchini, 1995) and *The Creative City: A Toolkit for Urban Innovators* (2000).

service sector but rather around the creative industries and the overall creative capacity of cities' inhabitants, which bring forth new technology and innovation-rich growth.[3] Cities need to attract the members of this "creative class" and jobs will follow. In order to come out on top of the creative city ranking and to ensure a flourishing economic prosperity, urban centers must attract as much human capital as possible. This means that cities compete for the supposedly highly flexible and finicky members of the creative class, who move wherever the urban atmosphere caters best to their lifestyle choices. Tailoring entire neighborhoods around the three Ts (technology, talent, and tolerance, as proposed by Florida), cities now try to provide all kinds of cultural amenities (e.g., art galleries, cafés, festivals, museums, music scene, cycling, etc.) to increase the productivity of their creative dwellers.

This, however, is the fallacy in this future-oriented tale of creative transformation. Rather than viewing creativity as an essential dimension of being human, its economic functionality and its exclusivity are foregrounded. Its narrative groundwork follows a logic of profit-oriented economic growth and profitability. Jamie Peck, one of Florida's harshest critics, warns against such an instrumentalization of creativity and its innovative force when he writes:

> rather than "civilizing" urban economic development by "bringing in culture," creativity strategies do the opposite: they commodify the arts and cultural resources, even social tolerance itself, suturing them as putative economic assets to evolving regimes of urban competition. ("Struggling" 763)

So just like Janna Banning, who asks for alternative approaches to creative city development, we want to propose a different understanding of the creative city script. In their analysis of creative rationalities at work in Frankfurt am Main, Germany, Iris Dzudzek and Peter Lindner define the creative-economy script as "the result of an ongoing collective (re-)writing and performing endeavour, to which not only 'partners in mind' contribute but also sometimes fierce opponents" (392f.).

Their definition of a script falls in line with our definition of a cultural narrative, which grounds itself in the theoretical thinking of Roger Betsworth. It entails a model of complex narrative investigation of stories that define the core of a culture's character. This definition equally implies the option to tell a story differently, indeed, even to disagree. Cultural texts and performances

---

3. The sociologist Andreas Reckwitz (2017) identifies this societal regime of innovation and newness as a distinct movement of the late modern age. His term *creativity dispositif* describes an aestheticization of society that is now mostly interested in the production and reception of aesthetically new experiences.

therefore may work both ways, affirmatively or in critical subversion to its cultural narrative (see Cortiel and Grünzweig 31). This text therefore reframes the creative city script and historically grounds it in a tradition of American cultural criticism by Ralph Waldo Emerson and John Dewey that Richard Florida conveniently disregards. The following text starts out with an analysis of the terminological origins of the "creative class," which was already coined by Emerson long before Richard Florida. It continues with a discussion on the conceptual relation between art and creativity by both cultural critics and ends on a political note while discussing the term of creative democracy introduced by Dewey. Overall, this ultimately leads to a different understanding of creativity in the city that is less standardized and more focused on the individual human creative ability detached from any value other than the creative process itself.

THE ORIGIN OF THE CREATIVE CLASS

In 2016, some fifteen years after *The Creative Class*'s initial publication, we presented a critique of Florida's model based on his notion of class. In an article entitled "Parasitic Simulacrum: Ralph Waldo Emerson, Richard Florida and the Urban 'Creative Class,'" we attempted to demonstrate that Florida's project was less concerned with creativity than with a "creative" simulacrum for the hyper-commercialization of the postindustrial city—or rather, some postindustrial cities—willing to undergo a transformation at the expense of its less privileged inhabitants and, of course, at the expense of other, less privileged cities (Grünzweig).

The starting point of this critique, which was part of a volume documenting the work of the predecessor project to *City Scripts,* funded by the German Mercator Foundation, was the realization that the term "creative class" was actually not coined by Florida. Rather, it was first introduced, like so many other innovative conceptions, by Ralph Waldo Emerson, the foremost cultural critic of the United States in the nineteenth century. In his later text "Power," which became a part of a collection of lectures and essays in *The Conduct of Life* (1860), Emerson wrote the following remarkable sentence: "In every company, there is not only the active and passive sex, but, in both men and women, a deeper and more important *sex of the mind,* namely the inventive or creative class of both men and women, and the uninventive or accepting class" (57f.). The surprising freshness of this sentence cannot be overestimated. Breaking through the binary gender stereotype traditionally associated with creativity, Emerson is, in fact, creating a third category: Beyond the fundamental, albeit since heavily criticized, differentiation between biological sex and social gender, he is defining a cultural or creative "sex of the mind," which naturally transcends the binary quality of the other two. Its polarity lies elsewhere, namely between creative and uncreative.

Whereas Florida focuses on the emergence of a new urban environment to attract his "creative class," Emerson deals with the creatives themselves and their creativeness. While the latter does not ignore the cultural value of an urban environment, he makes fun of an artificially designed "creative" bubble—the personalities supposedly making up an urban creative core amount to little: "New York is a sucked orange" (Emerson, *Conduct* 117).

In our previous study, the lack of a definition of creativity was our strongest criticism of Florida's narrative (Grünzweig 219). In his 2002 book, the chapter that comes closest to addressing the topic is "The Creative Ethos," a section missing in the second edition, the only concrete cue he provides is that "creativity involves the ability to synthesize" (*Rise* 31).

> Einstein captured it nicely when he called his own work "combinatory play." It is a matter of sifting through data, perceptions and materials to come up with combinations that are *new and useful*. A creative synthesis is useful in such varied ways as producing a practical device, or a theory or insight that can be applied to solve a problem, or a work of art that can be appreciated. (Florida, *Rise* 31)

Florida's mention of "creative synthesis" recalls German polymath Wilhelm Maximilian Wundt (1832–1920), often referred to as the father of modern psychology. Indeed, Wundt theorizes how the interaction of various perceptions, ideas, and emotions can lead to a creative impulse. Immediately, however, we see how Florida explains this creative impulse as a mechanical and functional *combination,* primarily "useful" in "producing a practical device" (*Rise* 31). His reference to a creative work of art that can be "appreciated" similarly shows a limited level of aesthetic reflection.

The final chapter of the 2012 edition of his book then calls for a "Creative Compact," which will be "dedicated to the *creatification* of everyone" (Florida, *Revisited* 385). This neologism has not yet made it into Merriam-Webster, but its very morphemic construction suggests it is not about agency. What at first deceptively sounds like the emergence of a universally creative society is turned into its passive opposite. The creative potential of the human being is commodified: "Every job can and must be *creatified*" (388).

The appendix then lists a series of professions making up a "Super-Creative Core": "Computer and mathematical occupations / Architecture and engineering occupations / Life, physical and social science occupations / Education, training, and library occupations / Arts, design, entertainment, sports and media occupations" (Florida, *Revisited* 401). There is little that is new about these professions. But by *subsuming* them into one "class" category, creativity becomes associated with a privileged group in society. Emerson's "creative class," on the other hand, is a deeply democratic and egalitarian concept, which was further developed into a model of democratic creativity and creative democracy by one of the most important Emersonians of the twentieth century, John Dewey.

CREATIVITY AND ITS DISCONTENTS

For Emerson, creativity is antagonistic to dominant society and culture:

> A true announcement of the law of creation, if a man were found worthy to declare it, would carry art up into the kingdom of nature, and destroy its separate and contrasted existence. The fountains of invention and beauty in modern society are all but dried up. A popular novel, a theatre, or a ballroom makes us feel that we are all paupers in the almshouse of this world, without dignity, without skill, or industry. Art is poor and low. (*Essays* 208)

Emerson's cultural criticism and that of the other Transcendentalists (including, but not limited to, Margaret Fuller and Henry David Thoreau), even though it was formulated at the *beginning* of the development of the capitalist-industrial complex, is amazingly accurate also for an evaluation of our contemporary situation. Art, as Emerson observes it in his time, is "poor and low" because it is commodified. It makes us "all paupers": "As soon as beauty is sought [. . .] for pleasure, it degrades the seeker" (Emerson, *Essays* 209).

Emerson's essay titled "Art" (1841) is a veritable mission statement of the meaning of creativity. He differentiates between "Art" as a fundamental human quality, and the practice of lowercase "arts" in the plural, which denies this claim:

> There is higher work for Art than the arts. They [the latter] are abortive births [!] of an imperfect or vitiated instinct. Art is the need to create; but in its essence, immense and universal, it is impatient of working with lame or tied hands, and of making cripples and monsters, such as all pictures and statues are. Nothing less than the creation of man and nature is its end. (Emerson, *Essays* 207)

Art is defined as the human "need to create," a process, rather, than a product. The artistic products, compared to the "essence" of art, which is "immense and universal," are not only imperfect, but an expression of an artistic practice that lacks agency and freedom ("lame and tied hands"). This is not a discriminatory metaphor of the (failed) artist as a "cripple," but of the products which include, notice the radicality of the statement, even "all pictures and statues." To reduce "Art" to its products thus destroys its task of the "creation of man and nature" (Emerson, *Essays* 207).

Art is thus equal to the creative drive and not its material results. Creativity in that sense is a means to fully realize human potential:

> A man should find in it an outlet for his whole energy. He may paint and carve only as long as he can do that. Art should exhilarate, and throw down the walls of circumstance on every side, awakening in the beholder the same sense of universal relation and power which the work evinced in the artist, and its highest effect is to make new artists. (Emerson, *Essays* 207)

Emerson's essays, from the beginning to his later work, emphasize the importance to overcome human division, separation, and alienation. The point here is that creativity is an expression of human beings' *whole* energy. Art is not something that can be *added* to "jazz up" a human, urban environment. It is at the center of a fully realized human life. Artistic activities such as painting and sculpture only meet these requirements if they liberate (provide an outlet for) the creative impetus. The walls of circumstance, which here we want to interpret as the gentrified sector of a "creatively" worked-over city, need to be overthrown so that the creative individuals can establish a relationship to all parts of life and all people around them. In the end, the purpose of art is not to end up in a museum, but to inspire creativity. That, indeed, is not Florida's "creatification" of the urban environment and urban profession by imposing the *label* of art on "circumstance," but instead present a challenge *through* art.

Through "creatification" of the human environment, Florida promises a merging of art and "circumstantial life," but it is a subordination of art to commercial interests, the total commodification of art in the public sphere. Instead, Emerson argues for a different relationship between creativity and everyday occupations at large: "Beauty must come back to the useful arts, and the distinction between the fine and the useful arts be forgotten":

> [People] reject life as prosaic, and create a death which they call poetic. They dispatch the day's weary chores, and fly to voluptuous reveries. They eat and

> drink, that they may afterwards execute the ideal. Thus is art vilified; the name conveys to the mind its secondary and bad senses; it stands in the imagination as somewhat contrary to nature, and struck with death from the first. (Emerson, *Essays* 209)

Instead, a creative life must bring creativity *into* the "useful arts," rather than embellishing them in the format of a creative death. In that sense, in "nature" (in the sense of a holistic life allowing human beings to come to their senses) "all is useful, all is beautiful" (Emerson, *Essays* 210).

What is important for our context of creative urbanism is that Emerson does not limit creativity to the traditional realm of high culture. The creative impetus will not "reiterate its miracles in the old arts [. . .]." In the New World (geographically as well as historically), it "will come, as always, unannounced, and spring up between the feet of brave and earnest men" (*Essays* 210).

> Proceeding from a religious heart it will raise to a divine use the railroad, the insurance office, the joint-stock company, our law, our primary assemblies, our commerce, the galvanic battery, the electric jar, the prism, and the chemist's retort, in which we seek now only an economical use. (Emerson, *Essays* 210)

The contrast between "divine use" and "economical use" requires a bit of an explanation. Emerson, who gave up his profession as a minister in Boston's tradition-laden Unitarian Second Church because of his inability to follow established dogmas of institutional practice and theological belief, continues to use religious terminology, but radically changes its semantics. According to this shift, which becomes characteristic of the whole Transcendentalist movement, divinity is now located inside the human individual rather than outside and especially above it. This does not mean a disavowal of metaphysics, but its grounding in the physicality of human life on earth. A "religious heart" will recognize everyday life as part of a unified world where the objects of nature "are not chaotic, and are not foreign, but have a law which is also a law of the human mind" (Emerson, "American Scholar" 86). It is the "opposite of the soul, answering to it part for part" (87).

Emerson and the Transcendentalists thus view their modern culture (which, in the preceding quote, is very much located in an urban environment) as having a higher meaning. The religious vocabulary is a lexical variable for a fulfilled, creative life, where human activities have a value for and in themselves and for the people engaged in them. The mode of seeking "only an economical use" of his modern culture then flattens out this symbolism; the activities in the world (in "Nature") are reified; the creative actor becomes an object. In his famous address "The American Scholar" he formulates this in a prototypical way:

> Man is thus metamorphosed into a thing, into many things. The planter, who is Man sent out into the field to gather food, is seldom cheered by any idea of the true dignity of his ministry. He sees his bushel and his cart, and nothing beyond, and sinks into the farmer, instead of Man on the farm. The tradesman scarcely ever gives an ideal worth to his work, but is ridden by the routine of his craft, and the soul is subject to dollars. The priest becomes a form; the attorney, a statute-book; the mechanic a machine; the sailor a rope of the ship. (Emerson, "American Scholar" 83f.)

This analysis of a commodified culture is very close to that of the early, "young" Marx, especially in his *Economic and Philosophic Manuscripts* of 1844 before the establishment of the economic prerogative in classical Marxism. Going beyond this "Marxist Humanism," which concentrates on the deficits in human existence, Emerson then goes on to develop a positive vision, namely that of human creativity, which interprets culture as constantly evolving. The creative mind thus progressively changes with the developments in the culture—not in dependence *from,* but in dialogue *with* these "useful arts." Translated into our contemporary situation, the creative mind would find ways to "throw down the walls" of a digital society that increasingly forces us to adapt our lives to them.

Emerson's essay "Circles" explains that the "key to every man is his thought." This thought is progressive, innovative, and inherently creative:

> In the thought of to-morrow there is a power to upheave all thy creed, all the creeds, all the literatures, of the nations, and marshal thee to a heaven which no epic dream has yet depicted. Every man is not so much a workman in the world, as he is a suggestion of that he should be. Men walk as prophecies of the next age. (Emerson, *Essays* 175)

In contradistinction to Florida, the task of Emerson's creative class is thus not to devise ways to adapt (but ultimately confirm and stabilize) the system, but to develop a progressive vision that will at first be resisted. Eventually, however, it will establish itself as a new paradigm, though not without a new "prophecy of the next age."

CREATIVE PARTICIPATION AND IMAGINATION

The pragmatist philosopher John Dewey brings Emerson, who strongly anticipated philosophers such as Charles Sanders Peirce, William James, and Dewey himself, into the modernist age. Herwig Friedl insists that the works of both Emerson and Dewey "have provided the most expansive and penetrating response to the specific call of Being in America" (133). In Emerson, Dewey saw a thinker and critic with a poetic vision that prepared the grounds for the pragmatist belief in human experience. In his 1903 essay, "Emerson—The Philosopher of Democracy," he quotes Emerson's conviction that "I am, [. . .] in all my theories, ethics and politics, a poet." Dewey adds that "we may, I think, safely take his word for it that he meant to be a maker rather than a reflector" (406). With this claim, Dewey appropriates "Emerson as the ancestor of the pragmatic turn from antecedents to consequences, as the initiator of a shift from a conception of truth as representation to an idea of truth as strategies of possible conduct" (Friedl 136). Dewey's emphasis on the poetic quality of Emerson's cultural criticism shows that Dewey understood philosophy as an act of creative practice.

John Dewey develops Emerson's concept of creativity in significant ways. Both thinkers approach it as a phenomenon that entails all-pervasive aesthetic expressions of human experience and future-oriented imaginative constructions constantly questioning the status quo. Dewey equally sees creativity, much in opposition to Richard Florida and the current "creative city" discourse, as a noncommodified, holistic approach to life. Critically anticipating Florida's version of the "creative class," Dewey draws on Emerson when he says

> against creed and system, convention and institution, Emerson stands for restoring to the common man that which in the name of religion, of philosophy, of art and of morality, has been embezzled from the common store and appropriated to sectarian and class [!] use. (Dewey, "Emerson" 411)

Emerson's division between a creative and an "uninventive" class emphasized the importance for all human beings to develop their creativity and not the emergence of a hegemonic group in society. In line with Emerson, Dewey argues against a distinction between elitist notions of creativity since he believed that aesthetic or creative activity is constitutive of common experiences in everyday life.

In this vein, Dewey expresses the intrinsic connection of art and its creative practice to ordinary experience. To him, even the highest form of art will always be linked to everyday human activity (see Negus and Pickering

45). In his refusal to separate art from experience, the philosopher saw the "task to restore continuity between the refined and intensified forms of experience that are works of art and the everyday events, doings, and sufferings that are universally recognized to constitute experience" (Dewey, *Art* 3). Dewey's approach toward this *restored continuity,* Keith Negus and Michael Pickering argue, "made a major contribution to the development of a democratic conception of art" (43). This democratic assertion is grounded very much in the Emersonian maxim of the "creative class."

Dewey's insistence on the democratic relationship between art and creativity leads to his call to make "art more accessible to the common man" (Friedl 134). As a consequence, he strictly opposes a concept of fine art "requiring a highly cultivated disposition for its proper appreciation" or even worse "the appropriation of art by those claiming social exclusivity and a 'superior cultural status'" (Negus and Pickering 41). So, against popular beliefs, Dewey regarded "the museum concept of art" as outdated and false, amounting to a place promoting the "separation of art from the objects and scenes of ordinary experience" (Dewey, *Art* 6).

In a timely manner that anticipated contemporary cultural and urbanist debates, Dewey's antimuseum argument turns not only against the separation of art from its original place of creation but also against predominantly commercial motivations. Seemingly foreshadowing what has since become known as the "Bilbao effect,"[4] he remarks:

> The contents of galleries and museums testify to the growth of economic cosmopolitanism. The mobility of trade and of populations, due to the economic system, has weakened or destroyed the connection between works of art and the genius loci of which they were once the natural expression. (Dewey, *Art* 9)

His critique of "the growth of economic cosmopolitanism" thus critically anticipates Florida's concept of the "creative class" and its goal of an economically profitable "creatification." As the local experience is the origin of any artwork, the direct spatial localization of art in its original cultural background seems to be of essence to Dewey. A globalized economic understanding of art dilutes its purpose. For Dewey, art and aesthetic expression embody an all-embracing approach to life as a whole. It is inspired by experience and, in

---

4. The Bilbao effect describes a strategy of purposefully enhancing places through sensational architecture to attract outside attention and draw in commercial interest. This phenomenon is named after the outpost of the Guggenheim Museum in Bilbao, Spain, which was built by Frank O. Gehry in 1997.

turn, inspires new experience. It is a fundamental expression of culture and innovative thinking. Creativity is thus a decisive, and essential dimension of human life in an existential sense. Cities as condensed spaces of human life and culture very much depend on creative activity. Hence, Dewey's idea of creative urbanism anticipates and goes beyond the commercialized notion of Florida. He sees creativity as having an impact on inclusive social development, a concept he eventually characterizes as "creative democracy."

Dewey struggled to find an English word to fully capture the entirety of the reciprocal meaning of art and its underlying creative processes as a whole:

> We have no word in the English language that unambiguously includes what is signified by the two words "artistic" and "esthetic." Since "artistic" refers primarily to the act of production and "esthetic" to that of perception and enjoyment, the absence of a term designating the two processes taken together is unfortunate. (Dewey, *Art* 46)

In fact, he notes that this language deficiency results in a notion of art that oftentimes attributes all creative agency to the artist. This leads to the false "assumption that, since art is a process of creation, perception and enjoyment of it have nothing in common with the creative act" (46). However, the artwork equally calls for the *recipient* to become creatively active. The creative power of art therefore is not only channeled through the artist but also generated by the recipient. Like Emerson, who conceives the task of art to "make new artists," Dewey ascribes equal significance to the participatory reception of artistic work. Art, as an "active productive process, may thus be defined as an esthetic perception together with an *operative* perception of the efficiencies of the esthetic object" (Dewey, *Experience* 375).

Beyond the active and creative process of artistic work, its reception is equally productive, establishing *creative participation and imagination* for all of society. For Dewey art is "a matter of communication and participation in values of life by means of the imagination" (Dewey, *Art* 336). This interactive understanding of creativity as a dialogical experience through mutual acts of imagination and expression can also be found in the narrative contract between author and reader. According to Negus and Pickering, the "creative act," as Dewey calls it, "entails a communicative experience which is cross-relational. It is an intersubjective and interactive dialogue bringing its participants together in the activity of interpretation, exchange and understanding" (23).

What matters with regard to creativity is not the final product but its inherent stimulus to imagination and contemplation. The interaction with the material artwork causes aesthetic experiences that evoke processes of self-reflection. Consequently, any such exchange is very personal and, according to Dewey, "is not therefore twice alike for different persons even today" (Dewey, *Art* 331). As matter of fact, it even "changes with the same person at different times as he [or she] brings something different to a work" (331). So contrary to functional products or machines, art does not serve any instrumental purpose other than to challenge and question perceptions of the self and society in general. In John Dewey's words, "this fact constitutes the uniqueness of esthetic experience and this uniqueness is in turn a challenge to thought" (274). Or as Isobel Armstrong states in her book *The Radical Aesthetic* (2000), the aesthetic experience "crosses the boundaries between maker, art object, and response and reconfigures them" (162).

CREATIVE RECONFIGURATION

Art as Experience, a book based on a series of ten lectures on the thought of William James that Dewey gave at Harvard University in 1931 and published in 1934, develops the pragmatist view that society and culture are always fluid and never static. In this constant state of overcoming the given, creativity becomes an essential human ability for innovation and future-oriented agency. Dewey remarks that there is still a societal lack of flexibility and fear of the uncertainty of innovation since it leads to questioning prevailing principles. He states that "creative intelligence is looked upon with distrust; the innovations that are the essence of individuality are feared, and generous impulse is put under bonds not to disturb the peace" (*Art* 348).

In fact, Dewey shares Emerson's understanding that art represents one of the most radical acts of creativity, which brings forth innovative approaches that renegotiate existing structures and imagine alternative ideas. As indicated in the initial quote on art as "the beauty parlor of civilization" (*Art* 344), Dewey rejects the notion that art should serve merely aesthetic enjoyment, as entertainment, or as an indicator of social status, all of which results in the atrophy of Art. Dewey would strongly disagree with the mechanical concept of "creative synthesis" in Florida's meaning, which implies the creation of practical products and superficial, artistic entertainment. In opposition to Florida, Dewey understands Art as the continuous act of reinventing a society's status quo. The unique challenge of creativity to human thought is, therefore, all-embracing: "The act of creation involves grappling with the conventions, traditions, media and institutional conditions through which any experience can be given communicative form" (Negus and Pickering 4).

In the end, Emerson and Dewey understand creativity as an act of abandonment of and contradiction to the dominant social order. According to Friedl, both thinkers advocate "concepts of a persistent removal and the refusal to acknowledge 'settling' as an ultimate goal of human existence" (133). This short statement by Dewey condenses his approach perfectly: "Where everything is already complete, there is no fulfillment" (Dewey, *Art* 17). Consequently, creativity always constitutes an "opportunity for resolution" of existing structures and conventions (17). Creative acts of imagination therefore go beyond one's own horizon of experience.

In contrast to this subversive understanding of creativity, urban geographer Jamie Peck does not detect the same scrutinizing scope in the latter's approach to the concept. Quite to the contrary, he criticizes that Florida's deceptive sales pitch of "creative city"—development for economic revitalization—merely "(re)produces the dominant market order" and is by no means disruptive of the prevailing neoliberal imperative of market-driven competition ("Creativity Fix" 2). In his harsh critique of Florida's "creative" urbanity, he concludes that "entrenched problems like structural unemployment, residential inequality, working poverty, and racialized exclusion are barely even addressed by this form of cappuccino urban politics" (10). This image has become famous in the discussion of creative urbanism. Systematic plans to make cities more creative have mostly resulted in the continuation of, and often increase in, "socioeconomic inequality" (11). Even though Florida himself detects the gentrification driven increase of social inequality and segregation in his recent book *The New Urban Crisis* (2017), he hardly acknowledges his own role in contributing to these problems. His own economic interests as founder of the still up and running consulting firm Creative Class Group might be one reason for that.

The problem is that Florida's label gives a bad name to urban creativity. But the script of the "creative city" is not corrupt in itself. With the introduction of the Emerson-inspired concept of "creative democracy" in 1939, Dewey has proposed a creative concept that brings creative and innovative paradigms to the urban framework under the premise of social inclusivity and participation.

CREATIVE DEMOCRACY

For Dewey, Emerson was "the Philosopher of Democracy" (Dewey, "Emerson" 412). Both thinkers understand democracy as an experiment: "Always erasing precedent, they think America as always new and unapproachable" (Friedl 155). Dewey's "creative democracy" is thus essentially future-oriented and follows a progressive vision. He formulates this vision as follows: "Since it is one that can have no end till experience itself comes to an end, the task of democracy is forever that of creation of a freer and more humane experience in which all share and to which all contribute" (Dewey, "Creative Democracy" 230).

Facing the imminent threat of fascist regimes throughout Europe and the increasing aggressiveness of Nazi Germany, Dewey's famous speech titled "Creative Democracy—The Task Before Us," delivered on October 2, 1939, called for a passionate defense of democratic social structures and egalitarian political participation that "can [only] be accomplished [. . .] by inventive effort and creative activity" (225). His notion of creative activity is based on social cooperation and embracing the continuous creative reimagination by all members of society.

Especially with regard to future challenges, democracy, for Dewey, is directly linked to human creativity and inventiveness. It is thus both "the product and source of creative agency" (Breitenwischer 54). In short, human creativity and inventiveness in a democratic life entail the ever-evolving task to "[put] a new practical meaning in old ideas" (Dewey, "Creative Democracy" 226). The reciprocal relation of creative agency and democratic activity for Dewey is manifested in an act of continuous renegotiation of the self, making it everyone's task to challenge political decision-making and to propose better solutions.

Creative democracy is founded on the belief in the equality of the "Common Man," on the "faith in the potentialities of human nature as that nature is exhibited in every human being irrespective of race, color, sex, birth and family, of material or cultural wealth" (Dewey, "Creative Democracy" 226). In fact, for Dewey, creative potential exists in the people who inhabit cities undergoing structural change and crisis. He describes those people as "unused resources," which can be found in the "waste of grown men and women who are without the chance to work" (225). This view of the urban public can be easily applied to struggling postindustrial cities with their high unemployment rates. John Dewey's call for a creative democracy helps to constitute a more holistic and noncommodified understanding of creativity in the city, one that puts less emphasis on neoliberal intentions and understands creativity as a societal task of ongoing cultural reevaluation and political participation.

CONCLUSION: (IN)VOLUNTARY GENTRIFICATION

For the artist Janna Banning, the work "Art is only for the rich" embraces her alternative proposition of creativity (see fig. 10.1). In an Emersonian and

FIGURE 10.1. "Art is only for the rich." © Janna Banning, with anonymous response. Photo by Hanna Rodewald, December 26, 2019. Used with kind permission of the artist.

Deweyan sense, she places her artwork not in a museum but outside in the immediate context of public space: "out there, where the transformation is happening," as she notes ("Gentrifizierung"; our translation).[5] Originally the installation consisted of the sentence "ART IS ONLY FOR THE RICH" in bold, red, glow-in-the-dark letters hung between two trees on a former parking lot that belongs to an abandoned administrative building. This deliberatively provocative statement points to and simultaneously questions a narrowly capitalistic and commercialized understanding of art. This is an understanding, however, which Dewey also, almost a century earlier, denounces in *Art as Experience* when he says:

> The *nouveaux riches*, who are an important by-product of the capitalist system, have felt especially bound to surround themselves with works of fine art which, being rare, are also costly. Generally speaking, the typical collector is

---

5. "Die Arbeit findet im öffentlichen Raum statt—dort, wo der Wandel stattfindet."

the typical capitalist. For evidence of good standing in the realm of higher culture, he amasses paintings, statuary, and artistic *bijoux,* as his stocks and bonds certify to his standing in the economic world. (Dewey, *Art* 8)

With her work, Banning, therefore, invites the viewer to reflect on this exclusionary and socially rarefied conception of art and to participate in an alternative, less commodified version.

Her provocation fell on fertile ground when a few weeks into its installation, an unknown person felt inspired to add another, though less idiomatic, English-language line under the original sentence: "RICH OF IMAGINATION." While the artistic execution differed from the original, as it was written on pieces of paper and hung up with a neon-yellow cord, the answer expresses the inverted meaning behind the artwork. It reverses the literal, exclusionary message to a purpose of art that is again open to everyone. The installation now argues for the general human ability to think and to imagine. Looking out on the ruins of a former industrial site of the Hoesch steelworks (a company merged into the Krupp group in 1992), Banning's work and the contribution it has inspired propose a sense of future-oriented innovation and creative agency in the framework of urban development that is in line with Emerson's and Dewey's ideas about art. Through her art, she initiates a dialog that aims to think outside of the usually gentrifying box of creative urbanism. Evidently, Banning holds up a democratic understanding of art and creativity that is similar to the thought of Ralph Waldo Emerson and John Dewey.

Our reconstructions of subversive notions of creativity through Emerson's category of the creative class and Dewey's democratic understanding of creativity have reconnected the creative city script with its historical roots in American cultural criticism. An understanding of creativity in the city that is less concerned with its functionality and profitability than with the processes of (self-)reflection and innovative thinking. What counts with regard to creative acts is not the *outcome* but the ever-evolving *process* of creative work and its aesthetic perception. We hope to have shown that the creative city discourse therefore does not necessarily need to end in commodification and gentrification. The previous conceptualization of creativity by Emerson and Dewey has led to the conclusion that it needs to be recognized as the human potential of imaginative and productive experience and expression. This realization transforms the creative-city script into a more inclusive and ultimately more democratic endeavor.

WORKS CITED

Armstrong, Isobel. *The Radical Aesthetic*. Blackwell, 2000.

Banning, Janna. "Art Is Only for the Rich." *Wir arbeiten für Gentrifizierung ehrenamtlich*. 2019, https://gentrifizierung.org/orte/art-only-rich/.

———. "Gentrifizierung ehrenamtlich." *Wir arbeiten für Gentrifizierung ehrenamtlich*. 2019, https://gentrifizierung.org.

Betsworth, Roger G. *Social Ethics: An Examination of American Moral Traditions*. Westminster/John Knox Press, 1990.

Breitenwischer, Dustin. "Creative Democracy and Aesthetic Freedom: Notes on John Dewey and Frederick Douglass." *Democratic Cultures and Populist Imaginaries*, edited by Donald E. Pease, *REAL Yearbook of Research in English and American Literature*, vol. 34, 2018, pp. 47–63.

Creative Class Group. https://creativeclass.com/richard_florida/. Accessed 25 July 2021.

Cortiel, Jeanne, and Walter Grünzweig. "Das Erzählen in der Kultur: Narrativ, Religion und Kulturanalyse." *Kulturwissenschaftliche Perspektiven in Der Nordamerika-Forschung*, edited by Friedrich Jaeger, Stauffenburg, 2001, pp. 27–40.

Dewey, John. *Art as Experience*. 1934. Perigee Books, 1980.

———. "Creative Democracy—The Task Before Us." 1939. *The Later Works: 1925–1953*, vol. 14, 1939–1941, edited by Jo Ann Boydston, Southern Illinois UP, 1988, pp. 224–30.

———. "Emerson—The Philosopher of Democracy." *International Journal of Ethics*, vol. 13, no. 4, 1903, pp. 405–13.

———. *Experience and Nature*. 1925. Dover Publications, 1958.

Dzudzek, Iris, and Peter Lindner. "Performing the Creative-Economy Script: Contradicting Urban Rationalities at Work." *Regional Studies*, vol. 49, no. 3, 2015, pp. 388–403.

Emerson, Ralph Waldo. "The American Scholar." 1837. Quoted from Emerson, *The Complete Works of Ralph Waldo Emerson*. Vol. 1, Houghton Mifflin, 1903, pp. 81–115.

———. *The Conduct of Life*. 1860. Quoted from Emerson, *The Complete Works of Ralph Waldo Emerson*. Vol. 6, Houghton Mifflin, 1904.

———. *Essays: First Series*. 1841. Quoted from Emerson, *Essays: First and Second Series*. Library of America, 1991.

Florida, Richard L. *Cities and the Creative Class*. Routledge, 2005.

———. *The New Urban Crisis: How Our Cities Are Increasing Inequality, Deepening Segregation, and Failing the Middle Class—and What We Can Do About It*. Oneworld Publications, 2017.

———. *The Rise of the Creative Class: And How It's Transforming Work, Leisure, Community and Everyday Life*. Basic Books, 2002.

———. *The Rise of the Creative Class, Revisited*. Basic Books, 2012.

Friedl, Herwig. "Thinking America: Emerson and Dewey." *Negotiations of America's National Identity*, edited by Roland Hagenbüchle and Josef Raab, Stauffenburg, 2000, pp. 131–57.

Grünzweig, Walter. "Parasitic Simulacrum: Ralph Waldo Emerson, Richard Florida, and the Urban 'Creative Class.'" *Urban Transformations in the U.S.A.: Spaces, Communities, Representations*, edited by Julia Sattler, transcript, 2016, pp. 81–97.

Landry, Charles. *The Creative City: A Toolkit for Urban Innovators*. Earthscan, 2000.

Landry, Charles, and Franco Bianchini. *The Creative City*. Demos, 1995.

Negus, Keith, and Michael Pickering. *Creativity, Communication and Cultural Value.* Sage Publications, 2004.

Peck, Jamie. "The Creativity Fix." *Fronesis,* vol. 24, 2007, pp. 1–14, https://www.eurozine.com/the-creativity-fix/.

———. "Struggling with the Creative Class." *International Journal of Urban and Regional Research,* vol. 29, no. 4, 2005, pp. 740–70.

Reckwitz, Andreas. *The Invention of Creativity: Modern Society and the Culture of the New.* Polity, 2017.

Throgmorton, James A. "Planning as Persuasive Storytelling in a Global-Scale Web of Relationships." *Planning Theory,* vol. 2, no. 2, 2003, pp. 125–51.

CHAPTER 11

Forms, Frames, and Possible Futures

BARBARA ECKSTEIN AND
JAMES A. THROGMORTON

In 2003 we coedited a collection of stories and essays in a book titled *Story and Sustainability,* bringing together then, as now, our fields of inquiry: literary scholarship and urban planning. In it, we sought to juxtapose diverse essays by scholars and practitioners that addressed the interaction of story, sustainability, the (US) city, and democracy. We advanced three specific arguments concerning their interaction. First, sustainability is both necessary and difficult to achieve. Second, dense urban environments raise the human stakes of sustainability and make the balancing of environmental and public health, social justice, and economic growth through democratic means both more necessary and more difficult to achieve. And third, intensely privatized American cities that emphasize economic growth further heighten the importance and difficulty of pursuing sustainability. Storytelling, that is, an arrangement of events situated in time and space whether conveyed via words, numbers, images, or sounds by some interested party, is a central means of participating in all three arguments, we assumed. In short, we argued, with the help of the other contributors, "story, sustainability, and democracy are mutually constitutive" (Eckstein and Throgmorton 4).[1] In this essay we reflect on that 2003

---

1. Robert Beauregard's essay in the collection distinguished between representative, participatory, and discursive democracy and argued that discursive democracy would, in a perfect world, produce sustainable cities. He defined a discursive democracy as "one in which people's interests are formed through talk and deliberation" (75).

collection, what has changed, and the assertions about scripts put forth by the editors of this volume.

We introduced *Story and Sustainability* in 2003 with a scene from the classic American novel *Invisible Man* (1952) by Ralph Ellison. It is a scene in which Ellison's young protagonist, new to New York City, encounters a man pushing discarded blueprints in a cart. We saw in the scene the numerous discarded urban plans of "the man," those many developments, improvements, and designs to raze neighborhoods of low-income—which is to say, predominantly minority—residents and renew the real estate and revenue prospects of residents of means—which is to say, predominantly white. Though when newly arrived in the city, Ellison's invisible man believes he can make and enact a plan in the US and thereby manage his destiny, before long his story finds him living underground literally off the grid, that is creatively siphoning energy from the electric utility company. As a young African American new to one of America's most powerful urban spaces, he has learned quickly that his identity as a man, a human, is invisible behind his color and his caste. Recognition—not fame, but dignity—has been denied him. Without the fundamental agreement of mutual recognition, the invisible man feels no responsibility to the rules that govern urban society at street level. Indeed, without mutual recognition, no one feels responsibility for creating sustainable places for everyone, all life.

Ellison's view of American urban plans in 1952 that we reiterated in 2003 remains pertinent nearly a generation later. The fundamental national contradiction that brings democratic principles and a racialized hierarchy of residents head-to-head remains. Despite the expansion of legal rights over centuries, each the result of painful and prolonged insistence, the temptation for many residents—mostly white, more male than not—to evade the contradiction of our foundation persists. Development, improvement, design—these presumptions of urban, especially economic, progress—mostly follow the paths of evasion that continue to lead to profit for some and generations of disinheritance for others. These paths and their attendant stories have taken on and often still retain the mantle of inevitability.

In "Imagining Sustainable Places," Throgmorton argued that imagining a sustainable place requires becoming conscious of the ways in which city users displace the social and environmental costs of their actions onto distant places (39–61). City users displace those costs by importing consumer goods and energy produced at the cost of unlivable wages and pollution in those distant places via complex transportation networks. The electric power grid and global-scale container-ship supply chains provide two important examples of such networks. Because those costs are displaced to distant locations—

whether across town or across the globe—and because those costs (negative externalities) are typically not fully incorporated into the prices of energy and consumer goods, city users typically do not alter their behavior in light of those costs. In a localized sense, therefore, the people of a place might think they are developing their city sustainably but, in fact, they may be displacing many, if not most of the adverse social and environmental effects onto distant places, only to have the most significant of them (e.g., climate change) return to harm city users along with everyone else on the planet.

Throgmorton went on to argue that progress toward sustainability requires making space within one's own place for stories that draw attention to the magnitude of the displaced costs, ways to reduce those costs throughout supply chains, and ways to develop more sustainable patterns of land development at the regional scale ("Imagining" 58–61). Because the content of a city's story and the planning that contributes to it depend on who authors it, he concluded by emphasizing the need for inclusive processes and places.

Reading references to *Invisible Man* in 2021, we cannot help but hear the inclusive counternarrative: "Say their names." Across the US, across the world, the name and face of George Floyd have been made visible in these pandemic times. Not only he, and not only victims of police violence, but also the names and gifts of innumerable artists, scientists, writers, thinkers of color have become more visible on more—not all—media. Across color lines, the (willing) public has heard not just the stories but the interpretations by people of color of public and private life necessary for honest-to-God recognition. White Americans like us have been invited to recognize ourselves again in the large and small violence and evasions that are the daily life of American hierarchy and embrace our responsibility for untangling the contradiction at the heart of our democracy. We cannot do this by plans for development, improvement, and design that face some Americans' desired future and turn our backs on a history of racial scapegoating and usurpation of other people's towns and farms by Europeans in North America that precedes the republic by centuries. It is liberating to look up from one's feet following a path paved for us and find our eyes met by a history and a diverse citizenry with so much to teach us.

In proposing scripts as a useful means to understand story and planning together, our editors may be articulating a strategy for identifying alternative paths that lead to rather than away from the contradictions of the US and its cities. The main goal of the *City Scripts: Narratives of Postindustrial Urban Futures* collection is both to theorize and substantiate the notion of scripts for contemporary narrative and literary studies. This collection of essays is also intended to highlight the importance of storytelling and narratological analysis for urban studies and urban planning and to enable a greater role for literary and cultural studies methodologies in urban studies and in postindustrial urban futures. "Factual and fictional stories affect how we imagine our cities and life within them," our editors write in the introduction.

They define scripts as "a new conceptual framework for the study of the art of persuasion in urban development. Scripts are artful combinations of narratives" in a variety of media that, through "framing, inscription, description and prescription [. . .] establish contingent connective tissues between the past, the present and the future" of cities (Buchenau and Gurr 142). The words "artful combination of narratives" suggest one possible way out of the concern that launched Eckstein's essay in 2003, that is, the frequent deployment of story to defend boundaries and galvanize segregated communities. The root *script* nevertheless carries within it writing and so cannot evade the effort to formalize one's desires for the purpose of influencing others—that prescription the editors speak of. In 2003 Eckstein wrote of the "elusiveness of truth and complexity of desire" manifested in story ("Making Space" 14). That said, combining narratives can, if artful enough, heighten a public's awareness of what is elusive and complex in storytelling, though not without risking the truth about specific desires. All the more reason to share interpretive strategies and not just the narratives or scripts themselves. Such sharing of interpretive strategies is at the core of what transdisciplinary narratology has to offer urban development.

Political psychologist Molly Andrews posits one interpretive strategy when she helps us understand how diverse actor-storytellers imagine their cities and their lives within them. She reports that tellers of urban narratives are inclined to imagine futures that are consistent with their pasts, and they expect others to act in the future as they think those others have acted before; they assume "what has gone before, and what is about to follow, belong together" (2). And yet we storytellers are "forever revisiting our pasts, in light of changing circumstances of the present, and in so doing, our vision for the future is reconstituted" (3). Andrews argues that imagination enables us to construct the "and then" of the stories we tell; it addresses not just the "if only" of our pasts but also the "what if" and the "not-yet-real" of our futures, and thereby "gives us the ability to contemplate a world that might have been, as well as one which might still be" (4–5). The *New York Times*' Michelle Alexander puts a sharp cut on this when she asks, "What If We're All Coming Back?" What would each of us do now if we knew the odds were very high that we would be reborn as a poor person in a world ravaged by climate change?

US Victorianist literary scholar Caroline Levine specifically offers an interpretive strategy that considers literary and urban forms together as a means to get at how power works and that thereby enters conversations about scripts. In Levine's book *Forms,* she proposes that analysts of narrative and city attend to "numerous overlapping social, [political, natural, and aesthetic] forms" arguing it is in encountering one another that their "organizing power [is] compromised, rerouted, or deflected" (132). She identifies four major forms: wholes, rhythms, hierarchies, and networks. In addition, she borrows from design theory the concept of affordance: "the potential uses or actions latent in materials and designs" (18). For Levine, the usefulness of the concept of affordance particularly lies in its "cross[ing] back and forth between materiality and design" (18). That said, in her argument "literary forms are not analogies of social forms. As transgeohistorical designs and as participants in specific situated power relations, they exist in overlapping relation to social and political forms" (Eckstein, "Formal Encounters" 91).

In her book, Levine employs her theory to especially good effect in the reading of, for example, Charles Dickens's *Bleak House* (1852–53) and its Victorian London setting and in the reading of the US television series *The Wire* (HBO, 2002–8) and the millennial Baltimore it addresses. In Eckstein's essay in *The Routledge Companion to Urban Imaginaries,* Levine's new formalism frames the reading of Indra Sinha's novel *Animal's People* (2007) and the Bhopal defined by the 1984 catastrophic toxic release there, as well as her reading of Naomi Wallace's drama *The Hard Weather Boating Party* (2014) and Louisville (Kentucky) defined by its long history with the chemical industry. Eckstein argues, in part, that while a single monumental chemical leak and loss of life and health have made the very city of Bhopal and its name a *whole* that city leaders and literary representations must address as such, the smaller persistent chemical emissions of Louisville's Rubbertown over time have produced a *rhythm* that has elicited a different city and different story of toxic threat. Dominant forms, even stubborn ones, overlap with others in space and time that tinker in big and small ways with the meanings of those diverse forms, each with affordances particular to it.

Despite the considerable complexity Levine's new formalism entails, one of its values is the description and analysis of overlapping forms that are not all vectors, human desires with arrows on their chests heading toward the fulfillment of those desires that, along the way, collide with other vectors. Yes, toxic events in both cities have elicited strong human emotions and diverse ideas about addressing the problems at hand, but the interpretive tool of differing forms affords an understanding of events that is not just another participant in a clash of values, wills, and goals.

Another interpretive strategy with a similar virtue is developed in the doctoral work of Christopher Dolle in environmental humanities at the University of Iowa. Dolle posits that all interpretive activity at this point in the twenty-first century should be conducted with the understanding that the Earth's humans are immersed in two framing environments: the material world of the sixth extinction and the digital world of the internet 2.0, that internet governed by the machinations of social media. Dolle's project specifically attends to the animal stories and animal memes that circulate in these environments aside and through the lives of humans and their products. One influence on Dolle's work especially pertinent to the theorizing of scripts is Australian environmental philosopher and anthropologist Thom Van Dooren's *Flight Ways: Life and Loss at the Edge of Extinction* (2014). Van Dooren explains extinction not as a cliff but as an unfolding story for each species, each flock or herd, over time. Animals—birds in this case—lead, he shows, storied lives connected to particular places. Little Penguins, for example, have a relationship with a specific rocky shoreline in Sydney that is not "interchangeable, but deeply storied, carrying the past experiences of individuals and the generations before them" despite human construction of walls and upscale housing (64). Apprehending, in the environments of both mass extinction and human social media, the storied lives of animals with their own scripts on their own terms enables an understanding of sustainability and democracy different from the anthropocentric frames usually deployed.

In considering the efficacy of scripts and their relationship to stories, we have pondered the significance of overlapping narratives, artfully combined narratives, as well as the persistence of prescription in the rhetoric of storytelling that our editors offer by way of definition. We have also offered new formalism and the interplay of affordances as well as the coexistence of environments of accelerated extinction and accelerated electronic media as interpretive means to think differently about the interface of cities, stories, sustainability, and democracy. To close our chapter, we turn to the significance of narrative framing in various media that, our editors propose, can "establish contingent connective tissues between the past, the present and the future" of cities (Buchenau and Gurr 142). We offer our own frames as examples. Throgmorton begins with the public frame of city governance. Eckstein finishes with the private frame of the human heart. Together we recognize the sinews that connect each script to the other.

Throgmorton: It is one thing to imagine sustainable cities, but it is quite another to transform any particular city into a sustainable place. Over the past ten years, I have learned a great deal about those requirements by serving as a member of my city's city council from 2012 through 2019 and, simultaneously, as mayor from 2016 through 2019. As mayor, I tried to lead my city toward becoming a more inclusive, just, and sustainable place (Throgmorton, *Co-Crafting*; "Planners"; "Storytelling").

In my capacity as an elected council member/mayor, I saw many instances of individuals, private businesses, nongovernmental organizations, elected officials, governmental entities, and others using stories and storytelling to report their experiences, to strengthen their claims about what city government should do in response to specific issues and to convey their visions for the city's future. My experience revealed a great deal about how, specifically, stories (and scripts more broadly) influence what people advocated, what city councils do, and what external constraints and incentives affected a city's actions.

In what follows, I draw upon my experience, recognizing that it was one elected person's experience in one city, yet emphasizing a few key points that I think apply to all city governments in the US and to the relationship among storytelling, democracy, and the ability of city governments to craft sustainable futures for their cities.

Often when people use the words *the city*, they conflate two different understandings of what *the city* means. One refers to *the city* as a territorially bounded municipal corporation, whereas the other understands *the city* to be a complex multijurisdictional place in which people live, work, and play. As a municipal corporation, the city has the legal right to take specific types of action on behalf of the city's residents and businesses. The formal structure of city governments varies from place to place, but they usually have a chief executive (e.g., a *mayor*), a legislative body of elected representatives (e.g., a *council*), and other officers having special functions.

The second use of *the city* manifests what urbanist Jane Jacobs called "problems in organized complexity—organisms that are replete with unexamined, but obviously intricately interconnected, and surely understandable, relationships" (438–39). In addition to this internal complexity, individual cities are typically enmeshed in urbanized regions with a complex array of multiple overlapping governmental jurisdictions. Moreover, cities depend upon various networks (e.g., transport, energy, and finance) and flows (e.g., water, consumer goods, and displaced environmental costs) to function. These networks and flows typically extend far beyond the legal territorial limits of the city, often to the global scale. In this sense, cities can be thought of as nodes in a global-scale web, a web that consists of a highly fluid and constantly changing set of relationships.

In the United States, city governments vary in institutional structure primarily because they are "creatures of the state"; that is, they derive all their powers from the individual states.[2] In some states, local governments can do only that which states explicitly permit them to do. In other states, some cities are granted the authority to govern themselves within constraints established by their state governments. This "Home Rule" status notwithstanding, states can still preempt local governments' authority to act on particular issues. Moreover, in the US, the role of the mayor varies from city to city. Some cities have a "strong mayor" form of government in which the mayor has the power to appoint and replace key department heads and to veto ordinances passed by a majority of the city's legislative body. Think Mayor Daley's Chicago. Other cities, mine included, have a council/manager form of government in which the mayor's powers are considerably less.

Beyond the formal structures of their governments, cities also vary considerably in history, size, economic base, ethnic diversity, political leanings, environmental conditions, and many other ways. Some are very large, whereas the rest are considerably smaller. Some have been withering economically, others have been booming. Some have relatively homogenous populations, whereas others are quite diverse. Some are severely threatened by specific environmental risks and hazards (e.g., hurricanes) that are irrelevant to other places. Some are red (Republican) cities in red states, whereas others are blue (Democratic) in blue states, and still others are either blue in red or red in blue.

The elected leaders of a city cannot make their place more sustainable simply by proclaiming their support for the characteristics of an ideal sustainable city. Making a turn toward sustainability requires working with a large and diverse array of other people to transform the city's policies, plans, budgets, capital improvement plans, codes, and practices where necessary. This can be arduous. To do it successfully, the city's mayor and other elected leaders must understand the contexts and constraints within which they operate, and they must be skilled at crafting the step-by-step actions required to move a city in that more sustainable direction.

As they act (whether to promote sustainability or not), city leaders (mayors, council members, and professional staff) routinely tell themselves continually unfolding stories about what they have been doing with regard to the key issues confronting their cities. These stories consist of a mix of ordinances, resolutions, plans, budgets, programs, and projects. Wanting to redevelop part of their city, for example, they might hire a consultant to help the professional staff devise a plan, conduct public outreach and engagement, produce a draft plan, have the local planning and zoning commission review the draft

---

2. Frug and Barron (2008) report that states shape city structures in three key ways: regulations, laws, and financing. By limiting or prohibiting more proactive or innovative ideas, states can constrain cities' actions considerably.

plan and propose amendments, and have the city council review and adopt the plan. With the plan in hand, city staff would then use various tools (e.g., tax increment financing, height and density bonuses, transfer of development rights, and capital improvement programs) to enable and encourage private investment in the area. Over time, investment would occur and ribbons would be cut. All this, plus related action, would become part of the city leaders' continually unfolding story. If one has not been tracking the unfolding, one will have a very hard time influencing the city leaders' next steps.

In my experience, there can be a massive gap between the stories city officials tell themselves and the stories that other residents tell about the city and their lives within it. Most members of the general public know very little about the flow of action pertaining to specific topics or the background information that city staff and council members draw upon when making decisions in that flow. Standard ways of informing the public through the news media about the complexities of this flow provide little help. Consequently, the general public remains largely in the dark until some particular issue grabs their attention. And when the general public becomes involved, they typically frame their advocacy either in terms of testimonial storytelling based on their own lives and those of their close relatives, friends, and neighbors or else in terms of generalized opinion only loosely connected to the specific decisions at hand. The sequence of actions elicits a familiar substantive and narrative path dependency that can be very hard to change.[3] But change is possible, within constraints.

With that in mind, I want to highlight three stories that are currently intersecting with and potentially influencing such continually unfolding stories in US cities. One, surely the predominant one, derives from conventional urban theory. Ever since political scientist Paul Peterson published *City Limits* back in 1981, the conventional reasoning has been that cities inevitably must compete with one another to attract private investment and highly educated residents, and hence must adopt business- and development-friendly policies. This reasoning limits democratic engagement within cities to relatively inconsequential matters, makes city politics mostly irrelevant, and goes a long way toward explaining why, at least in my city, residents typically know more about national than local politics and why only a very small percentage of registered voters vote in city council elections. Enacting this story, city leaders defer to the policy priorities of the local "growth machine" while city staff enacts a neoliberal, entrepreneurial form of planning that is highly unlikely to lead

---

3. For detail about path dependency, see Pierson; Sorensen. See also Haef and Gurr's chapter 4 in this book for more detailed discussion of "narrative path dependency."

the city toward becoming a more equitable and sustainable place (Molotch 309–32).

The second story focuses on the need to eliminate racial inequities. Although the underlying history of efforts to eliminate them is quite deep, the most recent manifestations have been generated by the murders of Trayvon Martin in 2012, Michael Brown in 2014, George Floyd in 2020, and many others. In each case, the murders stimulated stories that circulated in social media, sparked protests and demonstrations in cities throughout the US, and, at least in my city, persuaded city leaders to make incremental changes in local policies and practices. In my city, we created an "Ad Hoc Committee on Diversity Issues"; began monitoring and reporting on disproportionality in traffic stops, searches, and arrests; required police officers to wear and use body cameras; required all city employees to participate in implicit bias training; mandated training for city staff in crisis intervention and de-escalation techniques; hired more Black police officers; instituted greater diversity on the city's boards and commissions; and more. City officials, myself included, renarrated these incremental steps as a story about how we had been making important changes to reduce racial inequities.

Conversely, many (if not most) Black residents either thought we were taking only "baby steps" and needed to do much more, or else were completely unaware of the changes city government had been making. The 2020 demonstrations following the killing of George Floyd by a Minneapolis police officer dramatically increased pressure on city leaders to make deeper changes in policies and practices. This pressure included calls for defunding the police and shifting funding to programs that would help communities of color, especially Black communities, overcome structural racism. In my city, just a few months after I had retired as mayor, large multiethnic crowds of protestors led by Iowa Freedom Riders (IFR) peacefully but loudly marched for weeks through different city neighborhoods every night (at times to city council members' homes) while chanting "Say their names! George Floyd," carrying signs, and tagging buildings and streets with markers such as "BLM," and "Fu*k 12."[4] At least twice protestors marched from downtown to (and onto) Interstate 80. IFR subsequently presented the city council with a set of twelve demands for action, many of which displayed a lack of knowledge about what the city had actually been doing or had the legal authority to do. The city council responded by passing a seventeen-point resolution addressing systemic racism and law enforcement policies, and by later establishing a Truth and Reconcili-

---

4. The latter is a slang term, a meme, which basically means "Fuck the Police." Black rappers and others began using it around 2014, and the subsequent deaths of Black men at the hands of the police greatly increased its usage.

ation Commission. The story continues, the BLM story having disrupted and, at least temporarily, transformed the city's continually unfolding story.

The third story focuses on climate change. Empowered by scientific studies and stories that have circulated internationally, this story calls on local governments to play their part in minimizing climate change by reducing and eventually eliminating their reliance on fossil fuels. In many cases, cities have responded by adopting climate action and adaptation plans. Our city adopted such a plan in 2018 when I was still mayor. Crafted with the help of a consultant and a climate action advisory committee, it indicated a set of actions to reduce citywide greenhouse gas emissions by the percentages called for in the 2016 Paris Accord. Immediately after we adopted that plan, the International Panel on Climate Change (IPCC) released a new report that indicated the situation had become worse than what had been expected just a few years earlier and deeper cuts in emissions would be required. Over the succeeding months, student climate strikers began pressuring city leaders to ensure their cities (ours included) would do what the IPCC's report said was necessary. In our case, the pressure continued through the middle of 2020 as the climate strikers who were acting as part of a global social media–based movement held a couple of demonstrations, berated us for "doing nothing," and demanded that we take specific actions: Proclaim a "climate emergency," significantly accelerate the amount and pace at which carbon emissions would be decreased, and hire a new Climate Plan Action Coordinator charged with developing community partnerships that would lead to net-zero carbon dioxide (CO_2) emissions by 2050. The city manager and I met with a group of local climate strikers, listened carefully to them, and made sure they knew what we had been doing. I also tried to ensure they understood two key constraints we operated under: First, state government had preempted local government's ability to adopt carbon emission standards for new buildings that were stricter than the state's standard, and second, we had no authority over MidAmerican Energy and, though it is in our city limits, the University of Iowa.[5] Even so, after three work session discussions in midsummer, and after an inspiring visit by sixteen-year-old Swedish climate activist Greta Thunberg, we approved a resolution declaring a climate crisis, adopting the more demanding 45 percent and 100 percent reduction goals, and directing the staff to recommend within one hundred days actions we could take to achieve the 45 percent reduction by 2030.

---

5. MidAmerican provides almost all of the electric power and natural gas used in Iowa City and accounts for well over half of the city's CO_2 emissions. The university's power plant accounts for another 15 percent.

Greta Thunberg's visit early in October proved decisive. She had sailed across the Atlantic Ocean, spoken to the US Congress, and driven halfway across the country in an all-electric car prior to arriving in our city. I had the opportunity to introduce her to a crowd of four to five thousand people at a key intersection in the heart of our city. Looking at the joyful, excited, and hopeful faces of students, parents, and other adults in the crowd, and hearing them react to Greta and what she said, I finally knew that we had a strong constituency for climate action. Early in October, we created a new Climate Action Commission to help us accomplish our climate action goals. In mid-November, the staff presented us with an outstanding report identifying actions the city should consider taking to achieve our new goals.

Racial inequities and greenhouse gas emissions have accumulated over generations, and bills have come due—overdue. It is up to us now to pick up the tab.

Eckstein: In 2003 I turned to an Inuit definition of storyteller to help unravel the question of who or what authorizes the author of a story.

> The Inuits say that the storyteller is the one who makes space for the story to be heard. As I see it, this definition of the traditional storyteller cum author may be especially useful for planners, for it assumes that the stories storytellers tell are not their own. It is their knowledge of traditional stories and local conventions; it is their skill as narrators, as "hosts," for stories they hear and retell; it is their demeanor, their voice, their ordering, their shaping, their ability—literally—to create an amiable narrative and physical space, that allow their telling, retelling, and thus transformation of the community's stories to be heard. (Eckstein, "Making Space" 21)

On one hand, an ability to make space for stories to be heard is more important than ever as, for example, US cities grapple with calls to defund the police. On the other hand, amiability in narrative or in place is an insufficiently urgent affect in a transformative and necessary discussion such as this one. Nevertheless, the suspension of the planner's ego and the cultivation of patience by all players as they listen to as well as narrate the past remains important. Peace negotiator John Paul Lederach writes of the generative energy to be found in the past if decision-makers do not too quickly implement instrumental solutions born of well-worn paths and long-established infrastructure perpetually promising a different future that never arrives (147).

That generative energy may be sparked by disruptions in the usual expectations of a story and indeed of the storyteller. In 2003, I pointed to literature and literary theorists who use and analyze techniques of disruption and thus can teach their readers or listeners how to read or hear differently. In disrupted habits may be found the will to change. A generation before the 2020 pandemic and the unfolding assaults on US democracy and environmental stewardship during the Trump presidency, I wrote as though I knew what disruption of habits and will to change were. Maybe I did, then. But more recent events have brought new opportunities for knowledge and understanding. The life in suspension that the pandemic has required together with the witness of repeated escalating injustice driven by powerful political will targeting especially people of color and crucial biomes created a space and time for old understandings of familiar stories to be disrupted and new modes of thinking and even being to take their place. A professional life of studying African American, American Indian, and Asian American literature and history as well as environmental humanities; a public life of marching, chanting, writing, lobbying, organizing, and arguing were not enough for this white woman to understand at heart what it would mean to live one's life—one generation among many—in a regime of violent injustice.

But the pause of the pandemic and the relentless violation of every political and moral value I embrace completely turned the interpretive frame around for me. As white friends and colleagues were bewailing every day the violations I too saw, my frame of reference became not my own life but a long, long life lived in the jurisdiction of a Bull Connor or a slaveholder before him. My frame of reference became Mamie Till, the mother of Emmett Till, who had the stunning emotional courage to insist her fifteen-year-old son's body, mutilated by his murderers, be displayed in an open casket as witness to centuries of terror—not terrorism defined by 9/11 but centuries of terror. Strange to say, this shift in my interpretive frame that turned the horror I knew into the horror I, as a fellow American, am, made me calmer than many around me. The brevity of the disastrous use of power before us diminished in comparison to the time endured and the alternatives presented by generations of African Americans, American Indians, Asian Americans, and others. The disregard for other species has also, most often, occurred alongside the assaults on people of color. Externalities all. I don't know that I can prescribe conditions for this sort of reframing of how one sees, hears, feels—pandemics and the abuse of the US presidency are not the answer—but I know that it is necessary for everyone in the US who is white and some who are not.

If I try to imagine what scripts would produce this change of frame to a frame of heart, I would begin with humility close to home, among intellectuals and academics. In 2003 I quoted the wonderful Italian scholar of oral history Alessandro Portelli writing of the necessarily difficult encounter of an academic researcher with a storyteller from the laboring class different from himself: "Reopening a dialogue between two human worlds which long ago ceased to speak to each other is a difficult enterprise, and it causes many burning humiliations [for the researcher, for everyone]" (27). But there is no turning away from these humiliations if we mean to shape improvements of a genuinely just and sustainable kind. Portelli recommends dealing with power openly. That's a start.

But justice and sustainability, as elusive as they are, are insufficient. The future contingent upon this present reframing of the past is one that recognizes justice is only "the minimal standard of love." Making this claim in a lecture, ethicist Scott Bader-Saye goes on to explain, "love itself exceeds justice in its mode of giving and forgiving." In every council chamber, in every chamber of our hearts, there is much reframing work to do. Luckily there are scripts of love from every generation, every culture, every territory, even every species to inform the work.

WORKS CITED

Alexander, Michelle. "What If We're All Coming Back?" *New York Times*, 29 Oct. 2018, https://www.nytimes.com/2018/10/29/opinion/climate-change-politics-john-rawls.html.

Andrews, Molly. *Narrative Imagination and Everyday Life*. Oxford UP, 2014.

Bader-Saye, Scott. Unreferenced lecture cited in Alan Scarfe. "Second Sunday in Lent. February 27, 2021." The Episcopal Diocese of Iowa. https://www.iowaepiscopal.org/news-blog/second-sunday-in-lent. Accessed 27 Feb. 2021.

Beauregard, Robert A. "Democracy, Storytelling, and the Sustainable City." *Story and Sustainability: Planning, Practice, and Possibilities for American Cities*, edited by Barbara Eckstein and James A. Throgmorton, MIT Press, 2003, pp. 65–77.

Buchenau, Barbara, and Jens Martin Gurr. "'Scripts' in Urban Development: Procedural Knowledge, Self-Description, and Persuasive Blueprint for the Future." *Charting Literary Urban Studies: Texts as Models of and for the City*, by Jens Martin Gurr, Routledge, 2021, pp. 141–63.

Dolle, Christopher V. *Inter / -Species / -Net / -Sect: Biology. Technology. Promise. Perversion.* 2021. U of Iowa, PhD dissertation.

Eckstein, Barbara. "Formal Encounters in Two Tales of Toxicity: Bhopal, *Animal's People*, Louisville, *The Hard Weather Boating Party*." *The Routledge Companion to Urban Imaginaries*, edited by Christoph Lindner and Miriam Meissner, Routledge, 2019, pp. 90–102.

———. "Making Space: Stories in the Practice of Planning," *Story and Sustainability: Planning, Practice, and Possibilities for American Cities*, edited by Barbara Eckstein and James A. Throgmorton, MIT Press, 2003, pp. 13–36.

Eckstein, Barbara, and James A. Throgmorton. "Introduction Blueprint Blues." *Story and Sustainability: Planning, Practice, and Possibilities for American Cities*, edited by Barbara Eckstein and James A. Throgmorton, MIT Press, 2003, pp. 1–7.

Ellison, Ralph. *Invisible Man*. Random House 1952.

Frug, Gerald E., and David J. Barron. *City Bound: How States Stifle Urban Innovation*. Cornell UP, 2008.

IPCC—Intergovernmental Panel on Climate Change. "Summary for Policymakers." *Global Warming of 1.5°C. An IPCC Special Report on the Impacts of Global Warming of 1.5°C above Pre-Industrial Levels and Related Global Greenhouse Gas Emission Pathways, in the Context of Strengthening the Global Response to the Threat of Climate Change, Sustainable Development, and Efforts to Eradicate Poverty*, edited by Valérie Masson-Delmotte, Panmao Zhai, Hans-Otto Pörtner, Debra Roberts, James Skea, Priyadarshi Shukla, Anna Pirani, Wilfran Moufouma-Okia, C. Péan, Roz Pidcock, Sarah Connors, J. B. Robin Matthews, Yang Chen, X. Zhou, M. I. Gomis, E. Lonnoy, T. Maycock, M. Tignor, and T. Waterfield, Cambridge UP, 2018, https://www.ipcc.ch/sr15/chapter/spm.

Jacobs, Jane. *The Death and Life of Great American Cities*. Vintage, 1961.

Lederach, John Paul. *The Moral Imagination: The Art and Soul of Building Peace*. Oxford UP, 2005.

Levine, Caroline. *Forms: Whole, Rhythm, Hierarchy, Network*. Princeton UP, 2015.

Molotch, Harvey. "The City as a Growth Machine: Toward a Political Economy of Place." *American Journal of Sociology*, vol. 82, no. 2, 1976, pp. 309–32.

Peterson, Paul E. *City Limits*. U of Chicago P, 1981.

Pierson Paul. *Politics in Time: History, Institutions, and Social Analysis*. Princeton UP, 2004.

Portelli, Alessandro. *The Death of Luigi Trastulli and Other Stories: Form and Meaning in Oral History*. SUNY Press, 1991.

Sorensen, Andre. "Taking Path Dependence Seriously: An Historical Institutionalist Research Agenda in Planning History." *Planning Perspectives*, vol. 30, no. 1, 2015, pp. 17–38.

Throgmorton, James A. *Co-Crafting the Just City: Tales from the Field by a Planning Scholar Turned Mayor*. Routledge, 2022.

———. "Imagining Sustainable Places." *Story and Sustainability: Planning, Practice, and Possibilities for American Cities*, edited by Barbara Eckstein and James A. Throgmorton, MIT Press, 2003, pp. 39–61.

———. "Planners in Politics, Politicians in Planning." *Planning Theory & Practice*, vol. 22, no. 3, 2021, pp. 495–502.

———. "Storytelling and City Crafting in a Contested Age: One Mayor's Practice Story." *Planners in Politics: Do They Make a Difference?*, edited by Louis Albrechts, Edward Elgar Publishing, 2020, pp. 174–97.

Van Dooren, Thom. *Flight Ways: Life and Loss at the Edge of Extinction*. Columbia UP, 2014.

CONTRIBUTORS

LIEVEN AMEEL is university lecturer in comparative literature at Tampere University, Finland. He holds a PhD in Finnish literature and comparative literature from the University of Helsinki and the Justus Liebig University Giessen. He has published widely on literary experiences of the city, narrative planning, and urban futures. His books include *Helsinki in Early Twentieth-Century Literature* (2014) and *The Narrative Turn in Urban Planning* (2020) and the coedited volumes *Literature and the Peripheral City* (2015), *Literary Second Cities* (2017), and *The Materiality of Literary Narratives in Urban History* (2019).

JULIANE BOROSCH is a doctoral researcher in the Scripts for Postindustrial Urban Futures: American Models, Transatlantic Interventions research group at the Department of Anglophone Studies at the University Duisburg-Essen. Her dissertation project investigates landmarks of the former industrial city in Detroit, Michigan, and the Ruhr Area, Germany, at the conjunction of creative and sustainable development. Her research combines literary, cultural, and media studies. Further research interests include questions of seriality, television, and history of the nineteenth and twentieth centuries.

BARBARA BUCHENAU is professor of North American literary and cultural studies at the University Duisburg-Essen and the speaker of the Scripts for Postindustrial Urban Futures: American Models, Transatlantic Interventions interinstitutional research group, funded by the Volkswagen Foundation (2018–23). Her publications address socio-spatial imaginaries in early modern and contemporary times, Atlantic cultural transfer, as well as figurations of approximation in pragmatic texts and maps.

With Lieven Ameel and Jens Gurr, she is the author of *Narrative in Urban Planning: A Practical Field Guide* (2023).

FLORIAN DECKERS is a doctoral researcher in the Scripts for Postindustrial Urban Futures: American Models, Transatlantic Interventions research group at the Department of Anglophone Studies at the University Duisburg-Essen. His research interests include contemporary popular culture, literary urban studies, and transnational American studies. His dissertation project, "Raising Ethnic Voices," explores contemporary reimaginations of the city by Latinx artists and activists in New York.

BARBARA ECKSTEIN retired as a professor from the English Department and the Center for Global and Regional Environmental Research at the University of Iowa (US) in 2019. Her teaching and research were in environmental humanities with an emphasis on justice for humans and other species. Her work, such as the book *Sustaining New Orleans* (2006), most often attends to specific places and histories. A recent publication is "Empires' City-Building and the 1792 Intervention of Aupaumut's Book," *Urban History* (2021). In retirement, she retains these interests as she pursues action on climate change.

KORNELIA FREITAG is the chair of American studies at Ruhr-University Bochum. Her major areas of research are American poetry and cultural and literary theory. She has published *Cultural Criticism in Women's Experimental Writing: The Poetry of Rosmarie Waldrop, Lyn Hejinian and Susan Howe* (2006), has coedited *Another Language: Poetic Experiments in Britain and North America* (2008) and *Modern American Poetry: Points of Access* (2013), and edited *Recovery and Transgression: Memory in American Poetry* (2015). Currently she is serving as vice rector for academic affairs at her home university.

WALTER GRÜNZWEIG is professor of American literature and culture at TU Dortmund University. A native of Austria, he received his BA in English at Ohio University and his subsequent degrees at Karl-Franzens-Universität Graz. He has taught at universities in Austria, Germany, Hungary, Italy, Slovenia, and the United States. He specializes in nineteenth-century American literature as well as transatlantic literary and cultural relations and international student exchange. His interest in urban American studies is related to his years of work on Walt Whitman and his literary urbanism.

RANDI GUNZENHÄUSER is professor of American studies and the media at TU Dortmund University. Her research interests and teaching range from literature, the arts, and performative cultures since 1800 across the aesthetics of the affects in transatlantic popular cultures to remediation in video games. She is author of *Automaten—Roboter—Cyborgs: Körperkonzepte im Wandel* (2006) and *Horror at Home: Genre, Gender und das Gothic Sublime* (1993). She takes a special interest in medial aspects of city planning and building discourses, be they modes of narration, color schemes, or the structures of web pages.

JENS MARTIN GURR is professor of British and Anglophone literature and culture at the University of Duisburg-Essen, Germany. He is the cofounder and speaker of the Metropolitan Research competence field at the University Alliance Ruhr. Research interests include literary urban studies, theories and methods of interdisciplinary urban research, and the theory of models as well as literature and climate change. He is the author of *Charting Literary Urban Studies: Texts as Models of and for the City* (2021) and coeditor of *Understanding Complex Urban Systems: Multidisciplinary Approaches to Modeling* (2014).

ELISABETH HAEFS is a postdoctoral researcher in the Scripts for Postindustrial Urban Futures: American Models, Transatlantic Interventions research group at the Department of Anglophone Studies at the University Duisburg-Essen. Her dissertation engaged in a comparison between narratives of community-building gardening in the former "European Green Capital"—Essen, Germany—and in the alleged ecological model city of Portland, Oregon. Further research interests include the field of literature and science, specifically the narrativity of scientific writing.

CHRIS KATZENBERG is a doctoral researcher in the Scripts for Postindustrial Urban Futures: American Models, Transatlantic Interventions research group at the Department of American Studies at Ruhr University Bochum. His PhD project traces the transatlantic trajectories and transformations of "Collective Impact," an influential American city script for inclusion at the intersection of urban education and social reform. His research interests reach from contemporary US literature and (literary) urban studies to transnationalism, globalization, race, and ethnicity.

JOHANNES MARIA KRICKL is a doctoral researcher in the Scripts for Postindustrial Urban Futures: American Models, Transatlantic Interventions research group at the Department of North American History at Ruhr University Bochum. His current work investigates inland port cities and their logistics industry, river- and lakefront revitalizations, as well as the cultural, environmental, and public urban history of postindustrialism. His research also addresses the nexus between the US history of ideas and transatlantic urbanism, covering matters of metahistory (*Historik*), semiotics, and narrative theory.

RENEE M. MORENO is professor in the Chicano/a Studies Department at California State University, Northridge (CSUN), where she teaches composition and literature courses. She holds a joint PhD in English and education from the University of Michigan and has held postdoctoral fellowships at the University of California, Los Angeles, and the University of Notre Dame. Dr. Moreno directs the Chicano Studies Writing Center and supervises part-time faculty teaching composition courses in the department; she cochairs CSUN's Writing Council. She is working on a book-length project recovering an early history of Chicano artists in Denver and counternarratives documenting gentrification in her home neighborhood of Swansea in Denver.

HANNA RODEWALD is a doctoral researcher in the Scripts for Postindustrial Urban Futures: American Models, Transatlantic Interventions research group. She is currently working on her PhD in American studies at TU Dortmund University, where she finished her BA and MEd in English and American studies, fine arts, and educational science. Looking into the implementations of the creative city script in postindustrial cities from a transatlantic perspective, her dissertation combines three of her major fields of interest: art, urban imaginaries, and transatlantic American relations.

JULIA SATTLER is assistant professor of American studies at TU Dortmund University. She studied English, American studies, and Protestant theology at TU Dortmund and Hamilton College, New York. She is the author of *Mixed-Race Identity in the American South: Roots, Memory, and Family Secrets* (2021) and the editor of *Urban Transformations in the U.S.A.: Spaces, Communities, Representations* (transcript, 2016). Her ongoing research investigates the narration of urban transformation processes in the German and American Rust Belts. Following this trajectory, Julia Sattler is currently studying the negotiation of radical urban change in American poetry.

MARIA SULIMMA is junior professor of North American literature and cultural studies at the University of Freiburg. Prior to this, she was the postdoctoral researcher of the Scripts for Postindustrial Urban Futures: American Models, Transatlantic Interventions research group at the University Duisburg-Essen. She is the author of *Gender and Seriality: Practices and Politics of Contemporary US Television* (2021). Her recent work is on storytelling and gentrification as well as the urban pastimes of nineteenth- and twenty-first-century fiction.

JAMES A. THROGMORTON is emeritus professor, School of Planning and Public Affairs, University of Iowa. He is the author of *Planning as Persuasive Storytelling* (1996), *Co-Crafting the Just City* (2022), and dozens of articles in scholarly journals and edited books. In collaboration with Barbara Eckstein, he also coedited *Story and Sustainability* (2003). As an active resident of Iowa City, Iowa, he served as an elected member of its city council from late 1993 through 1995 and again from 2012 through 2019. During the last four years of his council term, he also served as mayor.

MICHAEL WALA teaches North American history at Ruhr-University Bochum. He spent a year at Stanford University as visiting scholar and taught in Great Britain as well as in the United States before coming to Bochum. His research focuses on various aspects of American history, on international relations, and on the history of intelligence services. He has written and edited a large number of books, most recently *Otto John*, cowritten with Benjamin Carter Hett (CUNY) and published in 2019, and he coauthored a comprehensive history of the United States, *Geschichte der USA*, published in 2021 in an updated edition by Reclam.

KATHARINA WOOD is a doctoral researcher in the Scripts for Postindustrial Urban Futures: American Models, Transatlantic Interventions research group at the Department of Cultural Studies at TU Dortmund University. In her dissertation, she dissects transatlantic green city scripts used to build a greener future as brought forth through visionary approaches in green building standards and projects. Further research interests include green cultural studies, urban studies, and sustainability studies.

INDEX

addiction, 143, 147–48, 149

affordance, 216

African American communities: Albina gentrification, Portland, Oregon, and, 90–96, 91n4; Ellison's *Invisible Man*, 164, 213; Flournoy's *The Turner House*, 130–35; Markovits's *You Don't Have to Live Like This*, 127–30; May's "There Are Birds Here," 109–12; murders against, 27, 28n1, 214, 221, 224; redemptive scripts and, 163–66; Underground Railroad, 63–65, 63n8; US hostile relationship with BIPOC populations, 37–38. *See also* Black Lives Matter graffiti in Denver; Black Lives Matter (BLM) movement; Civil Rights Movement; gentrification

Agathocleous, Tanya, 165

AIDS, 148

Alderman, Derek, 51, 56

Alexander, Michelle, 215

Amato, Joseph A., 46n2

Ameel, Lieven, 6, 7, 72, 93, 99

American Rust (Meyer), 122

American studies, 7–8

Amy, Stan, 94

Anderson, Laurie, 168–69

Andrews, Molly, 215

Angelo, Hillary, 88, 89

Animal's People (Sinha), 216

architecture, 72, 73. *See also* tiny architecture

Aristotle, 157

Armstrong, Isobel, 205

art: Emerson on Art vs. "the arts," 198–99 (*see also* creativity scripts); Felski's liveliness of, 10

"Art is only for the rich" (Banning), 207–9, 208 fig. 10.1

Assmann, Aleida, 61, 186

Association for Literary Urban Studies, 5

atonement. *See* redemptive scripts

attachment, 10, 13, 44, 44n1, 53

Auerbach, Erich, 45, 46, 48, 50, 50n3, 66

Austin, J. L., 56

authenticity, 41, 139, 144–45, 146, 158–59

authorship, 9, 11, 13–14, 17

"Autres Temps . . ." (Wharton), 162–63

Azaryahu, Maoz, 8, 11–12, 30, 36–37, 148

Bader-Saye, Scott, 225
Baker, Keith Michael, 10–11
Baldwin, James, 164
Balzac, Honoré de, 166
Banning, Janna: "Art is only for the rich," 207–9, 208 fig. 10.1; *Wir arbeiten für Gentrifizierung ehrenamtlich*, 193–94
Barr, David, 60 fig. 2.5, 61
Barron, David J., 219n2
Barzak, Christopher, 122
Batiashvili, Nutsa, 188
Beauregard, Robert, 212n1
Benjamin, Walter, 6, 46n2
Bernstein, Robin, 8, 10n12, 44n1, 65
Betsworth, Roger, 195
Bilbao effect, 203, 203n4
Bildungsroman plot, 93, 99, 162
Black and Indigenous People of Color (BIPOC) populations, 37–38. *See also* African American communities; Indigenous communities
Black Lives Matter graffiti in Denver: aesthetics of, 35–36, 39, 39n12, 40; commodification and, 33, 35, 41; as counterscript, 28, 29, 34–35, 36, 38; Elijah McClain mural, Aurora, 29–35; as "tactic," 28–29, 34, 41; tagging of the state capitol, 35–40
Black Lives Matter (BLM) movement, 27–29, 56, 148n6, 221–22
Black Skyscraper, The (Brown), 6
Blazing Paddles Paddlefest (Cleveland), 175, 186–90, 187 fig. 9.1
Bleak House (Dickens), 216
Bode, Christoph, 48
bodegas. *See* gentrification microscripts in fictional bodegas and cafés
Braxton, Lisa, 122
broken windows theory, 40
Brooklyn gentrification novels, 131, 133
Brown, Adrienne, 6
Brown, Michael, 221
Brown/Freemaninov, Dumar, 33
Brown-Saracino, Japonica, 139
Buchenau, Barbara, 108–9, 156, 159, 188–89, 215

Butler, Judith, 30

Cadillac, Antoine Laumet de la Mothe, Sieur de, 62, 62n7, 63 fig. 2.6
cafés. *See* gentrification microscripts in fictional bodegas and cafés
Call It Sleep (Roth), 161–62
Cameron, Deborah, 71–72
"Can Detroit Save White People?" (Foley), 115
capitalism. *See* gentrification; neoliberal capitalism; property ownership
Charley, Jonathan, 70–71
Chauvin, Derek, 27
Chicano Civil Rights Movement (*El Movimiento*), 39n11
city, meaning of, 218
City after Abandonment, The (Dewar and Thomas), 135n1
City in American Literature and Culture, The (McNamara), 7
City Limits (Peterson), 220
City of Dispossessions (Mays), 6–7
city scripts: conflicts and contradictions between, 87; definitions of, 2, 4, 46; motivations or urban challenges for, 14–16; narrative and, 4; operations and analysis of, 9–10; story and, 4; urban memoirist scripts, 108–9. *See also* narratives; scriptivity; scripts; *and specific topics, such as* tiny architecture
City We Became, The (Jemisin), 147, 151–53
Civil Rights Movement, 54–55
Clark, Anna, 105–6
class: in Markovits's *You Don't Have to Live Like This*, 126, 127, 130; memoirs and, 107, 115–16; mobile homes and, 73; in Orange's *There There*, 143–46; race in US vs. class in Europe, 38. *See also* gentrification; inclusion/exclusion scripts
Cleaveland, Moses, 179
Cleveland waterfronts: Blazing Paddles Paddlefest, 175, 186–90, 187 fig. 9.1; Cleveland Waterfront Coalition, 182; Cuyahoga River fire (1969) as symbol and myth, 175, 183–89; founding myth and, 179–81; Great Lakes Exposition (1936–37), 178; historical thinking and, 176–77, 180–82, 184–86; narratives

as catalyst of change, 175–76; Native Americans, erasure of, 182; North Coast Harbor promotion, 178–83; oppositional narratives, 176; planning history, 177–78

climate change, 15–16, 222–23

Cohen, Daniel, 89

Cole, Alyssa, 122

colonialism: Detroit historical narratives and, 45–51, 56, 58, 62–64, 136; Detroit's Saginaw Trail and, 49; *figurae* and, 48–49; Kelley on racialized attacks and, 37–38; in Markovits's *You Don't Have to Live Like This*, 125–30; in Orange's *There There*, 142; tagging as deconstruction of, 39

Colorado State Capitol, tagging of, 35–40

Columbus, Christopher, 62

"comeback city" moniker, 54, 183, 183n2

commemoration. *See* memorialization and commemoration

commodification: of art and creativity, 195, 197, 198–201, 209; Black Lives Matter graffiti and, 33, 35, 41; as depoliticization of "tactic," 41

constructivist historical narratives, 184–86

counterscripting: Black Lives Matter graffiti as, 28, 29, 34–35, 36, 38; in digital space, 34–35; as inseparable from scripts, 10; in memoirs, 112, 119; memoirs and, 119; in Orange's *There There*, 152n10

Couser, Thomas, 107

COVID-19 pandemic, 1, 27, 59, 168

Cox, James, 142n4

cradle-to-cradle principle, 83

creativity scripts: Banning's "Art is only for the rich," 207–9, 208 fig. 10.1; Banning's *Wir arbeiten für Gentrifizierung ehrenamtlich*, 193–94; commodification, cultural criticism of, 198–201; "creatification," 197, 199; creative class in Emerson vs. Florida, 196–98; creative participation and imagination in Dewey, 202–5; creative-economy script, defined, 195; *creativity dispositif*, 195n3; cultural narrative, defined, 195–96; democracy, creative, 206–7; enigma of the creative city, 193–96; in Markovits's *You Don't Have to Live Like This*, 124; reconfiguration, creative, 205–6; as urban challenge, 14–15

Crèvecœur, J. Hector St. John de, 127

critical historical narratives, 185

cultural urban studies, 6–7

Cuyahoga River. *See* Cleveland waterfronts

Danielewicz, Jane, 107–8, 116

Davis, Charles L., II, 2

de Certeau, Michel, 6, 28, 34, 39, 41, 47

De Giusti, Sergio, 60 fig. 2.5

degrowth script, 69, 69n1, 71, 74–75, 77, 82, 84

deindustrialization: Cleveland and, 176, 179–81, 183, 184–85; defined, 14n13; Detroit and, 123–24; future imaginaries and, 3, 4; narratives and, 98–99. *See also* Rust Belt

democracy, creative, 206–7

Denver. *See* Black Lives Matter graffiti in Denver

deserted cities script, 1–2

Detroit: as "comeback city," 54; Detroit Future City plan (2012), 136; Detroit Utopia narrative, 123; Flournoy's *The Turner House*, 130–35, 136; Foley's "Can Detroit Save White People?," 115; historical transitions, 65; Kickert map (1911), 49, 50 fig. 2.1; Markovits's *You Don't Have to Live Like This*, 124–30, 135–36; May's "There Are Birds Here," 109–12; Music's "The Kidnapped Children," 115–19; Nethercott's "The Detroit Virus," 112–15; seals of Detroit and Wayne County, 58; whipping post site, 59; Woodward Plan (1805), 49–51, 52. *See also* figural walking on Woodward Avenue, Detroit

Detroit 300 Conservancy, 54

Detroit Anthology, A (Clark), 105–6

"Detroit Virus, The" (Nethercott), 112–15

Dewar, Margaret, 135n1

Dewey, John, 193, 196, 202–9

Dickens, Charles, 216

Didden Village, Rotterdam, 76–78, 76 fig. 3.1

Dietrich, Rainer, 48

"digital ups," 35n7

disnarration, 139

Dodge, Horace E., 61

Dolle, Christopher, 216–17

Dortmund-Sölde, Germany, 82–83

Drügh, Heinz, 145

Dwight, Ed, 63
Dzudzek, Iris, 194, 195

Eakin, John, 107–9
Eckstein, Barbara, 12, 13–14
ecological scripts: city narrative of environmentalists, 98; Cleveland waterfronts and, 176, 179–80, 184, 186–87; climate change, 15–16, 222–23; cradle-to-cradle principle, 83; gentrification and, 88–91; self-reliance in, 18; sufficiency script, 69, 69n1, 74–75, 79, 81, 83; tiny architecture and, 77–78. *See also* sustainability scripts
economy: circular, 83; Cleveland and, 183, 185, 189–90; creativity and, 194–95, 203, 206; degrowth script, 69, 69n1, 71, 74–75, 77, 82, 84; in Flournoy's *The Turner House*, 132, 134, 136; gentrification and, 90, 96–97; legacy cities and, 3n3; in Markovits's *You Don't Have to Live Like This*, 125–30, 136; of singularities, 14. *See also* creativity scripts; neoliberal capitalism; property ownership; Rust Belt; sustainability scripts
Edelstein, Dan, 10–11
Eisinger, Peter, 54
Elijah McClain RIP mural, 29–35, 31 fig. 1.1
Ellison, Ralph, 164, 213
Emerson, Ralph Waldo, 74, 196–202, 204–6, 209
Englert, Klaus, 78
Erdrich, Louise, 142n4
Evans, Krista, 73
Evans, Thomas "Detour," 30, 31 fig. 1.1, 32–34, 41
exclusion. *See* inclusion/exclusion scripts
exemplary historical narratives, 181

Felski, Rita, 2, 3n2, 10, 12, 13
Ferraro, Thomas J., 159
Fessenden, Tracy, 159
figurae, 45–46, 48, 50n3, 57–58, 65–66
figural walking on Woodward Avenue, Detroit: Auerbach's *figurae* and, 45, 46, 48, 50n3, 57–58, 66; Campus Martius, 51–54, 62; Dodge and Son Memorial Fountain, 61; Ford Motor Company historical marker, 61; *Gateway to Freedom: International Memorial to the Underground Railroad* (Dwight), 63–65, 64 fig. 2.7; Hart Plaza, 60–65; Kickert map (1911), 49, 50 fig. 2.1; *The Landing of Cadillac* (Kieffer), 62, 63 fig. 2.6; map, 52 fig. 2.2; *Michigan Soldiers' and Sailors' Monument* (Rogers), 53–54, 64; *Monument to Joe Louis* (Graham), 59–60, 60 fig. 2.5; *Power to the People* (Massey), 55–57, 55 fig. 2.3; Saginaw Trail and, 47, 49, 56; *The Spirit of Detroit* (Fredericks), 57–59, 57 fig. 2.4; Spirit Plaza, 57–59; storytelling, narrativity, scriptivity, and, 44–46, 65, 66; street names, commemorative, 51n4; *Transcending* (Barr and De Giusti), 60 fig. 2.5, 61–62; Walk to Freedom (1963), 54–55; walking as language, 46n2; walking as urban practice and figural interpretation, 46–48; Woodward Plan (1805), 49–51, 52

figures, urban, 46–48, 51–53, 61–62, 65–66. *See also* figural walking on Woodward Avenue, Detroit
Finch, Jason, 7
Fitzgerald, F. Scott, 160–61
Florida, Richard, 135, 194–99, 201–6
Flournoy, Angela, 123–24, 130–35
Floyd, George, 27, 214, 221
Fludernik, Monika, 12
Foley, Aaron, 115, 115n3
Foote, Kenneth, 8, 11–12, 30, 36–37, 148
Ford Motor Company, 61
formalism, new, 216
Förster, Hannah, 75
Four Souls (Erdrich), 142n4
framing, narrative: Dolle's two framing environments, 217; generative energy, disrupted habits, and frame of the heart, 223–25; public frame of city governance, 217–23
Franklin, C. L., 54
Fredericks, Marshall, 57–58
Friedl, Herwig, 202, 206
Frishman, Richard, 70
frontier myth: in Flournoy's *The Turner House*, 130–32; in Markovits's *You Don't Have to Live Like This*, 124–30
Frug, Gerald E., 219n2

Fugitive Slave Act, 63n8
Fuller, Margaret, 198
futures, 98, 123, 188, 190, 215
futures, urban. *See specific topics, such as* gentrification
futurity and *figurae*, 46–49, 57–58, 66

Gamper, Michael, 4n6
Garud, Raghu, 97
Gateway to Freedom: International Memorial to the Underground Railroad (Dwight), 63–65, 64 fig. 2.7
Gelfant, Blanche, 162
generative energy, 223–24
genetic historical narratives, 184–85
gentrification: Albina District, Portland, 90–96; antigentrifier's dilemma, 95; authenticity and, 146; Banning's *Wir arbeiten für Gentrifizierung ehrenamtlich*, 193–94; Brooklyn gentrification novels, 131, 133; creative urban development and, 194; in Detroit, as unique, 123; environmental, 89; in Flournoy's *The Turner House*, 130–35; genres, plot structures, and, 147; macro and micro approaches to, 139; in Markovits's *You Don't Have to Live Like This*, 124–30; of the mind, 153; spiritual, 148; struggle to represent, 138–40; as term, 138n1
gentrification microscripts in fictional bodegas and cafés: about microscripts, 140–41; Jemisin's *The City We Became*, 147, 151–53; Moshfegh's *My Year of Rest and Relaxation*, 142–46, 149, 150, 151, 152; Orange's *There There*, 142–46, 152; Schulman's *Maggie Terry*, 147–51; Staley on bodega fetishism, 149–50; the subnarratable and, 139–40
Gentrification of the Mind, The (Schulman), 148
ghost narratives, 131, 133–34
Gibson, Karen, 92n6
Gilbert, Dan, 54
Glass, Ruth, 15, 138n1
Go Tell It on the Mountain (Baldwin), 164
Goodling, Erin, 91
graffiti: aesthetics of, 35–36, 39, 39n12, 40; forms of, 31; memorial traditions

adapted to the street, 30–31; as rewriting the city, 28; RIP murals, 30–35; tagging, 35–40
Graham, Robert, 59, 60 fig. 2.5
Great Gatsby, The (Fitzgerald), 160–61, 162, 163, 167, 169
Green, Jamaal, 91
Greenberg, Jonathan, 144
greenwashing, 88–89
Gurr, Jens Martin, 108–9, 156, 159, 188–89, 215
Guterres, António, 1

Hard Weather Boating Party, The (Wallace), 216
Harris, Tracy, 83
Hart, Francis Russel, 107
Hart, Philip A., 60
haunting narratives, 131, 133–34
heart, frame of, 224–25
Heidegger, Martin, 39n12
Heise, Thomas, 15, 147
Henryson, Hanna, 15
Hern, Matt, 92
Herron, Jerry, 125
Hill, Lamont, 146–47
historical thinking, 176–77, 180–82, 184–86
historicizations, 176–77
homeownership. *See* property ownership
HQE approach (Haute Qualité Environnementale), 79
Huber, Martin, 4n6
Hurm, Gerd, 6
Hurricane Sandy, 168–69

In the Heights (Miranda), 150
Inauri, Tinatin, 188
inclusion/exclusion scripts: art and, 209; creativity and, 203–4, 206, 209; Detroit memoirs and, 111, 119–20; in Ellison's *Invisible Man*, 213–14; gentrification and, 91–96, 138n1, 194; microaggressive attention, 152; in Moshfegh's *My Year of Rest and Relaxation*, 145–46; Nethercott's "The Detroit Virus" and, 119–20; in Orange's *There There*, 143–46; redemptive

scripts and, 169; sustainability scripts vs., 88–90; Throgmorton's five city narratives and, 98–99; as urban challenge, 15
Indigenous communities: Cadillac and, 62n7; Cleveland waterfronts and, 182; Detroit's Woodward Avenue and, 47, 49, 51, 62; in Orange's *There There*, 142–44; US hostile relationship with BIPOC populations, 37–38
inequality, narrative, 105, 111
International Panel on Climate Change (IPCC), 222
Intuitionist, The (Whitehead), 164–66, 169
Invisible Man (Ellison), 164, 213, 214
Iowa Freedom Riders (IFR), 221–22

Jacobs, Jane, 218
Jaeger, Stephan, 186
James, William, 202, 205
Jameson, Frederic, 138
Jemisin, N. K., 151–53
Jonas, Andrew E. G., 88, 89

Karnøe, Peter, 97
Katz, Vera, 92
Kelleter, Frank, 4n7, 13
Kelley, Robin D. G., 27, 37–38
Kelling, George L., 40
Kellogg, Wendy, 175–76
Kickert, Conrad, 47, 49
"Kidnapped Children, The" (Music), 115–19
Kieffer, William, 62
King, Martin Luther, Jr., 54
Knauer, Lisa Maya, 38
Koschorke, Albrecht, 4nn5–6, 9n11, 95, 100
Kronos Quartet, 168–69
Kumaraswamy, Arun, 97

Lahusen, Christiane, 106–7, 108, 109
Lake Erie. *See* Cleveland waterfronts
land speculation. *See* property ownership
Landfall (Anderson and Kronos Quartet), 168–69
Landing of Cadillac, The (Kieffer and Feeley), 62, 63 fig. 2.6

Landry, Charles, 194n2
Le Corbusier, 78
Leary, John Patrick, 123
Lederach, John Paul, 223
Lefebvre, Henri, 6
legacy cities, 2, 3n3, 182. *See also* Rust Belt
Levine, Caroline, 215–16
Lindner, Peter, 194, 195
Linkon, Sherry Lee, 14n13
Literary Geographies journal, 5–6
Literary Second Cities (Finch, Ameel, and Salmela), 7
literary urban studies, 5–7
Litt, Steven, 177
living labs (*Reallabore*), 74–75, 77, 82
Logements à Poissy (Virtuel Architecture), 78–80, 80 fig. 3.2
logos and seals of cities, 58–59
Lotman, Juri, 177, 187–88
Louis, Joe, 59–60
Love Medicine (Erdrich), 142n4
Löw, Martina, 175
Lukács, Georg, 159

Maggie Terry (Schulman), 147–51
Markovits, Benjamin, 124–30, 135–36
Markus, Thomas, 71–72
Martin, Trayvon, 28n1, 221
Marx, Karl, 201
Mask, Deidre, 56
Massey, Hubert, 55–56
May, Jamaal, 109–12, 119
Mayer, Ruth, 4n6, 140–41
Mays, Kyle T., 6–7
McClain, Elijah, 29–35, 36, 41
McClintock, Nathan, 91
McNamara, Kevin R., 7
memoirs in Detroit: about memoirs, 107–9; the anthologies, 105–6; autobiography vs. memoir, 106–7; Foley's "Can Detroit Save White People?," 115; May's "There Are Birds Here," 109–12; Music's "The Kidnapped Children," 115–19; Nethercott's "The Detroit Virus," 112–15

memorialization and commemoration: Dodge and Son Memorial Fountain, Detroit, 61; *Gateway to Freedom: International Memorial to the Underground Railroad,* Detroit (Dwight), 63–65, 64 fig. 2.7; HIV/AIDS crisis and lack of, 148; *Michigan Soldiers' and Sailors' Monument,* Detroit (Rogers), 53–54, 64; removal of statues and busts, 62; RIP murals and, 30; scaling of memory and, 56; street names and, 51n4. *See also* figural walking on Woodward Avenue, Detroit

memory: autobiographical, 108; history vs., 185–86; myth and, 186; scaling of, 56, 61; selective, 62–63; symbols as mnemonic constellations, 187

Metahistory (White), 98

Meyer, Philipp, 122

Michaels, Lloyd, 162

Michigan Soldiers' and Sailors' Monument (Rogers), 53–54, 64

microscripts: about, 140–41; architecture and, 72; fictional bodegas and cafés and, 145–47, 153–54; *Power to the People* street mural (Massey) as, 55; tiny homes and, 75

minimalist narrative, 83

Misch, Georg, 107

modernity, 156, 158–61, 164, 166

Möglichkeitsräume (spaces of possibility), 74–75, 77

Molina, Natalia, 10, 110

Monument to Joe Louis (Graham), 59–60, 60 fig. 2.5

Moshfegh, Ottessa, 142–46

Moya, Paula M. L., 2, 3n2, 12–14

Muhammad, Khalil Gibran, 38

murals, 30–35, 56–57

Music, Marsha, 115–19, 120

MVRDV, 76–78

My Year of Rest and Relaxation (Moshfegh), 142–46, 149, 150, 151, 152

Myers, Elijah E., 38

Narrating Space / Spatializing Narrative (Ryan, Foote, and Azaryahu), 8

narrative framing. *See* framing, narrative

narrative inequality, 105, 111

narrative path dependencies, 87, 96–99

narratives: architecture, language, and, 70–73; as catalysts of change, 175–76; city scripts and, 4; cultural, defined, 195–96; definitions of, 4n5; as formatting templates, 95; haunting, 131, 133–34; historical narratives, constructivist, 184–86; historical narratives, teleological, 180–82; minimalist, 83; redemptive, 157–60; scripts and, 11–14; serial, 13; Throgmorton's five urban narratives, 98–99; in urban planning, 89–90, 89n2, 95, 98–99

narrativity: anthropological base of, 4n6; architecture, narrative, and, 70–73; architecture and, 72; Detroit's Woodward Avenue and, 44–45, 65–66; figural, 45, 66; naturalization of, 66; possessing, 11–12; transdisciplinary methodology and, 8

narratology, transdisciplinary, 4, 8–16, 20, 215

Native Americans. *See* Indigenous communities

Negus, Keith, 203, 204

neoliberal capitalism: creative city and, 206; in fiction, 134–35, 135n1; in Jemisin's *The City We Became,* 151; "right to the city" and, 124; sufficiency narratives and, 74–75. *See also* gentrification

Nethercott, Shaun, 112–15, 119–20

Neuman, Bernd, 107

Neumann, Tracy, 4

New Cleveland Campaign, 178–79

New York City: Ellison's *Invisible Man,* 164, 213, 214; Jemisin's *The City We Became,* 147, 151–53; Moshfegh's *My Year of Rest and Relaxation,* 142–46, 149, 150, 151, 152; planning, redemptive scripts in, 166–68; *Reclaiming the Edge* waterfront plan, 167; *Vision 2020* waterfront plan, 167–68, 169

Nielsen, Cecilia Schøler, 39

Nietzsche, Friedrich, 39n12

Noguchi, Isamu, 60–61

Norris, Frank, 140

"North-East Passage: The Inner City and the American Dream" (documentary; Swart), 94–95

Oakland, CA, 142–46

Öko-Institut, 75
On the Waterfront (film), 168
One for Sorrow (Barzak), 122
Orange, Tommy, 142–46

Pabón-Colón, Jessica Nydia, 35n7
Patch, Jason, 146–47
path dependencies, narrative, 87, 96–99
pattern-script-interrelations, 188–89
Peacock, James, 15, 131, 133, 146
Peck, Jamie, 194, 195, 206
Peirce, Charles Sanders, 202
performativity, 2, 8, 10n12, 44n1, 56, 119–20, 154
Peterson, Paul, 220
Phelan, James, 157
Pickering, Michael, 203, 204
Pielack, Leslie, 47, 49
Pillaud, Laurent, 78
Poissy, France, 78–80
Portelli, Alessandro, 225
Portland, Oregon: Albina Community Plan (ACP) and gentrification, 90–96; Albina Vision Community Investment Plan, 96; historical racism in, 92n6; narrative path dependencies and, 99; sustainability script and, 87–88; Urban Growth Boundary (UGB), 89–90
Power to the People street mural (Massey), 55–57, 55 fig. 2.3
praefiguratio, 57
Prince, Gerald, 139
property ownership: in Flournoy's *The Turner House*, 130–35, 136; in Markovits's *You Don't Have to Live Like This*, 124–30, 135–36; postindustrial novels and, 122–23; tiny homes and, 74. See also gentrification
Psarra, Sophia, 72

queer communities, 147–48

"racial scripts," 10, 110. See also African American communities; Indigenous communities
Rauert, Roderick, 78

realist fiction, 140
Reallabore (living labs), 74–75, 77, 82
Reckwitz, Andreas, 14–15, 195n3
redemptive scripts: about, 156–57; African American literature and, 163–64; in films, 168; Fitzgerald's *The Great Gatsby*, 160–61, 162, 163, 167, 169; gentrification and, 91–95; *Landfall* album (Anderson and Kronos Quartet), 168–69; meanings of redemption, 157–58; in Music's "The Kidnapped Children," 118–19; narrative structures and redemptive plots, 157–60, 159 table 8.1, 169; in New York City planning, 166–68; Roth's *Call It Sleep*, 161–62; Smith's *A Tree Grows in Brooklyn*, 162; tiny homes and, 75, 77, 83; Wharton's "Autres Temps . . . ," 162–63; Whitehead's *The Intuitionist*, 164–66. See also urban planning
Reinburg, Virginia, 52
Richard, Gabriel, 58
Ridge, Jim, 186–87
"right to the city," 124
RIP murals, 30–35
Rogers, Randolf, 53
Roth, Henry, 161–62
Rotterdam, 76–78
Rowe, John Carlos, 7
Rowlandson, Mary, 48
Rüsen, Jörn, 176–77, 180–85, 188
Rust Belt: creativity scripts and, 15; memoirs and, 105–6, 107, 111, 120; Neumann on, 4; ownership debates in, 122; storytelling and, 2–3; transformation processes in, 123. See also deindustrialization; *and specific cities*
Ryan, Marie-Laure, 3n2, 8, 11–12, 30, 36–37, 45, 148
Ryberg-Webster, Stephanie, 3n3

Salmela, Markku, 7, 162
Samanta, Aritree, 175–76
Santayana, George, 140
Santino, Jack, 30
Sattler, Julia, 7
"Say their names" and #spraytheirnames, 34–35, 214, 221
Schacter, Daniel, 108

INDEX • 239

Schacter, Rafael, 36
Schlichtman, John Joe, 146–47
Schmid, Benedikt, 74–75, 77, 82
Schmid, Wolf, 4n6
Schulman, Sarah: on gentrification of the mind, 153; *The Gentrification of the Mind*, 148; *Maggie Terry*, 147–51
Schulz, Christian, 74–75, 77, 82
Scripting Revolution (Baker and Edelstein), 10–11
scriptivity: defined, 2n1, 10n12; Detroit's Woodward Avenue and, 44–45, 44n1, 65–66; figural, 66; iconic sculptures, lemmatas, and epigrams as, 58; naturalization of, 66
scripts: figural dimension of, 51–52; meanings and definitions of, 2, 3, 9–10, 10n12, 215; as method in social sciences and humanities, 9; narratives and, 11–14; storytelling and, 9; three functions of, 156. *See also* city scripts
scriptures, 159
semiotics, cultural, 188
serial narratives, 13
Share the River, 175, 186–87
Shepherd, Jessica, 45
Siegele, Claudia, 80
Simmel, Georg, 6
Sinha, Indra, 216
Smith, Betty, 162
Smith, Neil, 124, 130
Sölde, Germany (Dortmund), 82–83
Sonntag, Susan, 145
Souther, J. Mark, 183
"space of the other," 41
spaces of possibility (*Möglichkeitsräume*), 74–75, 77
Spirit of Detroit, The (Fredericks), 57–59, 57 fig. 2.4
#spraytheirnames, 34–35
Staley, Willy, 149–50
Steffen, Arne, 69
Stein, Gertrude, 142
Stewart, Fred, 94
Story and Sustainability (Eckstein and Throgmorton), 212–14

storytelling: the "and then" of, 215; city scripts and, 4; Detroit's Woodward Avenue and, 44–45; disnarration, unnarration, and, 139; dynamization in, 4n5; frame of city governance and, 220–23; interpretive strategies, 215–17; Inuit definition of storyteller, 223; rust belts and transformation engines, images of, 2–3; scripts and, 9
Stradling, David, 183–84, 186
Stradling, Richard, 183–84, 186
street names, 51n4
Strohmaier, Alexandra, 4n6
Su, Shia, 83
subnarratability, 139–40, 153
sufficiency script: cradle-to-cradle principle, 83; tiny homes and, 69, 69n1, 74–75, 79, 81, 83
Sulimma, Maria, 13
supranarratability, 139–40
sustainability scripts: Eckstein and Throgmorton's *Story and Sustainability*, 212–14; Iowa City and frame of city governance, 217–23; three-pillar model of sustainability, 79; tiny homes and, 78, 82, 83; as urban challenge, 15–16; urban renewal and inclusive script vs., 88–90
Swart, Cornelius, 94–95
symbols, semiotics of, 179, 183, 184, 186–89

"tactic," 28–29, 34, 41
Talking Drum, The (Braxton), 122
Taylor, George, 53
teleological historical narratives, 180–82
"There Are Birds Here" (May), 109–12
There There (Orange), 142–46, 152
Thomas, June Manning, 135n1
Thoreau, Henry David, 74, 81, 198
Throgmorton, James A., 95, 98–99
Thunberg, Greta, 222–23
Tighe, J. Rosie, 3n3
Till, Mamie, 224
tiny architecture: about, 69; Didden Village, Rotterdam, 76–78, 76 fig. 3.1; Dortmund-Sölde, Germany, 82–83; historical perspective, 73–74; Logements à Poissy (Virtuel Architecture), 78–80, 80 fig. 3.2;

narrative, language, and architecture, 70–73; redemptive scripts, 75–76, 83; sufficiency narratives, degrowth, and, 69, 69n1, 74–75; Wohnwagon caravans, Austria, 80–82, 81 fig. 3.3

Tracks (Erdrich), 142n4

traditional historical narratives, 181

tragedy plot, 91–95, 97

Transcendentalism, 74, 198, 200

Transcending (Barr and De Giusti), 60 fig. 2.5, 61–62

Tree Grows in Brooklyn, A (Smith), 162

Trubek, Anne, 105

"TukeOne," 30, 31 fig. 1.1, 32–33

Turner, Frederick Jackson, 130–31

Turner House, The (Flournoy), 123–24, 130–35

Underground Railroad, 63–65, 63n8

United Farm Workers, 39n11

unnarration, 139–40

urban (white) flight script, 1–2, 117–18

Urban Growth Boundary (UGB), 89–90

urban memoirist scripts. *See* memoirs in Detroit

urban planning: Albina District, Portland, Oregon, 87–88, 90–96; *Bildungsroman* plot in, 93, 99; "green as good" formula, 88; narrative path dependencies and, 87, 96–99; narratives in, 89–90, 89n2, 95, 98–99; public frame of city governance and, 217–23; redemptive, in New York City planning, 166–68; sustainability/inclusive and renewal/gentrification scripts, 88–90. *See also* Cleveland waterfronts

urban scripts. *See* city scripts

urban studies, literary and cultural, 5–7

Urban Transformations in the U.S.A. (Sattler), 7

utopianism: Detroit Utopia narrative, 65, 123; in Markovits's *You Don't Have to Live Like This*, 126, 129; racist, in Oregon, 92n6; scripts, utopian and dystopian qualities of, 9; urban planning, sustainability, and, 18

Vail, Thomas, 178

van Buren, Diane, 46

Veiga, Hiero, 31 fig. 1.1, 32–34

Virtuel Architecture, Poissy, France, 78–80, 80 fig. 3.2

Vivien, Béatrice, 78

Voices from the Rust Belt (Trubek), 105–6

Voinovich, George V., 178–83, 190

Wachsmuth, David, 89

Wacquant, Loïc, 48

Walden; or, Life in the Woods (Thoreau), 74

Walk to Freedom (1963), 54–55

walking. *See* figural walking on Woodward Avenue, Detroit

Walkowitz, Daniel J., 38

Wallace, Naomi, 216

Warhol, Robyn, 139–40

Washington, John, 91

Weck, Sabine, 74–75, 77, 82

Wertsch, James V., 188

Westwell, Guy, 168

Wharton, Edith, 162–63

When No One Is Watching (Cole), 122

White, Hayden, 98

white (urban) flight script, 1–2, 117–18

Whitehead, Colson, 164–66, 169

Williams, John, 48

Williams, Nikki, 95

Wilson, James Q., 40

Wir arbeiten für Gentrifizierung ehrenamtlich (Banning), 193–94

Wire, The (HBO), 216

Wirth-Nesher, Hana, 161–62

Wohnwagon caravans, 80–82, 81 fig. 3.3

Woloch, Alex, 98, 145

Woodward, Augustus B., 49–51, 56

Wundt, Wilhelm Maximilian, 197

You Don't Have to Live Like This (Markovits), 124–30, 135–36

Zachary, Ernest, 46

Zell-Ziegler, Carina, 75

Zimmermann, George, 28n1

Zukin, Sharon, 146